Also by Frank Wal

Maralinga

'An amazing tale – utterly gripping, it reads like a thriller.' *Jon Faine, ABC Radio Melbourne*

'The story reaches out and grabs you by the throat.' *Dr Clare Wright, historian*

'Shocking revelations . . .' *Margaret Throsby, Midday Interview, ABC Classic FM*

'An extraordinary story – there are things here that would make your hair stand on end.' *Philip Clark, ABC Radio Canberra*

'This account . . . sparks a rage in the reader that human beings could be treated with such contempt, such cold-blooded, Nazi-like calculated evilness.' *Law Society Journal*

The Tiger Man of Vietnam

'One of those great untold stories . . . Walker tells it with verve and excitement and with meticulous attention to detail.' *Sydney Morning Herald*

Ghost Platoon

'Walker and others like him are doing their country a great service by bringing both the good and bad deeds of Aussie diggers out of the shadows and into the open.' *Sunday Age*

Commandos

'Amazing stories.' *Mark Colvin, ABC Radio PM*

'A cracking read . . . forget those thriller novels, this is the real thing and the stories are incredible.' *Scott Levi, ABC Central Coast*

'Incredible stories . . . a great book.' *Miranda Devine, 2GB*

Frank Walker has been an Australian journalist and foreign correspondent in Germany and the United States for 40 years, covering wars and coups, floods and fires, terrorist attacks and political brawls, movie stars and street crime. This is his sixth non-fiction book. His first two bestselling books, *The Tiger Man of Vietnam* and *Ghost Platoon*, revealed uncomfortable truths about Australia's actions in the Vietnam War. His third bestselling book, *Maralinga*, lifted the veil of secrecy thrown over the British atomic bomb tests in the outback and shocking human experiments in Australia in the 1950s and 1960s. His fourth book, *Commandos*, examined the most daring secret raids behind enemy lines by Australians and New Zealanders in World War II. In 2017 Frank wrote *Traitors*, an exposé of how Australia and its allies betrayed our Anzacs and let Nazi and Japanese war criminals go free.

He can be contacted via his website, www.frankwalker.com.au

The SCANDALOUS FREDDIE McEVOY

FRANK WALKER

hachette
AUSTRALIA

hachette
AUSTRALIA

Published in Australia and New Zealand in 2018
by Hachette Australia
(an imprint of Hachette Australia Pty Limited)
Level 17, 207 Kent Street, Sydney NSW 2000
www.hachette.com.au

10 9 8 7 6 5 4 3 2 1

 A catalogue record for this
book is available from the
NATIONAL LIBRARY OF AUSTRALIA   National Library of Australia

ISBN: 978 0 7336 3987 6 (paperback)

Cover design by Christabella Designs
Cover photograph courtesy of Walter Carone/Paris Match via Getty Images. Freddie McEvoy (right)
acting as best man at the wedding of Errol Flynn (left) on the French Riviera in 1950.
All internal photographs were collated by the author from the public domain.
Typeset in 12/17.6 pt Simoncini Garamond Std by Bookhouse, Sydney
Printed and bound in Great Britain by Clays Ltd, Elcograf S.p.A.

 MIX
Paper from
responsible sources
FSC
www.fsc.org   FSC® C104740

For Esther and Hannah

CONTENTS

PROLOGUE

Freddie McEvoy was many things: the first Australian to win a medal at any Winter Olympics, world bobsledding champion several times over and amateur racing car driver who mixed it with the best in the world. He was also a bounder, cad, scoundrel, rascally rapscallion, rake, lover, brawler, black-marketeer, smuggler, suspected Nazi spy and suspected Allied double agent. He was a playboy who cavorted with the rich and famous of the 1930s and 40s, a dashing charmer who always seemed to have money although he never worked for a living, and the best mate of Hollywood star swashbuckler and fellow Aussie larrikin Errol Flynn. Armed only with his charm, wit and his skills in the bedroom, Freddie set out to win the hearts – and money – of wealthy women to support his extravagant and scandalous life. And they couldn't pay up fast enough.

As his best friend Errol Flynn said of Freddie: 'Freddie was one of the great livers of life. He lived it the way he saw it. He didn't give a hoot.'[1] Adventure writer Robert Ruark said Freddie was one of the 'true swashbucklers, just as wild as Errol Flynn, just as handsome, just as reckless and just as careless of public opinion . . . both tall, handsome gentlemen [were] striking figures at any place where the sun shone warm, there was booze to be drunk and women to chase'.[2]

This is the incredible true story of Freddie McEvoy, Australian international Casanova, daredevil, speed freak and card shark, whose last gamble proved deadly.

CHAPTER 1

FREDDIE EYEBALLS ADOLF HITLER

1936 Winter Olympics
6 February 1936, Garmisch-Partenkirchen, Germany

Frederick Joseph McEvoy tightened his grip on the flagstaff and leaned forward into the driving snow. The big Australian – 6 feet 2 inches (1.87 metres) of solid muscle, broad shoulders bulging against the white Olympic uniform – shook the flag to rid it of the gathering crust of snow. The red, white and blue British Union Jack fell free. It fluttered slightly in the falling snow that was getting heavier by the minute. The Melbourne-born athlete's thick moustache – the must-have facial accessory of every dashingly handsome man in the 1930s – collected snow that drifted into his face.

Freddie turned around to the 37 men and women lined up behind him. They looked at him expectantly. Freddie winked at them, put his head back and laughed. Here he was, an Aussie, about to lead the British Winter Olympic team into the opening ceremony of the 1936 Games, where they would march past a rabid dictator. The madness of the moment didn't escape him. Six days short of his 29th birthday, Freddie already had a Europe-wide reputation as a dashing high-society playboy with an eye for the ladies. The ladies certainly had eyes for the ruggedly hand-some Australian. Freddie's reckless pursuit of speed on mountain slopes and in fast cars had earned him the nickname 'Suicide Freddie', and a place leading the British Olympic bobsled team into Nazi Germany's Winter Olympic Games.

British Olympic selectors recognised that Freddie had a steely determination to win, and that he was utterly fearless. His daring tactics on bobsleds had won him races in the past few years in Switzerland. He'd invented a couple of innovations on the bobsled that were considered bold, but extremely dangerous, even deadly. Bill Fiske of the American bobsled team later wrote: 'Freddie McEvoy has invented one of the most lethal toboggans ever seen on the run. He had a toboggan constructed of hollow ground runners . . . [they were] tremendously fast on a straight course, but impossible to manoeuvre around corners.'[1] In the months leading up to the February Olympics in Garmisch-Partenkirchen Freddie had driven the British four-man and two-man bobsled teams hard, training on this new type of bobsled, and he'd whipped them into real contenders against the Alpine winter sport superpowers.

Instead of picking the usual upper-crust society amateur English competitor to lead the Olympic squad, the British team managers decided to appoint Australian Freddie to the honoured position of standard bearer of the British Winter Olympic team. Eighteen years after the devastating Great War and the horrors of the trenches, the British were determined to beat the Germans in their Bavarian backyard. They wanted to show that jumped-up corporal who was now German Chancellor, ranting and raving to cheering crowds, that Britain was strong and not to be threatened. The 1936 Olympics were far more about power and politics than sport, and Freddie was leading the British team right into the thick of it.

Freddie watched the 32-strong French team march ahead into the driving snow. Now it was the turn of *Grossbritannien*, the German name for Great Britain carried on a placard in front of the team by a pretty German woman. She smiled coquettishly at Freddie as she motioned him to follow her, showing the way into the parade ground. That's a prospect for later, thought Freddie, who regarded life as one long, determined pursuit of women, preferably those with money. Freddie hoisted the British flag higher and stepped forward. The snow had only started falling last night, but it was already 6 inches deep and crunched under his feet as he began the march that would take the British team past the roaring crowds, towards the waiting German Führer, Adolf Hitler.

The British team, the fifth largest in the Games, followed in his footsteps, some talking excitedly. They were fast approaching the stands holding the German public. Freddie heard a burst of laughter behind him. Someone had made a smart comment. Freddie turned around and glared.

'Silence!' he shouted. Freddie didn't want the team to think this was all a jolly holiday. He knew that every German would be watching the British team with mixed emotions. Many men in the crowd would have been in the trenches just 18 years ago, shooting at the British, Australians, Canadians, Americans and French. Many more would have lost family members in that long war. This was deadly serious. No laughing, particularly in front of the Nazi fanatics surrounding the podium.

As Freddie reached the entry to the makeshift parade ground, a German military band struck up a new marching tune for the British. Freddie didn't recognise it, but the Germans in the stands seemed to see a joke in the choice, and burst out in collective laughter. Freddie looked up at the stand to his right. Twenty thousand people in heavy coats, snow settling on their fur hats, waited in the stands to see the opening ceremony. Would they jeer or boo the British? Freddie had earlier told the British team that no matter what happened, they were to stare straight ahead and march behind him in unison as best they could in the driving snow.

The team and managers had discussed and argued for a long time over what sort of salute to give as they passed the podium where Hitler would be standing. They figured the Austrians and Italians would give Hitler the Nazi salute, and there was considerable pressure from Olympic officials to honour the German hosts with an outstretched arm salute. The Olympic officials argued it wasn't so much a Nazi salute, but an Olympic salute that had been introduced at the Paris Games in 1924. It involved holding the right arm forward and horizontal from the body, with palm down, then bringing it across the chest. The difference to the Nazi elevated right arm salute was only slight, but it allowed British officials to argue they weren't giving Hitler the Nazi salute.

Through the driving snow Freddie saw the ranks of the French team in front of him reach the balcony of the hotel

Olympia Haus, where Hitler and his cronies stood to take the salute. The French flag dipped and the crowd roared out its delight as the French team extended their right arms parallel to the ground in front of them. Technically it might be the correct Olympic salute, but to the Germans watching it sure looked like the French team had just given their Führer the Nazi salute. They were ecstatic.[2]

Freddie was under strict orders from British team officials to dip the British flag and give the Olympic salute as he passed under Hitler's gaze. Freddie wasn't politically minded, and didn't care much whether he saluted Hitler or not. He'd lived most of his adult life in the Swiss Alps at the rich playground of St Moritz, and spoke both German and French fluently. He'd mixed socially with the wealthy of Germany, as well as the rest of high society, on the Alpine slopes. He'd heard many rich German holiday-makers and aristocrats speak admiringly of Hitler, saying he had dragged Germany out of economic destruction, that he was restoring German pride and that he had crushed the communists.

As Freddie came abreast of Hitler and his inner circle, he dipped the British flag and briefly held out his arm parallel to the ground in the Olympic salute. Freddie looked up at the balcony and for a moment his eyes locked with the cold black eyes of Adolf Hitler, standing bare headed in the falling snow in a thick black leather coat.

Hitler briefly nodded to accept the salute, but there was no warmth in the gesture. Hitler didn't smile at the giant Australian dipping the British flag. Hitler's face was haughty, stiff and unemotional. Hitler broke his brief eye contact with Freddie, and turned to make a comment to the weasely-looking man standing behind him, who quickly nodded his agreement. That was Joseph Goebbels, Minister for Propaganda, who had planned this spectacle. Freddie turned his head to the front, and continued the march into the parade ground. As the British team behind Freddie gave the Olympic salute, the crowd roared its approval. They took the salute to demonstrate that their former wartime enemy was honouring their Führer.

The official German propaganda film made of the opening ceremony showed much of what happened as Freddie and the other flag bearers marched past Hitler, but they cut out what came next.

The 55 Americans, who were second last in the parade just before the German hosts, did not dip their flag or give any salute as they passed Hitler. The proud Americans to this day are adamant their flag will never dip in salute to any mortal. Besides, the American Olympic team had come close to boycotting the 1936 Olympics because of the Nazi treatment of Jews. According to non-German media reports of the time, the only other Olympic competitor nations to join the small anti-Nazi protest of not dipping their flag to Hitler were Bulgaria and Iceland. Australia, which was second onto the parade ground with its one athlete, speed skater George 'Ken' Kennedy representing the land Down Under, did dip the flag.[3]

The last country to enter the parade ground was the host, Germany, marching under the red, white and black swastika of the Nazi flag. The 77-strong team's synchronised Nazi salute and loud shout of 'Heil Hitler!' as its members passed the Führer was greeted with a massive roar from the crowd. As one, the entire audience saluted back with a sea of arms extending the Nazi salute.

From the very start of Hitler's push to power, southern Bavaria had been a stronghold of the Nazi Party, and the traditional holiday region of Garmisch-Partenkirchen was particularly hard-core Nazi.

The national teams continued their march into the open field at the bottom of the ski jump, where they stood in their allotted spots for the swearing-in ceremony. Hitler didn't display any of his notorious bombast as he declared the 1936 Winter Olympics open. The band played a martial tune and cannons fired in salute. Church bells rang. A massive Olympic flag was unfurled on a hill overlooking the town. The Olympic flame burst into life on a high tower. The flag bearers were ushered to stand in a semi-circle around the elevated platform where German champion skier Willy Bogner took the Olympic oath, holding the Nazi flag in one hand and giving the Nazi salute with the other.

That night Goebbels wrote in his diary:

Thursday. Garmisch covered in snow. Wonderful entry to the town. Big opening ceremony following an old-fashioned ritual. But perhaps it has to be so. The Führer conducted the official opening. Endless cheering from the public. Nearly all nations gave the Hitler salute as they marched past the Führer.[4]

With the official ceremony over, Freddie and the other flag bearers led the athletes out of the parade ground to a stirring victory tune from the military band. By now the snow was almost a foot deep, and the 756 Winter Olympic competitors were keen to get somewhere warm rather than suffer from hypothermia before they even started.

Hitler knew the eyes of the world were on him and his new German Reich during this Winter Olympics. The Propaganda Ministry had gone all out to portray Nazi Germany as an open and welcoming country. There had been a strong possibility that some nations, particularly the United States, would boycott the games. Olympic bosses had awarded Germany the 1936 Olympics – both winter and summer games – in April 1931. At that time Germany was ruled from the historic town of Weimar by a democratic government that was seen as cultured and enlightened, if somewhat chaotic. Nazi brownshirts were still regarded as thugs on the fringe. However, two years later the Nazis emerged from successive elections as the largest party in the Reichstag. Even though the Nazi Party did not have a majority to form government, President von Hindenburg appointed Adolf Hitler as Chancellor on 30 January 1933. Two months later Hitler seized dictatorial powers with the passing of the Enabling Act. So by late 1935, the International Olympic Committee (IOC) faced a very different Germany from the one to which it had awarded the 1936 Olympic Games.

The IOC had to face down Nazi racist ideologues demanding that only Aryans – meaning white men and women – be eligible to compete in the 1936 Games, arguing that they were the only ones who embodied the Olympic ideal. Shortly after the Los Angeles 1932 Olympics, at which several black athletes blitzed track-and-field events, the Nazi newspaper *Völkischer Beobachter* editorialised:

Blacks have no place in the Olympics . . . unfortunately these days one often sees the free white man having to compete with blacks, with Neger [negroes] for the victory palm. This is a disgrace and a degradation of the Olympic idea without parallel. The ancient Greeks would turn over in their graves if they knew what modern men were doing with their sacred national Games. The next [summer] Olympics will be held in Berlin. Hopefully the men in control will do their duty. Blacks must be excluded. We demand it.[5]

The Olympic committee feared widespread boycotts of the 1936 Olympics if the new Nazi government tried to instigate a 'black-free' or 'Jew-free' German Games. Hitler had earlier accused the Olympics of being a secret plot by Jews and Freemasons to spread notions of multiculturalism and athletic equality. Propaganda Minister Joseph Goebbels said in 1933 that sport in Germany had just one task: 'to strengthen the character of the German people, imbuing it with the fighting spirit and steadfast camaraderie necessary in the struggle for its existence'.[6]

However, Goebbels immediately saw the propaganda possibilities of turning the German Olympics into a Nazi spectacular. Through lavish pageantry and overblown martial parades, the world would see the might and power of the new Nazi Germany. So when Olympic officials came to seek the new Nazi regime's attitude to hosting the 1936 Olympics, they were pleasantly surprised to find them receptive to holding back the usual anti-Jewish rhetoric; they even promised to stem the bashings while the Games were underway. After the Enabling Act, German sporting organisations and clubs expelled all Jews, so there was little chance of Hitler being embarrassed by a German Jew winning medals. Hitler told Olympic officials there would be no demand for blacks to be banned from the German Games. The Nazi leaders pledged to be the perfect host for the 1936 Olympics, and to outdo all previous Olympic host nations in welcoming the world to the Games. Olympic officials, particularly IOC president,

DEUTSCHLAND 1936
IV·OLYMPISCHE WINTERSPIELE
GARMISCH-PARTENKIRCHEN
6-16.FEBRUAR 1936

The official poster for the 1936 Winter Olympics
suggests the athlete is giving the Nazi salute.

Henri de Baillet-Latour, were relieved. De Baillet-Latour wrote to his predecessor Baron de Coubertin that at a time when Europe was falling apart with the threat of communism, at least the Nazis had 'an effective plan and method' to hold the Games.[7]

While there was little chance of any black athletes appearing at the Winter Olympics in Garmisch-Partenkirchen, the southern Bavarian town had a long history of hatred of Jews. Hermann Göring lived there after the failed 1923 Nazi coup, and the town made him an honorary citizen. Hitler had wanted to buy a mountain retreat mansion in the area, but when the owner wouldn't sell he built in nearby Berchtesgaden. As soon as Hitler's anti-Semitic Nuremberg Laws were passed in 1935, many Jews were rounded up and expelled from the holiday resort, their shops and businesses seized by local Nazis. For years before the Winter Olympics arrived in Garmisch-Partenkirchen, signs declaring 'Jews not wanted' were posted in the local region. It was forbidden to do business in Yiddish and Jews could not buy or rent property in the town. At night brownshirt *Sturmabteilung* (SA) thugs did their dirty work in lanes and alleys, bashing anyone they thought might be Jewish.

British and American journalists who ventured to Garmisch-Partenkirchen in late 1935 found anti-Semitic signs all over the town. On the highway leading into the town from Munich, signs were posted on the side of the road telling Jews to turn around because they were not welcome. Speed-limit road signs warning of dangerous curves said this didn't apply to Jews; the Nazi joke was that it encouraged Jews to kill themselves. Copies of the Nazi newspaper *Der Stürmer* stood on stands on every street corner and shop counter. Several hotels declared they would not rent rooms to Jews. One British journalist took a photo inside the Partenkirchen ski club that declared, 'No Jews Allowed Here', and the image went around the world.[8] In November 1935 the French Winter Olympic managers announced champion bobsledders Philippe de Rothschild and Jean Rheims, both Jewish, would not compete at Garmisch-Partenkirchen. They chose to boycott. Protest marches were held across France against joining the German Olympics. The French government dismissed the demonstrations as the work of communists. In the United States, Jewish groups called for a boycott of the German Olympics because of the anti-Semitic actions brought in under the Nuremberg Laws. The US Olympic committee argued that this was a domestic political issue, and the Olympics were above politics.

The head of the German Olympic organising committee, Karl Ritter von Halt, was so concerned that these protests could end in failure for the Games that he warned Berlin, 'if the slightest disturbance occurs in Garmisch-Partenkirchen . . . it will not be possible to hold the [Summer] Olympic Games in Berlin because all other nations will then withdraw from the event'.[9] Halt stressed that his only motive was to have a successful Olympics, and that he was 'not expressing these concerns in order to help the Jews'.

His message got through. In December 1935 the order went out from Berlin to remove all anti-Semitic signs from the town, and for the SA not to wear their brownshirt uniform with swastika armbands in the streets. Instead locals were to wear traditional Tyrolean clothing of dark green and hats with feathers. The town council was told to delay plans to expel all Jews from the region until the winter Games were over. Frescoes of Christian scenes painted on the side of buildings were touched up. The

Nazi regime knew it had to suppress the ugly side of Germany for the duration of the Winter Olympics. It was to be the curtain raiser for the much more important Summer Olympics in Berlin six months later. Leni Riefenstahl, the filmmaker who made the ground-breaking 1935 propaganda film *Triumph des Willens* (Triumph of the Will), which helped elevate Hitler to godlike status, wanted to use the Olympics to take Nazi propaganda to the world. The winter Games were to be a dress rehearsal for her documentary team, experimenting with new cameras and filming the athletes from angles she could later use in the larger summer Games in Berlin. The pressure was on the small Bavarian town to be on its best behaviour for the few weeks of the Winter Olympics.

By mid-January 1936, when the American team arrived, the town had been stripped of all anti-Semitic signs. Locals were dressed in traditional clothing, looking as Bavarian as possible. Copies of *Der Stürmer* were placed under shop counters. International journalists were housed together where the Gestapo could keep an eye on them. All film footage of the Games would be taken by Germans from the Propaganda Ministry. It wasn't an easy transformation for the locals. Bavarian police ordered houses, hotels and restaurants run by Jews not to display the German colours of red, white and black. Two dark-skinned members of the Spanish delegation were cursed and assaulted in the street by Nazi SS men. The SS thugs got off with a reprimand from their superiors after they said they were provoked and thought their victims were Jews rather than 'ordinary foreigners'.[10]

Experienced foreign correspondents weren't fooled for a second by the façade presented in Garmisch-Partenkirchen.

Famed American reporter William L Shirer wrote a week before the Olympics began that removing the anti-Semitic signs he'd seen earlier in the town was an attempt to cover-up 'the kind of treatment meted out to Jews in this country'.[11] Shirer said he was then summoned to the local propaganda officer and berated for printing lies. German radio denounced him as 'a dirty Jew trying to torpedo the Winter Olympics at Garmisch with false stories about the Jews and Nazi officials there'.[12] Shirer was not a Jew. After World War II he wrote the international bestseller *The Rise and Fall of the Third Reich.*

A day before the opening ceremony the Propaganda Ministry threw a party for the international press who had come to cover the Winter Olympics. The head of the ministry, Walter Funk, welcomed the men – there were no women reporters at the time – and tried a bit of humour, saying the world only listened to propaganda 'when it convinces them and creates enthusiasm'.[13] Funk told the foreign reporters that the Winter Olympics would give them the opportunity to report on the real Germany, the Germany that loved sport and hosting international athletes, and urged them not to criticise politics 'as they usually do'. A correspondent for the *Wisconsin Jewish Chronicle* wrote that the German Winter Olympics was a 'classic example of irony, anomaly and duplicity'. The anti-Jewish signs that were all over Garmisch-Partenkirchen just a week earlier were 'conspicuous by their absence'. The correspondent noted that when the American Olympians did not give the straight-arm salute as they marched past Hitler the crowd suddenly fell silent. Later in the day when the American ice hockey team defeated Germany, they were booed. 'The Olympic Games should never have been held in the foul Nazi atmosphere,' the American Jewish newspaper stated.[14]

•

As Freddie McEvoy and all the other Winter Olympic athletes arrived in Garmisch-Partenkirchen and settled into their billeted accommodation around the town, it appeared the Games were going to be a disaster, not because of Nazi ideology, but due to the weather. Just one day away from the opening ceremony the mountains and ground around Garmisch-Partenkirchen were completely bare. There was no snow; not a skerrick of the cold white stuff necessary for skiing, skating or sliding. It meant Freddie and his bobsled crew had not been able to practise on the Garmisch-Partenkirchen run. Of course, the German teams had had all winter to practise.

Hitler was due to come into the town by train from Munich the morning of the opening ceremony, 6 February. Panicked organisers were trucking in snow from mountaintops to pack on the ski runs and bobsled course. But then, as darkness fell, a blizzard descended. Locals and Olympians woke to a solid snow cover right across the town and the surrounding mountains. It continued to fall throughout the day. Organisers announced it was 'Hitler weather', a twist on the term that usually described warm sunny days.

For the 28 nations that had turned up for the largest winter Games so far, Garmisch-Partenkirchen looked like a winter fairytale. The façade painting over the evil of the Nazi regime was complete.

CHAPTER 2

FREDDIE FINDS PLEASURE
IS HIS BUSINESS

Freddie's path to leading the British Winter Olympic team at Garmisch-Partenkirchen in 1936 was a winding and extraordinary story. It goes back to the start of the twentieth century.

Freddie's father was Frederick Aloysius McEvoy, a wealthy farmer and considerable landowner in the Gundagai district of New South Wales, where he bred cattle and racehorses. In August 1900 Frederick married Violet Coral Healy, who had been born in Nelson, New Zealand before moving to Australia. Violet was an energetic woman who loved to sing and dance. She performed in the popular Edwardian musical comedy *Florodora*. The production required a chorus line of six pretty 'Florodora Girls', and their fame meant that they invariably married very rich men. Violet and Frederick's son Freddie was born on 12 February 1907 in Melbourne, where his parents had moved to the big city to be among the elite of the horse-breeding and racing society.

A second son, Theodore, was born a few years later. Frederick was a popular man in Melbourne's exclusive clubs. He was accepted for his money, his racing tips and his bonhomie. He was a good all-round sportsman, a golfer and a top cricketer who in 1877 had been a spin bowler for the Victorian state team. Frederick made a fortune from racehorses and was expanding his horse-racing empire, partnering with racehorse owners in Chicago. However, Frederick died in November 1913 when Freddie was just six years old.

It seems that, as a widow, Violet didn't get on well with the grazier's family, because within six months of Frederick dying she sold up his 20,000 acres, 19,000 head of livestock and horses and decided to take Freddie and his younger brother Theodore and leave Australia for the excitement of Europe. She had received a considerable fortune from her late husband's estate, and aside from the sale of assets she inherited a £10,000 trust fund ($1.2 million in today's money) that provided a monthly allowance for Violet and her two sons. Violet was attracted to Europe's high-living society set, and even though she didn't have the aristocratic family background, she did have a small fortune. In high society, as anywhere, money opens doors. Violet took the boys to Switzerland and settled into the exclusive Badrutt's Palace, a swank hotel for the rich and famous perched high on the mountain above St Moritz. Built in 1896, it looked like a mountaintop stone castle. The Palace was the epitome of elegance and exclusivity. No expense was spared in building glittering ballrooms, exotic bedrooms, and luxurious reading rooms and bars; it also had one of the best kitchens in the Alps. The rich flocked to the hotel. This was a playground for the fabulously

E. Feely, G. F. Blake, G. H. Charlton, T. F. Burns, R. Trappes-Lomax, D. P. Hickey, F. J. McEvoy, B. E. Baile, G. St, L. Berkley, F. I. de Caires, A. J. d'Almeida, R. M. Léotaud, G, R. Bird, J. J. Moran, P. Taunton.

Freddie (seated middle row left) in Stonyhurst's 1925 Second XV.

wealthy to carry on as disgracefully as they wished in discreet surroundings. Many made it their home, a retreat from the hurly burly of the lesser classes below.

When World War I broke out in 1914, Freddie, Theodore and Violet found themselves trapped in the Swiss hotel. They couldn't get to England where Violet had intended to put the boys into school. So, while war raged on lands surrounding the Swiss Alps, seven-year-old Freddie played on in neutral Switzerland. His mother's money would last the duration. Badrutt's Palace became their home, a place of unreality, a Shangri-La of peace and fun high in the mountains, far above the death and destruction tearing the world apart below. Young Freddie's skills on the ski slopes improved rapidly. The Palace hotel insisted on carrying on as if the slaughter of millions in the trenches down below was happening on some distant planet. In 1917 White Russian aristocrats arrived as refugees from the communist revolution. The hotel continued its famous balls and dances. By the time the war was over, Freddie was 11 years old. He'd gone through a childhood hidden from the reality of the horrors in the world. Freddie the boy had learned that life was for having fun and pursuing desires.

With the war over, Violet sent the boys to England and enrolled them in the exclusive Jesuit school, Stonyhurst. Freddie was now encased in the heart of British Catholic high society. Founded in 1593, the school looked more like a feudal mansion estate than a school. It was here that Freddie was to make friends with young Englishmen who would later provide his entrée to British upper-crust society. On his arrival, the school noted Freddie spoke excellent French and German, but his academic record was to be mediocre throughout his years at the school. Study and scholastic achievement just didn't interest Freddie. At a time when Latin was the mark of academic success, the school disregarded Freddie's ability in living languages. But Freddie did excel in competitions and sport. In his first year he won chess and ping-pong contests. He did well in athletics, breaking the school record for the long jump. The next year he was in the school tennis team. By his senior school years he was in the soccer firsts, the seconds rugby team and the seconds cricket team.

While sport was clearly Freddie's forte, he also threw himself into the school's theatre club, performing the comic role of Sir Andrew Aguecheek in Shakespeare's *Twelfth Night*. The

Stonyhurst Magazine reported that Freddie presented a 'doleful silly ass rather than a mercurial silly ass . . . the inane laugh, admirable when heard, was heard all too rarely.' The reviewer said Freddie's voice lacked carrying power, but he had a presence on stage. 'He contrived to rouse laughter simply by standing still and letting his silly self be seen.'[1] While acting obviously wasn't Freddie's strong point, he seemed to know how to project himself to make an impression on an audience. In 1925, his final year, he finished school with a flourish on the sporting field, if not academically, winning the school tennis tournament.

Released from the confines of an upper-class English Catholic boarding school, he emerged into the middle of the Roaring 20s. Eighteen-year-old Freddie immediately embarked on a hedonistic life of parties, fast sleds, fast cars and somewhat slower women – those he could catch to help him learn the art of lovemaking. He was a young man at a time when there was a shortage of young men after the devastation of war. Having left Australia at the age of six, Freddie decided he needed to visit his homeland, because he had little memory of the land Down Under. He landed in Sydney aged just 19, and found himself a fish out of water. Sydney lads with whom he tried to strike up friendships ridiculed him for his accent and mocked his airs of refinement. He did make friends with a young tearaway who had been expelled from the exclusive Shore school and who was ploughing his way through the young women of Sydney. His name was Errol Flynn, and for a while Freddie and Errol had a great time. But Freddie realised the rough Sydney of 1926 was not his home, and after just six months he decided to return to the place he knew best.

In 1927 he stepped back into St Moritz and the luxurious confines of Badrutt's Palace. While his mother lived in Lausanne caring for his sickly and shy brother, Freddie was now 20 years old and dashingly handsome and athletic. Freddie rapidly acquired a reputation not only for athleticism on the alpine slopes, but also in the bedrooms of the fabulously rich. He was surrounded by glamour, parties and wealth, but Freddie himself had no means of income, no profession, no inherited fortune and no highly paid career to walk into. He was energetic and poor, surrounded by the idle rich. Somehow Freddie needed to acquire money to live in the style to which he had become accustomed.

He quickly recognised that opportunities were there to be had among the rich and fatuous in the mountain-top playground of St Moritz and on their yachts on the French Riviera. Still fresh to society, Freddie was no doubt inspired by the example of the Badrutt's Palace dancer Maurice Mouvet. Debonair, handsome, smooth talking, immaculately dressed, permanently polite and boasting impeccable manners, Maurice was a welcome fixture at the Badrutt's Palace balls, dances and festivities. Maurice was dance partner extraordinaire for the myriad wealthy widows and divorcees who flocked to Badrutt's for just such activities. He had introduced the tango to Europe, and was an acclaimed dancer. After the war there were many rich widows circulating, and even more cashed-up divorcees whose war-profiteer husbands had made a fortune selling arms and oil, and felt they now deserved a new, younger wife. In 1926 one such visitor to Badrutt's was Eleonora Ambrose, young divorcee and heiress to a Kansas oil baron's fortune. Maurice proved to be an excellent dance partner for her. He literally swept her off her feet on the ballroom floor ᴗed where he impressed with the horizontal

ᴜs was quite the norm at Badrutt's, this particular

ᴗp fling developed into something more serious. They

ᴗed, and overnight Maurice became a millionaire.[2]

Maurice provided Freddie with a vision: a wealthy wife would be the path to finance his life. It was easy, and better than working: find a rich widow or divorcee, impress her with his charm and adventurous spirit as well as his skill in the boudoir, and bingo, marriage and money would fall into his lap. While Freddie wasn't a great dancer, he certainly had all the other qualifications – he was dashingly handsome, charming, considerate, well mannered, immaculately dressed, impeccably mannered, multilingual, a good listener and a young man with an air of danger about him that ladies of leisure couldn't resist. He was also becoming quite adept with the cards at the casino and was able to provide profitable returns on the tables – provided a lady could be persuaded to provide some start money.

But not everything went Freddie's way. The Great Depression hit, and Freddie's cash cows started to dry up. It was a tough time, even for wealthy widows and divorcees. In 1930 Freddie was down on his luck, but he was an eternal optimist and always on the lookout for adventure. He caught a ship to New York City, the city of dreams. He had no assets except for his charm and a suitcase full of fine clothes. Broke and friendless in a strange city, he got a job selling books door to door. Friends said later that he was so destitute he sometimes had to sleep in the subway. But no matter how bad things got, Freddie always kept his appearance sharp and immaculate. His moustache was properly trimmed and his clothes pressed and clean. His tie was always straight and his shoes highly polished. And there was always a cheeky smile on his handsome young face, the kind of smile and glint in the eye that women couldn't resist. A friend at the time, Niccolò de Quattrociocchi, said that even in poverty Freddie cut an elegant figure. 'He would go without breakfast in order to buy [shoe] polish,' he said.[3] Another friend recounted the story of Freddie once telling him that he'd been invited to a lunch. The friend replied, 'That's great, now you won't be hungry for a while.' Freddie shook his head sadly. 'I declined the invitation,' he told his friend. 'If I were to eat lunch today I might acquire a bad habit and want to eat lunch every day.'[4]

Freddie proved to be an adept salesman. Despite the poor economic times, he was so successful at persuading people to buy the books he presented that his employer gave him a medal for excellent work. Freddie treasured the medal – his first. After struggling on the fringes at Stonyhurst and living a precarious life since school as a party boy, it was the first real recognition of his ability. By the time Freddie returned to Europe, he had developed a new gritty determination to succeed. He had tasted poverty, and he didn't like it one bit. He'd learned that the only person who was going to really provide him with a living was himself. The experience left a new ruthless streak in the young man. He was determined to secure money by whatever means necessary.

When he came back to Europe after four hard years in New York, Freddie's return was immediately welcomed by the high-society party scene. Everybody loved Freddie. Freddie was back in his element. He added fast cars to his reckless need for speed – whenever he could find someone to let him behind a wheel. Freddie was also building a reputation as a skilled card player, enjoying considerable success at the baccarat tables in the ritzy casinos of Monte Carlo and Cannes.

Liberated ladies with fortunes had their own network, swapping tips on who among the good-looking young men in acceptable social circles could perform in the bedroom, which of them was discreet and who could be trusted. Some went through husbands like a cat lapping up milk. Having a title certainly helped a penniless count or baron desperately trying to be snatched up by a rich American heiress. Freddie had no title, whether it be phony or real. He had only his physical attributes. As an Australian with a polished but relaxed and irreverent air about him, he was unique among the stuffy European upper crust. He worked hard to perfect his amorous skills and staying power in the bedroom, just as he trained to be the best and fastest in the new sport of bobsledding. This was an era when single women could not attend functions or go out to nightclubs without a male companion. Freddie set up an exclusive niche business supplying a tight-knit stable of trustworthy, good-looking, single young men who could be relied on to hold their fork correctly and entertain ladies needing company or as escorts to social functions. And, of course, to provide other more intimate services if required.

Chronicler of high society ins and outs, Dean Jennings, wrote that Freddie was:

> either a satyr or a saint – a satyr if he moved into your home and made love to your wife or mistress, and he seems to have been singularly successful in such nocturnal pursuits. He was a saint if he happened to be your friend, for one could be

assured of his unswerving loyalty. He had plenty of friends and few enemies.[5]

Jennings wrote that Freddie became skilled with a gun and boxing, and he knew how to defend himself. Irate husbands and jealous boyfriends of enthusiastic female volunteers for Freddie's attention learned to keep out of his way. But it rarely came to blows, or even raised voices. Freddie charmed them all. 'There were rumours, that he had been a smuggler, a high-priced gigolo, a swindler in a genteel way, and who could beguile and befriend the husbands he had betrayed,' Jennings later wrote.[6]

It was during one such adventure in London that Freddie again ran into a dashing fellow Australian who was to have a major impact on his life. In 1934 Errol Flynn was just starting to act on the provincial stage in England after having tremendous adventures sailing around the Pacific and South East Asia. The two men met at a party and realised they had crossed paths eight years earlier in Sydney when they were both teenagers. They immediately recognised that they had grown up to become as alike as peas in a pod, even looking like each other. For a while in London the two young Aussie rakes sought to outdo each other in their pursuit of willing women. They became firm friends, a friendship that was to be renewed years later when Errol Flynn became a major Hollywood movie star.

But the key to the big money that would finance his expensive lifestyle still eluded Freddie. There were plenty of enthusiastic admirers among the wealthy women willing to support him, including Barbara Hutton, the richest woman in the world. But as for marriage, Freddie didn't have the European aristocratic title the American millionairesses desired. Barbara Hutton was to marry a succession of counts, barons and princes, but not Freddie. Freddie was now in his late 20s and while he was having fun, he was starting to grow concerned that he hadn't snared one of the rich women he'd been aiming to inveigle into a wedding ceremony.

Freddie threw himself into bobsledding. He loved speed and risking his neck to get down the slope faster and faster. To survive and emerge alive from such death-defying acts was the greatest thrill. Freddie was an adrenalin junkie. In 1935 he won the European bobsled championship held at the highly dangerous Cresta run at St Moritz. That brought him to the attention of the British Olympic officials, and they offered the Australian the leading place in the British bobsled team for the 1936 Winter Olympics.

It was the breakthrough Freddie had been looking for. That recognition threw off any doubts he might have had about the path he had taken. He couldn't give a stuff about the future and how he would earn a living. The world was his oyster, and he was having a ball.

As Freddie told anyone who asked him what he did for a living: 'Pleasure is my business.'[7]

CHAPTER 3

FREDDIE, OLYMPIC BOBSLED CHAMPION

Six teams of bobsledders had already shot down the 1525-metre run before it was the turn of Freddie McEvoy's team. Freddie knew they were already up against it. The French team had turned up to the Olympics with a revolutionary new enclosed sled; Freddie could see it would reduce air drag and provide a huge advantage. Freddie and his team had a sled design that hadn't changed much in 20 years. It was a crude machine, like a go-kart on skates that careened down the mountain run at speeds hitting more than 80 miles an hour (129 kph). Each team had four starts at the run – one in the morning and one in the evening when the ice was hardest, the same again the second day. The four runs would be added together and the team with the lowest aggregate time over the four runs declared the winner.

Freddie's task as skipper of the four-man team was to steer the sled to find the fastest path down the ice tunnel to the end. He had to decide when to steer up the curved walls to slingshot their way out of the bends. Too far and the sled could fly over the top of the rim. Too low and they would lose valuable speed. Turn at the wrong time and it could tip over the sled, sending the men crashing head on into the ice wall at tremendous speed. The sled was crude with little real control, but Freddie was determined to get them down the 1.5 kilometre run without crashing.

The score of the previous team's run went up on the scoreboard. Schweiz II had just completed the run in an extremely fast 1 minute 22.45 seconds. Freddie knew the Swiss bobsled team very well. He'd grown up with the Schweiz II skipper Pierre Musy at St Moritz, and they'd competed on the famous long Cresta run that took more than 3 minutes to zoom down the mountain. He was the one who gave fearless Freddie the name 'Suicide' Freddie. Freddie turned to his three team-mates.

'Right, that's the time we have to beat. Let's do it,' Freddie said calmly. He knew them well. They'd trained together for months. It was a motley crew with only one bona fide Englishman among them. The brakeman Charles Green was 21 and built like a bull rhino from his native South Africa. The third man, Guy Dugdale, aged 31, was from British aristocracy. Born in Stratford-upon-Avon, he was the grandson of the Earl of Warwick and had the family money to play with the wealthy at Swiss ski resorts. The second man, James Cardno, aged 24, was a Scot and a good friend of Freddie's. They'd teamed up on bobsleds for the past few years in races across Switzerland. The team had learned to react instantly to Freddie's signals to lean to one side or the other to balance the sled in turns, to bob forward to speed up the sled, and lean back to slow it down. The rest was just hanging on for grim death as they rocketed down the steep icy run, bones rattling from the rutted ice inches below them. Their lives were literally in Freddie's hands – the hands of a crazy speed freak called Suicide.

Two members of the team slid the sled back and forth to make sure the skates were clear of any ice. Freddie was already sitting in the driver's seat, his thickly gloved hands gripping the small steering wheel, heavily booted feet on the pedals that helped shift the front of the sled. Guy Dugdale was seated in the third position where Charlie Green could push on his shoulders at the start. Officials signalled that the course was clear. Freddie took a deep breath and shouted: 'Go!'

The two sprinters ran alongside the sled, pushing hard against the shoulders of the seated men. James gave Freddie's shoulders one last heave and leapt in behind him. The sled was picking up speed quickly as it tipped over the edge and began the steep downhill run, the track running straight down for the first few hundred metres. Finally, Charles gave one last tremendous push on Guy's shoulders and hopped into the last seat. This was the most dangerous spot on the sled. The bucking sled sometimes threw the last man off, sending him crashing into the ice wall. Sometimes the last man got left behind at the start, unable to keep up and jump into his seat as the sled accelerated down the slope.

Faster and faster the sled sped down the first hundred metres. It was almost straight down and they picked up tremendous speed. The running skates were shrieking now. Freddie's skilled driving kept them from touching the sides of the run. Every touch would slow them down. One slight turn at 200 metres, then a steeper turn to the left called the Enders Curve at 400 metres.

Freddie took the curve in the middle of the 3-metre-high bank, picking up more speed as they hurtled on towards the slalom section. The force of the turn crushed the four men into the canvas seats – no suspension in this rattler. A slight turn to the right, then an immediate hard turn to the left, a sharp turn to the right, then a deceptively hard turn to the left. The sudden turns snapped the men's heads from side to side. Freddie's grip on the steering wheel tightened even more as he worked hard to keep the sled's skates in the best groove in the ice that he was picking out just ahead of them.

This swerving slalom section slowed down less skilful bobsledders, but Freddie's team leaned slightly down from the banks at each turn so they didn't waste valuable time scraping the top of the bank. They were really moving now, over 125 kilometres

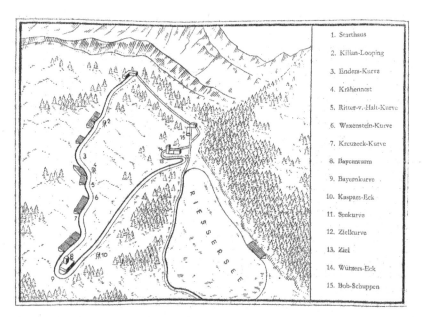

1. Starthaus
2. Kilian-Looping
3. Enders-Kurve
4. Krähennest
5. Ritter-v.-Halt-Kurve
6. Waxenstein-Kurve
7. Kreuzeck-Kurve
8. Bayernturm
9. Bayernkurve
10. Kaspars-Eck
11. Seekurve
12. Zielkurve
13. Ziel
14. Würzers-Eck
15. Bob-Schuppen

Map of the 1936 Olympic bobsled run.

an hour. The sled's skates shrieked on the ice and freezing spray sliced into their faces, forcing tears from their eyes right through the goggles. The wind and ice burned through their gloves gripping the bucking sled. The jagged ice flashed by just centimetres from their bodies. The wood and metal sled rattled, shook, swerved, bounced and ground along the ice as Freddie searched for the fastest rut in the pitted ice.

Now came the most dangerous section of the course – the *Bayernkurve*, the Bavarian Curve. It wasn't a curve so much as a hairpin bend, a complete 180-degree U-turn. Get it just slightly wrong and the sled and its occupants would hurl over the top of the bank and fly into the snow-covered bushes beyond. This was the most spectacular spot to watch the bobsleds. The international press contingent was packed into a grandstand with a good view, but Nazi VIPs were in a far better spot in a building right in the middle of the *Bayernkurve*. All were waiting to see a sled hit the bank and fly over the edge, or bounce back with an overcorrection and crash into the opposite wall. They weren't to be disappointed. The carnage was coming. There would be blood on the ice this day.

But not due to Freddie. He hit the bank sweetly, the sled flashing to the top of the steep 4-metre-high bank. This was the critical moment. Too fast and the sled would hit the top and the uppermost skate would flap over the lip, throwing the crude speed machine out of control. Too slow and the sled wouldn't make use of the slingshot effect at the end of the U-turn, and the race would be gone. Freddie saw the best groove in the ice that would hurtle the sled around the U-turn, and he used all his strength to stick in it. The G force going around the hairpin bend against the steep bank was enormous, grinding the four big men into their seats, forcing the air out of their lungs as they gripped the leather and steel sides of the sled, desperately holding on so as not to be thrown out. It took sheer muscle power and gritty determination to get around this bend without sliding off the frail seats.

As the *Bayernkurve* came to its end, Freddie pulled hard on the wheel and the sled bucked and surged back towards the centre of the track. He counter-steered to avoid hitting the wall on the other side and the British sled shot out of the curve and flew down the next straight faster than it had entered the deadly turn. The four men seized the chance to get their breath back, heaving in the freezing air as the sled flashed on at 130 kph. The centrifugal force had just about crushed them as they leaned into the curve, clinging to the leather straps inside the sled.

Faster and faster still the sled rocketed on. Seven hundred metres of dead-straight run – an opportunity to pick up incredible speed as they raced towards the end. But it was also a lethal trap. Up ahead was one final hairpin turn before the finish line. The Czechoslovakian team, on the second start of the day, had hit this final turn too fast and crashed out just 10 metres before the finishing line. A chaotic jumble of men and sled slid over the line. Several of the Czech team were rushed to hospital.

Suicide Freddie wasn't going to slow down. The sled hurtled towards the *Zielkurve*, the finishing curve. Freddie had a good line to the last steep bank of ice. Bugger caution. He roared in at full speed, wrestling the bucking steering wheel to keep the sled from accelerating to the top of the bank. Behind him, his team gripped the sled firmly with their right hands while leaning left and sticking out their left hands, touching the ice bank as the three men fought the sled to stay inside the run. Higher and higher rose the sled as it swept around the hard curve. With just centimetres to spare from the top of the bank, the sled whipped around out of the curve and back into the straight. Almost out of control now, Freddie wrestled with the wheel to keep the front skates on the middle groove. Half a second later, the four-man British bobsled team raced through the electric light beam that recorded the time at the end of the run.

One minute 23.38 seconds. Almost a whole second behind Schweiz II. Freddie was furious with himself. In the world of bobsledding this was a huge lead. He knew his team would have to do a whole lot better on their second run of the day. Yet as the remaining teams completed their runs, Freddie's hopes slowly rose. His team was almost two seconds faster than the two heavily favoured teams from the United States. Freddie's team was 0.09 of a second faster than Schweiz I.

Best of all for Freddie, Deutschland II, the third-last runner, was completely out of the contest – the team crashed at the *Bayernkurve*. And not just a minor accident. The waiting crowd had the spectacular crash they'd been waiting for. The number two German team got their approach wrong and their sled tipped over on the bank as they tried to stop hurling over the top and come spinning down the steep slope. The men crashed head first into the wall on the other side. Helmets, gloves, bodies and bits of sled flew into the air inside a cloud of snow and ice thrown up by the impact. As soon as the four Germans slid to a stop, rescue officials were there, deeply concerned that there might be fatalities. The four men were rushed to hospital. The watching

Nazi VIPs had their spectacular accident, but not with the team they wanted. The German team all survived.

It takes a lot of courage to go down the bobsled run after such a wipeout, and Czechoslovakia II had already seen their first team smash just short of the finishing line. Nevertheless, they bravely pulled in a good time – three seconds behind the British team. The final team to go down in that first run of the morning session was Deutschland I. This was a crack team who knew the Garmisch-Partenkirchen course like the back of their hands. They'd been practising on it all winter. Unperturbed by the loss of their comrades in Deutschland II, the Deutschland I team blitzed the course, coming in at a staggering 1 minute 20.73 seconds, the fastest so far. They were well out in front of the Swiss teams, and almost three seconds ahead of Freddie and his team.

The bobsledders had several hours to rest and recuperate before the afternoon run. The first run had started at 8am, and the weather had to remain cold enough for the ice to stay frozen through the middle of the day. The second run started at 4.30pm, just as the sun was starting to go down. Cold weather had swept in and the ice had firmed up a lot; workers had smoothed the track and replaced the blocks of ice on the high bends. Freddie's team would be among the last to go down on this second run of the day. He was happy about that. His main worry was visibility, and the ragged tracks carved out by the preceding teams.

Schweiz I had a superb run – chopping four seconds off their first run of the day. So did Schweiz II. The United States I team slashed an incredible six seconds off their first run. The next team to go down the run, Italy II, must have been inspired by the Americans to risk everything, but the Italians lost control at the *Bayernkurve* and had a spectacular spill over the top of the bank. Bodies flew everywhere, and the ambulance men once again rushed to what was becoming a death curve. The Italian driver suffered crushed ribs and a broken nose.

It took a bit of time to fix the bank of the *Bayernkurve*, and the delay may have put the men in Deutschland I off their rhythm. They flopped, coming in more than two seconds slower than their amazing first run of the day. Freddie thought his team might still be in it – maybe fourth or fifth if they had a good run.

Freddie and his men had long talks about where they could shave off a fraction of a second, how high they should run up the banks of the *Bayernkurve* and *Zielkurve*. Freddie decided they had to take a risk to get a faster start. All three men would now sprint alongside pushing the sled. Guy would jump in first after a few steps, secure his position, then James and finally Charlie. It was a risky manoeuvre because if one of them lost their footing or missed their seat when they jumped on the sled, it would be the end of their run. The French II team had already been disqualified when their fancy bathtub-looking sled took off and the final runner couldn't get into the sled properly and was dragged more than 50 metres. He ended up having his damaged leg amputated.

But Freddie had trained them hard for this and he was confident it would work. It had to. Sure enough, the extra push start worked like clockwork. The faster start got them away to a much better run, and they shaved a good three seconds off their first run. At the end of the first day the placements were: Schweiz II, Schweiz I, Britain, Deutschland I, United States I, France I and Belgium II. Freddie and his team in third place

Freddie and his team prepare for their second run.

were just 0.19 seconds behind second-placed Schweiz I, and 2.33 seconds behind first-placed Schweiz II. But the Germans were hot on their heels, just 0.22 of a second behind in fourth. It was still wide open. The second day of the competition was going to be a cliffhanger.

The next day, 12 February, was a far better day for bobsledding. At the crack of dawn Freddie looked out the window and saw with a thrill that it was overcast, with very little wind, and the temperature was hovering at just above zero. And it was his 29th birthday. It had to be an omen. Today would be a good day.

Deutschland I had the first run of the morning. Going first isn't good. There are no grooves carved in the ice by preceding sleds to follow. Any loose snow on the track will slow you down.

The Germans bombed it: a full second slower than the previous day. They were getting worse, not better. United States I were also one second slower than their last run. So were both Swiss teams. Freddie was surprised. He thought it would be a fast day. The British team were among the last runners of the morning. It wasn't too bad a run, at least not as bad as the others – just half a second slower than the previous evening. It would be tough to catch the Swiss team, but should be enough to hold their position in third or fourth place. It would all come down to the late-afternoon runs.

The draw for the fourth and final run in the afternoon put Freddie and his team as the third sled to kick off, just before Schweiz II. Schweiz I was to be the last runner of the day. United States I and Deutschland I were taking off in the middle of the pack. It wasn't ideal for the British team, but Freddie was confident they could hold their position and maybe even pass the Swiss team into second place.

It was now or never, and Freddie threw any remnants of caution to the wind. A huge push start, down the straight, through the slalom, zipping around the *Bayernkurve*, flawless acceleration down the last straight and a controlled final turn to the finish line. Everything fitted into place perfectly, allowing Freddie's team to pull off a tremendous run. They came in at 1 minute 19.11 seconds, a full 1.5 seconds off their morning run and their fastest run of the competition. Freddie had thrown down the gauntlet to the second-placed Swiss.

All they could do now was watch the results from the other teams roll in. Schweiz II did well, shaving 0.58 of a second off their morning run and cementing their gold medal. Once again

Deutschland I failed to pull off a medal-winning run – better than the morning run but not enough to catch the leaders. Now the real battle was for silver between Freddie's motley crew and Schweiz I. It would all come down to the final run of the day. Schweiz I would have to pull off a terrifically fast run to hold on to their second place against Freddie's strong challenge. In the fading light, the Swiss team got a great start and flew around the course, roaring in at 1 minute 18.61 seconds – the fastest time of the entire Olympic bobsled competition.

That miraculous last run by the Swiss pipped Freddie and his team for a silver medal by two-thirds of a second. The final combined times of the four runs were Schweiz II 5 minutes, 19.85 seconds, Schweiz I 5 minutes, 22.73 seconds, Britain 5 minutes, 23.41 seconds. Freddie's team had won Britain's first ever medal in bobsledding. They'd beaten the fancied United States into fourth by 0.72 seconds. To the host nation's embarrassment, the famous Deutschland I team ended up coming seventh. The French, with their snazzy bathtub-like sled, came ninth.[1]

Freddie McEvoy had just become the first Australian to win a medal at any Winter Olympic Games. It should have given him a place in Australia's sporting history. Unfortunately, because he was competing for Britain, his name isn't listed in the proud annals of Australian Olympic achievements. His feat barely got a mention in the newspapers in Australia. Bobsledding just wasn't on the Australian sports radar. The only other Australian at the 1936 Winter Olympics was speed skater George 'Ken' Kennedy. He carried the Australian flag into the opening ceremony for the first time in any Winter Olympics, but he bombed in his competition, coming 33rd out of 35. The official Australian

Olympic records say it wasn't until 1994 that Australia won its first winter Olympic medal, a bronze in relay speed skating. Freddie was wiped from history by the officials. It wouldn't be the only time.

That night Freddie didn't get the chance to celebrate his bronze medal and his birthday. He had to rest. The next day he started in the competition for the two-man bobsled. Once again Freddie was in the driver's seat. Behind him was his mate, the Scot James Cardno. There were four runs down the mountain over two days, just as for the four-man. Freddie was up against two-man specialists from the United States and Germany in the 23 teams. It was a big ask to have him back up for the two-man against such a huge field after the exhausting four-man, but Freddie was made of tough stuff and was in peak physical condition.

After the first day Freddie was coming fifth. The two American teams were first and third, with the Schweiz II team in second place. Freddie would have to do much better on the second day. He was just half a second behind the fourth-placed Schweiz I team, but two-and-a-half seconds behind United States II in third. He'd have to blitz the run on the second day to catch up to the medal contenders. The first run on the second day wasn't good: Freddie finished a good two seconds behind the bronze-medal contender. But the Schweiz I team in fourth place had an absolute shocker – a full 10 seconds slower than Freddie. The British team jumped into fourth place, but were now threatened by the Deutschland I team, who'd had a great morning run.

The United States II team were first down the mountain in the afternoon run. They pulled off a good 1 minute 22.16 seconds. It would take an enormous effort to dislodge them from the bronze-medal position. United States I and Schweiz II sealed their gold and silver positions with the fastest runs of the competition. Freddie was among the last runners of the afternoon. He and James agreed they would risk everything, hold nothing back. If they could shave three or four seconds off their run, they could squeak into a medal.

Freddie and James pulled off an amazing run, slashing an incredible six seconds off their morning run. But it wasn't enough. When the times for all four runs were compiled, Freddie and James missed out on a bronze medal by 6.29 seconds, a convincing margin. It was the morning run that had sunk them. Still, they came fourth, beating the German teams into fifth and sixth position. It was a very creditable performance by the Aussie and the Scot, up against highly trained full-time bobsledders.

That night Freddie and his team-mates celebrated hard, both belatedly for his birthday and because it was the day before the end of the Garmisch-Partenkirchen Olympics. Nearly all the athletes had finished their events and were ready to let off steam. Freddie was in his element. He loved women, and women loved him. Attractive Norwegian ice dancers, blonde French skiers, lithe Austrian downhill racers, even the German girl who'd carried the sign into the opening ceremony – all were targets for Freddie's Olympian bedroom efforts. His team-mates were staggered at Freddie's success in the unofficial Olympic event: the relay sexual pursuit. After years of training, young Olympic athletes are in peak physical condition. They want to unwind and partake of physical activities restricted during the discipline of training and being constantly watched by coaches and team managers. With those restrictions lifted at last, both male and female Olympians were keen to fulfil nature's urges.

With an Olympic medal to his credit, Freddie was determined to score new victories in the great fornicating fandango, one he hoped would end with another medal in the form of a wedding ring from a wealthy woman. When one of the bobsledders derided Freddie McEvoy as nothing but a playboy and asked American bobsledder Billy Fiske how he could admire such a man, Fiske replied: 'I admire anyone who can get away with something that I could not do myself.'[2]

CHAPTER 4

FREDDIE'S NEED FOR SPEED

The day after Freddie narrowly missed out on a second Olympic medal in the two-man bobsled, it was time for the closing ceremony of the Winter Olympics in Garmisch-Partenkirchen. Medals for the entire Games were to be handed out at the evening pageant. The Games had been a spectacular success, at least as far as organisation went, and had provided plenty of positive publicity for the Nazi regime.

One by one, the national teams marched behind their flags into the arena to tunes from the military band. The field was surrounded by massive Nazi flags, the red and black swastika contrasting with the white snow that covered the fairytale mountain scenery. Medal winners came in last – gold, silver and bronze winners for each event in their correct order. The Olympians stood in long rows, behind flags of the 28 competing nations fluttering in the gentle breeze.

Silence fell over the crowd. Outside the arena Freddie could hear a swelling of cheers and the cries of 'Heil Hitler!' growing to a crescendo. Then he saw the Führer walk into the arena. He was in a thick, black leather coat, army cap on his head. Just behind him in lockstep were his deputies Hermann Göring and Joseph Goebbels, then a long line of Olympic and Nazi high officials. The crowd instantly raised their right arms as one, and screamed out ecstatically, 'Heil Hitler, Heil, Heil!' The sound was almost deafening.

German soldiers in field grey with weapons shouldered lined up on the other side of the field came to attention with immaculate precision, stamped their feet and presented arms. This was the first time in the Games that Freddie had seen so many German soldiers. The organisers had held back on the militaristic element in the Olympic ceremony until this final moment. Freddie wasn't aware of it, but this was the work of Goebbels and filmmaker Leni Riefenstahl, who together saw the potential of the Olympic Games as a Nazi spectacular to impress the rest of the world in Berlin that summer. The Propaganda Ministry's film of the 1936 Winter Olympics, *Jugend der Welt* [Youth of the World] was shown 750,000 times in more than 40 countries of the world.[1]

Hitler strode to the podium and took his place above a massive red and black swastika banner. His deputies and Olympic officials spread out behind him. The medals were to be awarded by Olympic officials, not the Führer himself. Throughout the Games Hitler had kept himself very much to official Olympic duties. Foreign observers were relieved the Führer didn't use the Winter Olympics to deliver one of his bombastic crowd-stirring speeches.

He'd not gone to the huge dinners given for a thousand visitors and Olympic officials that were held in a giant hall in Munich. The Winter Olympics had been short on big-name guests such as Britain's newly crowned King Edward VIII, who had been a regular skier at Kitzbühel in Austria and was known to have pro-German views, but the Nazi hierarchy did welcome the crown prince of Sweden, a former crown prince of the old kingdom of Prussia, and Crown Princess Juliana of The Netherlands.

One noted VIP from Britain was Lord Londonderry, cousin to Winston Churchill, confidant of King Edward VIII and the most outspoken English aristocrat praising Hitler for his achievements in Germany. He had been British Secretary of State for Air until recently, and Hermann Göring took him under his wing at the Games so they could discuss Air Force matters. On his return to Britain, Londonderry declared that Hitler's aim was peace with France and Germany. Lady Londonderry was all atwitter over Hitler, saying he had an 'arresting personality' with wonderful far-seeing eyes. 'I felt I was in the presence of someone truly great, he is simple, dignified, humble. He is a leader of men.'[2]

The world's press gave a largely favourable report on Nazi behaviour at Garmisch-Partenkirchen. American journalist William L Shirer, who had a run-in with Nazi bureaucrats before the Games, said at the end of the Winter Olympics that it had been a 'pleasant interlude' in covering Nazi Germany, largely due to the beautiful scenery and 'rosy cheeked girls in their skiing outfits'. Shirer later interpreted the Winter Olympics as an artful snow job.[3] Another American journalist, Westbrook Pegler of the *Chicago Daily News*, wrote: 'It was a magnificent display of strong-arm authority, wholly corroborating the old tradition that

Hitler signs autographs for Olympic athletes as well as German crowds.

the German people's favourite sport is to be shoved around by men in uniform.[4] Pegler was refused a visa to cover the Summer Olympics in Berlin.

What the journalists and foreign officials didn't know was that behind the scenes Hitler was holding secret military talks with senior Nazi officials who had come to watch the Games. Goebbels, Göring, publisher of *Der Stürmer* Julius Streicher, Nazi Interior Minister Wilhelm Frick, senior army generals . . . all of Hitler's key lieutenants were at Garmisch-Partenkirchen. Buoyed by the positive publicity of a resurgent Germany emerging from the Winter Olympics, it was during the Games that Hitler made the decision to act on his long-simmering plan to reoc-cupy the Rhineland. The Treaty of Versailles ending the Great War had ordered all German troops to be expelled from the Rhineland, giving France a demilitarised buffer zone along its border. Hitler had long planned to send German troops into the Rhine Valley to regain military control over Germany's romantic heartland. On 12 February, while Freddie was winning a medal in the four-man bobsled on his birthday, Hitler secretly ordered the German army to get ready to move.[5] Hitler was taking a huge risk. It was possible France would resist the German army marching into the Rhineland, and if France decided to fight over the territory, the weak German army would easily have been beaten. Hitler would probably have been forced out of power. But with the success of the Olympics bolstering him, Hitler was confident France would do nothing to stop him. After all, he'd seen the British and French Olympians salute him as they'd marched past in the opening ceremony.

But all that backroom military plotting and the dark clouds that were gathering over Europe were far from the minds of the Olympic sportsmen at the closing ceremony. One by one, the event medallists stepped up on the three-tiered steps of the winner's box to receive their honours. German medal winners gave Hitler the Nazi salute and the crowd cheered 'Heil, Heil,

Heil' and joined the Führer returning the stiff-armed salute. When it came to the four-man bobsled event, Freddie took the stand in his white jumper marked with the Union Jack and stood stock still, arms by his sides, as did the Swiss gold and silver medal winners as their national anthem was played. Their team mates stood behind them; only the team captain got to stand on the victor's dais. The crowd was silent – there were no Germans to cheer and salute.

Germany didn't do as well as expected at the Winter Olympics. Norway was the clear winner of the Games with seven gold, five silver and three bronze medals. Germany came a distant second in the medal tally with three gold and three silver. On top of Freddie's bronze, Britain had won an unexpected gold medal in ice hockey. Nearly the entire British team lived in Canada and played in the ice-hockey league there, something that really annoyed the Canadians, who won only a silver. The empire had won Britain's medals for them.

The Austrians had a right to feel cheated. Their best skiers weren't allowed to compete at the Olympics because they earned a living as ski instructors. They were classified as professionals and therefore barred from the amateur Games. It didn't matter that German skiers were members of clubs that covered their living expenses, enabling them to ski full time; they were classified as amateurs. Austria ended up with one gold, one silver and two bronze medals. But when the military band came to play the Austrian national anthem it sounded to the crowd very much like they were playing the German anthem 'Deutschland, Deutschland Über Alles'. Nazi Germany had appropriated the melody composed by Austrian Joseph Haydn from the Austrian imperial anthem 'God Save Franz our Emperor'.[6]

It was dark by the time all the medals had been handed out. On the slalom slope hundreds of skiers with flaming torches descended the slope in long looping lines. At the end they lined the slope on two sides and turned their attention to the top of the hill. Lights on the field were suddenly extinguished and searchlights shot out to focus on the naval guard high on the hill where the Olympic flag was fluttering. Slowly the flag was lowered while the military band played a sad dirge. As the flag finally reached the ground, a series of cannons fired. The Olympic flame was gradually turned down until it was extinguished. The field was in darkness for several seconds until the lights went back on and the band struck up the *'Horst Wessel Lied'*, the Nazi anthem. Fireworks exploded out over the ski slope. Cannons fired around the parade ground. As one, the massive crowd roared 'Heil Hitler!' and went on and on giving the Nazi salute. The closing was far more militaristic than the opening ceremony. Goebbels and Leni Riefenstahl were trying out techniques for turning the Olympic Summer Games to be held in Berlin into a Nazi spectacular to dazzle the world.

For Hitler and his cronies, the Winter Olympics were a resounding success. Olympic officials, athletes and the world's press came away with positive impressions. All the athletes and officials were invited to a festive dinner in a Munich beer hall where the Germans showed how they could let their hair down. They put on cabaret acts mocking the strictness of Olympic organisers – but not the Nazis – with such witty songs as 'Ode to the White Sausage' (a staple food of southern Germany) and a comic dance troupe performing the snowflake ballet. The US Olympic Committee said its athletes found the 1936 Winter Games 'the nearest approach to fulfilling the ideas of the founders of the modern Olympic Games than any heretofore held'.[7] Any talk of boycotting the summer Games in Berlin disappeared. Shortly after the international journalists and athletes left Garmisch-Partenkirchen, the anti-Jewish signs went back up, SA uniforms went back on and *Der Stürmer* was selling on every street corner. Woe betide anyone who didn't pick up a copy.

While Nazi leaders got a huge boost from the winter Games, the effect on the life of Freddie McEvoy was enormous. The Australian playboy now had a deserved international reputation as a top-ranked sportsman, a phenomenal athlete with a need for speed. Freddie was the toast of the nightclubs of Paris. He was feted in the palatial mansions of the French Riviera. He was elevated beyond being a mere pretty party boy to a man of substance – even if he were still a man without money. Freddie increased his efforts courting wealthy female admirers. He was on the hunt for an available millionairess to whom he could hitch his speeding wagon.

Paris was the centre of world culture in the mid- to late 1930s. Europe's intelligentsia and upper-crust socialites were drawn like moths to the vibrant and decadent life of Paris. They filled the restaurants and cafes of the Left Bank talking of art, paintings, books, movies, theatre, fashion, music and sex scandals. There was an intoxicating air of excitement in the city. The French had been keen to put the horrors of World War I behind them, and many were determined to party like there would be no tomorrow. By 1936 Paris was starting to emerge from the hard times of the

Great Depression, and there was a mood of optimism. For the socialites it was vitally important to be up with the very latest news of who was sleeping with whom, which socialite had kicked which social climber out of their bed, and most important of all, who was about to marry whom and how much money would be fleeced before it ended in tears.

These were known as *les annees folles,* the crazy years, when writers such as Ernest Hemingway, WB Yeats, Henry Miller and Ezra Pound, artists such as Pablo Picasso, Max Ernst, Salvador Dali, Marc Chagall and Amedeo Modigliani, and musicians and composers such as George Gershwin, Erik Satie, Maurice Ravel and Igor Stravinsky all made Paris their home. Music halls such as the Moulin Rouge and Folies Bergère were packed. Maurice Chevalier charmed the international set with his so-very-French ways. Edith Piaf brought audiences to tears with her frail, heart-felt singing. Black dancer Josephine Baker shocked and delighted audiences with her risqué erotic performances and her notorious banana dress, earning acclaim she could never get in her native America.

Life in Paris was far more liberated than in the United States or Britain. Brothels were legal and sexual relations outside of marriage were regarded more as sport than a moral disgrace. Brothel madams were considered service providers and a crucial part of society. Their soirees attracted the elite citizens of France. Everyone was accepted and, unlike in America, no one was barred for the colour of their skin or their ethnic background. In discreet theatres, exhibitions of various sexual perversions were conducted live on stage. Invitations to orgies in palatial mansions were much sought after.

Tens of thousands of Americans made Paris their home as post-war prosperity in the United States gave the mighty dollar enormous purchasing power in France. Parisian politics were volatile and argued with passion. Fascist gangs roamed the city streets looking for communists or Jews to bash. Communist gangs returned the favour, and there were violent riots in the streets when the two groups clashed. Léon Blum, the Jewish leader of the Socialist Party, was prime minister of France. The Popular Front, an alliance of the Left and unionists, was a political force to match French fascist thugs backed by German Nazis.

On 7 March, just three weeks after the Winter Olympics, Hitler's troops marched into the Rhineland. Hitler was right – France and Britain did nothing. The violation of the Versailles Treaty threw a dark pall over the Parisian festivities, but the band played on as the storm clouds rolled ever closer. The outbreak of the Spanish Civil War in July 1936 and Nazi military backing for Franco's fascist rebel forces galvanised both the Right and the Left in Paris. Adventurers such as Ernest Hemingway packed their bags and headed off to join the conflict.

Freddie, the charming conquering hero, was welcomed back into this maelstrom of social activity. He was feted for his Olympic bronze medal which he – oh so reluctantly – brought out time and again to show the admiring beautiful people. Freddie didn't need a hunk of metal hanging around his neck to impress the ladies, but for him it had a far greater value. It was his entrée to a new professional life as a speed demon. He loved car racing, which was a huge sport in the mid-1930s, particularly in France and Italy. Freddie approached the major racing-car teams of Bugatti and Alfa Romeo, but he was rejected as an unknown. Most racing-car drivers of the time were wealthy amateurs, paying their own way for top supercars to roar around the track. Freddie didn't have that sort of money. In fact, despite his success at the Winter Olympics, Freddie was broke. If a wealthy woman did provide some financial support while he provided her company, he was off to the casino card tables. Freddie invariably had success at backgammon, but it was not enough to live the carefree sporty life to which he aspired.

Freddie then had a fortuitous meeting with two famed Parisian coachbuilders, Joseph Figoni and Ovidio Falaschi. They were designing a sensational revolutionary new sports car that was sleek, smooth and streamlined. They called the design *Goutte d'Eau* – a drop of water. In English it became known as the Teardrop Talbot. Light enough to race competitively, it looked like it was going fast when it stood still. Figoni and Falaschi had patented the curvaceous coupe, but were looking for some serious backing. They hired Freddie to be their frontman, their entrée to wealthy society and celebrities in the hope someone would invest in their dream. Freddie was ideal. He drove around a prototype vehicle called the Talbot-Lago Teardrop, receiving gasps of admiration as he guided the sexy-looking car to the swankiest hotels and holiday resorts, arranging to have it ostentatiously parked right out front. Dressed in his smartest casual wear, elegant man and feline machine cut quite a picture together.

Among the socialites and moneyed matrons in Paris who admired Freddie and the car was the undisputed queen of high society, the very attractive and still young Barbara Hutton. Renowned as the richest woman in the world as heiress to her father's Woolworth fortune, Barbara Hutton had an unfortunate tendency to marry the wrong man, something she did regularly. She was between husbands at a party in Paris when she saw a tall, muscular, virile-looking man staring at her from the other side of the room. The eye contact lingered but Barbara was confused when the man made no move to approach her. She was used to men swooning over her, trying to sweep her off her feet. This elegantly dressed man watched her intensely, obviously fascinated by her, but he made no move to seduce her. She looked him over. He was good looking, but not in the pretty-boy way of so many society men. He was ruggedly handsome: thick curly brown hair, pencil-thin moustache, full sensual lips and a long aquiline nose that she thought suggested a satyr. He was impeccably dressed in a double-breasted white dinner jacket with cabochon sapphires acting as buttons down his shirt front. This man had style, but she also detected an air of danger about him. Barbara Hutton was intrigued. She asked her friend Countess Dorothy Di Frasso who the man was.

'That's Freddie McEvoy, Olympic bobsled champion,' said the countess, one of the biggest party organisers and romantic matchmakers in high society in Europe and America. 'Be careful with that one, darling – he's a rogue. But he's not like the others. He has some integrity.'[8]

Barbara was intrigued. A rogue with integrity? Impossible, she thought. She looked at the spot where she'd seen him, but he was gone. She walked room to room looking for him in the large mansion, and eventually found him on the balcony, alone. Freddie turned to her with his most intense look. The fish had taken the hook. He immediately dropped his intensity, and smiled.

'Countess von Haugwitz-Reventlow, how do you do?' Freddie knew exactly who this pretty slip of a woman was. All of Paris knew. He deliberately used her titled married name. Rich Americans liked marrying European men with aristocratic titles, regardless of whether, as was often the case, they were penniless pretenders, turfed out of Russia after the Bolshevik revolution, or the youngest son of an East European dynasty with no castle, no lands and no prospects. Barbara Hutton's first marriage at age 21 was to 'Prince' Alexis Mdivani, who claimed to be heir to the throne of Georgia; actually he was a mere minor aristocrat of little importance, broke and intent on her money.

In 1935, after two years of an unhappy marriage, Barbara paid off the so-called prince for a genuine German-born Danish count in Kurt von Haugwitz-Reventlow. The count turned out to be even more ruthless than the phony prince in trying to get a grip on the Hutton fortune. Reventlow physically and mentally abused her. He once forced to her to join him at an orgy in Paris where girls as young as 13 were provided for the entertainment of the paying clients. Barbara was on her way to dumping the cruel count when she ran into Freddie.

Although he was an Australian with no title apart from an Olympic bronze medal, the richest woman in the world, known in the gossip newspapers as the 'poor little rich girl', was very much taken with the Antipodean hunk. Conversation turned to whom they knew on the French Riviera where Freddie spent his summers. It turned out they knew a lot of people in common. She was delighted with his tales of mansions and yachts in the sun, and pressed him on what it was like to go down a mountain at breakneck speed on a bobsled. She was entranced. Freddie seemed to be able to read her like a book, looking right into her with his intense gaze. She felt it was as though this man knew and understood her troubles with Kurt without her saying a word. She said something about how tiresome the long journey from Paris to the Riviera was, and Freddie saw an opening.

'I can drive it in under ten hours,' he said without any hint of bragging. It was said as though it were an established fact.

'Impossible,' she replied. The journey was 907 kilometres and usually took three days, two full days if the driver really pushed it.

'I can do it,' Freddie said.

'How?'

'In that,' he said, and pointed to the sleek maroon Talbot-Lago Teardrop parked in front of the mansion.

'That's yours? It's beautiful. But ten hours – it can't be done.'

'Wanna bet?'

'Ten thousand dollars – I'll give you ten thousand dollars if you get from Paris to Cannes in under ten hours.'

'You're on,' Freddie said, and offered his hand for her to shake on the deal.[9] Barbara accepted, and it was the start of a long and beautiful friendship.

Freddie planned the route meticulously. He didn't want a co-driver or navigator, because the weight would cost him speed. He also didn't want to share the prize money, which was a huge amount in the 1930s, enough to set him up for some time. In the very early hours of a spring morning, Freddie drove out of Paris at breakneck speed and roared his way south. There were no motorways, but Freddie knew the route well and all the short cuts to avoid traffic. He would have to navigate his way through a series of small towns and cities, along narrow winding roads and hairpin bends, up and down steep grades and over the Maritime Alps before arriving at the edge of the Mediterranean Sea. Freddie approached the long drive the same way he approached bobsledding – damn the brakes and full speed ahead. It would be tough. Very tough. The Talbot was still a test automobile. If

Freddie's Talbot-Lago Teardrop and thank-you card to the car's designers.

he managed to pull this off, it would send the reputation of the Talbot through the roof.

Incredibly, Freddie pulled into the parking lot outside the Cannes Casino precisely 9 hours and 45 minutes after he was clocked leaving Paris. The exhausted Aussie was cheered and applauded by French society and motoring fans. It was a phenomenal feat of driving and endurance. Barbara Hutton happily handed over the $10,000 – around $170,000 in today's money. Freddie promptly marched into the casino and doubled it. With that small fortune he bought a racing Maserati 6CM. Freddie's racing career was off to a roaring start. And there was the prospect of seducing Barbara Hutton. Sadly for both Freddie and Barbara, that would have to wait several years.

Freddie didn't ease himself into motor racing – he dived straight in the deep end. Motor racing in the late 1930s was still mostly an amateur affair, with drivers using their private wealth to pay for their cars and mechanic teams. Freddie aimed at getting his six-cylinder Maserati into the Voiturette class of cars under 1500 cc.

On 11 April 1936 Freddie entered himself in the Circuit de Monaco, 50 laps of a 1.9 mile (3.18 kilometres) course around Monte Carlo. The greatest drivers of the time were set to race. They included Robert Kohlrausch, a hard-line Nazi with a rank of *Untersturmführer* (Lieutenant) in the SS; Maurice Mestivier from France; Raymond Mays, one of Britain's most famous drivers; and 22-year-old B Bira, who was actually Prince Birabongse Bhanutej Bhanubandh of the Thai royal family. Bira won the Monaco race in dramatic fashion after the leaders crashed or were disqualified.

Freddie was one of those who crashed, but he emerged unhurt and determined to do better next time.[10]

On 21 June Freddie entered the Grand Prix de Picardie, two heats of 10 laps then a final 15 laps of a 6-mile (9.7 km) circuit near the city of Peronne, south of Lille. It was incredibly hot on race day and the engines suffered. Freddie in his Maserati 6CM finished in fourth position, two laps behind the first three. But Freddie impressed the crowd and other competitors by managing to keep his Maserati going while many more experienced drivers crashed or suffered mechanical problems.

A month later Freddie was off again. The Grand Prix de L'Albigeois, near Albi in southern France, was a triangular course of 5.5 miles (8.9 km). It was tough with three hard corners, two heats of 20 laps. The same rival drivers were there, looking a bit more askance at Freddie. They didn't see him as a real threat to the top drivers, but he was certainly one to watch because he tended to hang on to the bitter end. But this was a race that Freddie pushed too hard. His Maserati rolled over on one of the corners on his second lap and caught fire. Luckily Freddie was thrown clear and emerged shaken but unhurt. Once again Thai prince Bira collected the winner's trophy.

It took a while for Freddie's Maserati to be patched up and put back on the road. But on 2 August Freddie was back, entering the Coppa Ciano race in the Tuscan city of Livorno in Italy. Freddie nursed his beloved Maserati around the difficult mountain circuit and finished in eighth position in a time of 1 hour, 2 minutes behind the Italian winner Carlo Trossi.

Two weeks later Freddie lined up at the east Italian city of Pescara for the Coppa Acerbo. It wasn't a large field, but Freddie moved up the ladder, coming fourth, 6 minutes behind the English champion driver Richard Seaman. Freddie had barely a week to load his Maserati on a truck and get it over the Alps to the other side of Switzerland for the next race.

On 22 August, Freddie entered himself and his Maserati in the Swiss Grand Prix. This was a much bigger race on the European circuit and a major test for Freddie. The race was held at Bremgarten Circuit near Bern, on rural roads that were closed off to other vehicles during the 96 mile (154 km) race. The circuit was dangerous to take at speed – winding roads through villages and forests with trees on either side to slam into if the vehicle left the bitumen. Light was often poor as mountain mist and rain reduced visibility. It was a dangerous course, even deadly. Two years earlier British driver Hugh Hamilton had been killed during the Swiss Grand Prix when his car slipped off the track on his last lap and went straight into a tree.

Once again Freddie was up against wealthy aristocrats such as Britain's Earl Howe (whose actual name was Francis Richard Henry Penn, Viscount Curzon) in a Bugatti, and B Bira – alias the Prince of Siam. Richard 'Dick' Seaman, an old boy of Rugby School and Trinity College, Cambridge, had won the Swiss Grand Prix in 1934 and 1935 driving a Delage. Other wealthy drivers who had more money than sense included Italian Moris Bergamini and skilled British driver Raymond Mays.

Three out of four cars didn't finish the Swiss Grand Prix Voiturette 1500 cc race, but Freddie was one of the success stories. He finished a very creditable fourth behind the champion Dick Seaman, Carlo Trossi and Hans Ruesch – all far more experienced racing drivers. Freddie had done incredibly well, averaging 77 miles per hour (124 kph). Although the wealthy upper-crust motoring fraternity had initially looked with disdain upon the upstart from Australia, he'd proved himself to be a determined competitor and was now very much a part of this elite amateur club.

Two months later Freddie shipped his Maserati to New York to compete in the Vanderbilt Cup, an endurance race of 300 miles (480 kilometres) held on the Roosevelt Raceway near the town of Westbury on Long Island.[11] This was a huge race with big prize money put up by the multi-millionaire George Vanderbilt to attract the best drivers from Europe to take on the best American drivers. The Vanderbilt Cup, with first prize of US$20,000 (US$355,000 in today's money), was designed to encourage motor racing in the United States. It hadn't been run since 1916 and in 1927 the race track had been the site of a field airport where Charles Lindbergh took off in the *Spirit of St Louis*. The dirt-track course was twisty and bumpy, and included a dozen straight stretches of varying lengths and 16 different curves and turns requiring much severe braking and shifting of gears during the 75 laps. This made the course difficult for the powerful racing machines brought over from Europe for the big prize money. But they had a significant advantage over the Americans, whose cars were much less powerful and would struggle to keep up. Amateur Freddie was up against professional drivers backed by huge vehicle corporations. Ferrari, Bugatti and Alfa Romeo sent their best drivers.

Freddie didn't have the backing of a major racing-car team behind him, and he was unknown in America. The top European drivers still dismissed Freddie as a playboy driver who wasn't a

Freddie in his Maserati at New York's 1936 Vanderbilt Cup, proudly displaying the Australian flag.

serious threat – but Freddie was determined to give the Americans a show. He painted a large Australian flag on the side of his Maserati, and the word 'Australia' in bold letters over his garage on the racetrack. This time he wasn't competing for Britain against the Americans like he had in the bobsled; Freddie felt he was representing Australia, and for the first time in his life he grabbed the chance to shout to the world that he came from the land Down Under. The Aussie underdog was going to show this arrogant mob.

It took the Europeans and Freddie a while to get used to driving on the rough circuit. The race was more than 300 miles

(480 kilometres) long, 10 laps of a 28-mile circuit of dirt road, an exhausting distance that would test man and machine to the very limits. The hot favourite was Italian Tazio Nuvolari, dubbed 'the man with a contract with the devil' for the daredevil way he drove his Alfa Romeo. With speeds hitting 70 miles per hour (112 kph), Nuvolari blitzed the field, winning the trophy and the prize money. But in sixth position, well ahead of rivals such as the aristocrat Earl Howe, were Freddie McEvoy and his Maserati emblazoned with the Australian flag. Freddie finished in 4 hours, 57 minutes, 24.82 seconds – 25 minutes behind Nuvolari who, after all, had the devil riding beside him in his red rocket. Freddie won prize money of US$3000 (US$52,856 in today's dollars), enough to get himself back to the Swiss Alps just in time for the winter fun and games. He sold the Maserati in America, bringing his racing-car shenanigans to an end. Freddie was getting back to what he was good at: bobsledding and chasing rich women.

Ensconced once again in European high society, Freddie celebrated his winnings in London's Café de Paris, ordering his usual pink champagne and announcing to his cheering admirers that he was about to drink 'the blood of a wounded bookmaker'.[12] He'd earlier accepted a sizeable bet against him that he would not finish the New York race in the top 10, so it wasn't just the Vanderbilt prize money that was filling Freddie's pockets after his year-long jaunt racing cars. Freddie was on top of the world. Rich women were clamouring for his attention. He had a nice little earner in acting as a Mr Fixit, a middleman who brought together people seeking investments with celebrities and wealthy people. He could arrange the discreet sale of antiques or artworks from impoverished old European families to nouveau riche Americans. New York banking tycoon Henry 'Harry' S Morgan (founder of investment bank Morgan Stanley) hired Freddie as his personal assistant to arrange meetings with Europe's high society. He was also tasked with arranging beautiful women to attend dinners and parties for Morgan whenever he was in France and Switzerland.[13]

It was a role Freddie could play with *élan*. Everybody loved Freddie, and nobody begrudged him taking a sizeable cut from the deals he worked under the table. The Talbot car makers kept him on their payroll as a sort of ambassador to high society, persuading several very rich Americans to purchase a handmade Talbot-Lago Teardrop for their collections. The car that Freddie drove from Paris to Cannes was sold to an American collector. Today the deep-red wine-coloured Talbot occupies pride of place in the Mullin Automotive Museum in Oxnard, north of Los Angeles. It is worth upwards of US$10 million.

In January 1937 Freddie lined up again for the four-man bobsled. This time it was for the world championship held at St Moritz, virtually his home town. There simply weren't any other Australian bobsledders, so once again Freddie found himself leading the British team in the driver's position. Behind him was old Etonian and Trinity College, Cambridge upper-class chap David Looker. Like Freddie, Looker lived the playboy high life – winter in St Moritz, summer on the French Riviera. He'd been on a round-the-world yacht cruise the previous winter so had missed the Winter Olympics. Packing the rear of the four-man sled were two South Africans: Charlie Green, who had been part of Freddie's Olympic team, and Brian Black, a giant rugby forward who'd played for England in 10 matches between 1930 and 1933, as well as five matches for the British and Irish Lions. The four-man team completed their runs in 5 minutes, 9.7 seconds – 1.2 seconds faster than second-placed Germany. Freddie and his team were world champions, hailed in the London press as the first 'British' world champion bobsledders, ignoring the fact that only one of the four was English.[14]

A week later, Freddie and Brian Black became world champions in the two-man bobsled held at Cortina d'Ampezzo in Italy. The *Daily Express* heralded the achievement with the headline 'British pair world bobsleigh champions',[15] showing a picture of Freddie and Brian Black – a win for Britain even though they were an Australian and a South African. The *Express* excitedly reported that Britain's historic win was watched by Countess Ciano, the daughter of Italian dictator Mussolini, and several other Italian aristocrats.

Next winter Freddie was back at the 1938 world championship bobsled run. Brian Black was replaced by Chris MacKintosh, and once again Freddie's team won gold at the four-man bobsled at St Moritz. In the two-man, Freddie partnered up with Charlie Green, but this time they only managed silver.

In February 1939 Freddie once again led the British team in the four-man bobsled in the world championship. This time they won silver. For the third time Freddie had won a medal in the world championship for the four-man bobsled, an incredible achievement that should have been shouted from the rooftops by Australian sports fans. Sadly, it went unnoticed in Australia. Darker tidings were filling the newspapers. The spectre of fascism was growing increasingly menacing, and the threat emanating from Nazi Germany left little room for sport. Nazism even raised its ugly head in Freddie's bobsled. This time on his team was Peter Howard – journalist, playwright and captain of England's 1931 rugby team. Howard was also a British right-wing extremist, leader of the so-called Biff Boys, a brutal gang of British fascist blackshirt thugs who bashed opponents of the New Party headed by the aristocrat Nazi Sir Oswald Mosley.[16]

CHAPTER 5

GERMANY INVADES, FREDDIE
MARRIES MONEY

It's not clear whether Freddie listened to the fascist bobsledder in his 1939 four-man team. There is nothing in the official records of Freddie's life to indicate that fascist bovver boy and rugby star Peter Howard managed to divert Freddie's attention away from his dedicated pursuit of fun, speed, pink champagne and rich women long enough to become a fascist sympathiser. At age 33 Freddie was still chasing the hedonist life: girls, parties, yachts on the French Riviera, casinos, fast cars, tuxedos and other fine clothing. He was accommodating attractive women, and rich women however they might be packaged, and engaging in the never-ending pursuit of sources of money.

Freddie's discreet business as a wheeler-dealer middleman for Europeans fallen on hard times wanting to sell art, jewellery and other family heirlooms to wealthy Americans was doing well enough for him to live a sumptuous lifestyle. Freddie was like a wolf trailing a herd of deer, following the money wherever it went, looking for easy pickings. He appeared anywhere the big-time players congregated – be they princes or nabobs, wealthy widows and naïve young heiresses, swarthy South American millionaires, war profiteers and shonky tycoons, shady smugglers and mafia, glamorous celebrities, cool models or budding movie starlets. Throughout the late 1930s Freddie moved with the season – from the winter playground of St Moritz to Paris in the spring. Then summer on the Cote d'Azur with its luxury villas, and blossoming almond and mimosa trees. He played tennis, croquet and golf when not frolicking on yachts on the crystal blue water of the Mediterranean. The resident aristocrats turned their noses up at the cashed-up Americans who invaded the French Riviera in the late 1930s, dazzling locals with their ostentatious displays of wealth. The new arrivals built fantasy castles and parked luxurious giant yachts in the harbours of Nice, Cannes, Monte Carlo and formerly sleepy peaceful fishing villages such as St Tropez. Eccentric millionaire casino owner Frank Jay Gould entertained a stream of visiting celebrities, including Charlie Chaplin, Jean Paul Getty and Joseph Kennedy. Writers and artists such as Aldous Huxley, F Scott Fitzgerald, Jean Cocteau, André Gide and André Malraux made it their home. The crowd moved to Paris for the autumn.

Regulars at exclusive parties in Paris and Cannes before 1936 were Edward, Prince of Wales, and his American mistress Wallis Simpson. In mid-1930s France it was unremarkable that a married woman would openly engage in an affair. If anything, it would be remarkable if a married person of either sex wasn't busy canoodling outside wedlock, even if it were with their own sex.

Wallis Simpson's husband Ernest, a former Coldstream Guards officer, was proud of the arrangement his wife had with the future king. Business came his way, and the cuckold was included at parties among the royal chums. Besides, Ernest was busy having his own affair with his wife's best friend. Prince Edward was besotted with Wallis Simpson, following her around like a puppy. Some suggest Edward had a nanny fixation, stemming from his boyhood nanny who spanked him when he cried, then fondled and masturbated him to make him happy.[1] Edward certainly wasn't the only aristocrat to have a nanny crush, but Wallis must have had hidden talents, because she was by no means a beauty, or even particularly interesting to talk to. Like Edward, she was an admirer of Adolf Hitler and Nazi ideology. There were rumours that while living a wild life in China – during which she had an affair with a count who would later become Mussolini's son-in-law, thereby starting her long relationship with fascists – Wallis had learned sex tricks including oral skills that had the priggish prince coming back for more. She was certainly sexually active – during her affair with Prince Edward she was also having a secret affair with motorcar salesman Guy Trundle.[2] There were also suggestions that Wallis was some sort of hermaphrodite because of her angular features and raspy voice. That was never established either way, but she certainly was the stronger character, calling Edward her 'little man'.

Freddie was so charming and such excellent company that he was always welcome to join this elite circle in the social swirl of the Riviera and Paris. While Freddie was an entertaining, amusing and charming chap to have around, he also provided a needed rough edge to the perpetually smug aristocratic cafe society. The wealthy socialites didn't seem to mind that Freddie hardly ever paid back the loans they gave him. That was simply the price to be paid for having Freddie around. He was just so much fun.

'Freddie had the knack of knowing rich women who found him irresistible,' commented one friend to American social columnist George Frazier, who chronicled the life of the rich and fatuous.[3] However, they all knew Freddie was a commoner, a penniless adventurer from the remote Dominion of Australia who could never be accepted as an equal or a true member of the snooty aristocratic elite. Some critical observers of the social scene of the late 1930s remarked that Freddie was little more than a gigolo, a man with talents in the bedroom that were available for as long as the financial support lasted. That was unkind. Freddie certainly wasn't a prostitute who sold his body. It wasn't cash for sex. It was more that Freddie provided special services to women who were in need of intimacy, entertainment and male companionship. It was the full package, and Freddie certainly could provide that. In return Freddie accepted their sponsorship of his lifestyle of fast cars, sport, casinos, parties, sunshine and yachts. For women of means, having the gallant, handsome, polite, stylish and charming Freddie on their arm at a high-society function gave them a certain élan and respect. Not only was Freddie an excellent adornment who could smoothly introduce a newly arrived lady to the best people in society; his presence on a lady's arm commanded respect – it showed that she could afford him.

On top of that, making him even more irresistible was always the feeling that danger lurked just behind the smiling eyes of Freddie McEvoy. Everybody knew of his reckless driving and the fact that he risked his life over and over on the bobsled runs and in sleek fast cars. There was also a rumour, never quite confirmed, that he once killed a man in a brawl in a Marseille bar. Freddie did nothing to deny it, but nor did he ever concede that it was true. He certainly wasn't above engaging in a good old-fashioned bar-room brawl, whether it be to defend the honour of a lady, or simply because someone didn't like his manner. Like punk gunslingers in the Wild West, young rakes were keen to make a name for themselves by taking on the experienced veteran. Freddie didn't need boxing gloves to prove he could handle himself with his fists. To many, Freddie was an international man of mystery, a free man who never discussed how he earned the money to pay for his extravagant lifestyle. He freely admitted with a devilish grin to being a rogue, a rake, a rascal, a rapscallion. To many women, that not only made him even more attractive, but also irresistible.

One such ongoing arrangement with Freddie in the late 1930s was conducted with wealthy American widow Beatrice Cartwright. Thirty years older than Freddie, Mrs Cartwright was a formidable and strong woman who knew what she wanted and how to get it. Her grandfather Henry Huttleston Rogers was a founder of the Standard Oil Company – one of the biggest money-making machines in the world, which had made a huge fortune out of World War I. Mrs Cartwright had an income of $200,000 a year – more than US$10 million a year in today's money. By the time she crossed paths with Freddie, Beatrice had already put three husbands behind her. The first two ex-husbands – Alexander Pratt and Preston Gibson – were New Yorkers from good but dull families. The third was Captain Charles Cartwright

Freddie enjoying St Moritz.

of the British Royal Navy, with whom she had a young son who lived with the captain in England. By the time she met Freddie, she was estranged from the British navy captain, and so she was intrigued when she sat next to the handsome Australian at an elaborate Riviera dinner party. She'd heard of his skills, and had arranged the seating just so she could talk with him. The topic of conversation is not recorded, but it must have given Freddie an opening. During the course of polite dinner conversation, according to author Charles Higham, Freddie 'gently took Mrs Cartwright's hand and led it to a significant position under his napkin'.[4] Far from being shocked and horrified, Beatrice was impressed by what she found unfettered beneath Freddie's napkin. She kept her hand there throughout dessert, trying to make the up-and-down movement of her hand invisible to the other dinner guests. Over coffee she made it clear to the Australian speedster that as an aperitif she would like to further investigate what lay beneath his napkin. Freddie smiled. He had just hooked another moneyed matron – perhaps his biggest fish so far. Reports say that despite being somewhat of an invalid, Beatrice was sexually active – indeed, extremely sexually active. From that moment on, she required Freddie to attend to her desires at least three times a week.

Their time together was hardly a romance: Beatrice put Freddie on a retainer. It was virtually a business arrangement. She recognised that Freddie had to have a certain degree of freedom to play the field or he could lose interest in her. The arrangement was that Freddie would receive a substantial weekly allowance so long as he was available to her whenever she wished. Freddie told friends he was pleasantly surprised by the strenuous demands she made on him in the boudoir, which could leave him exhausted. He guessed that bit of news would circulate quickly and get back to her. In this society, that sort of gossip was good for her reputation as well as his. The 62-year-old Beatrice might not have been the one that Freddie would have chosen from the conga line of rich ladies with whom he was on intimate terms in Paris and the Riviera, but Beatrice was certainly one of the very richest. And she had serious connections.

Wallis Simpson was a regular guest at Beatrice Cartwright's beautiful Casa Estella villa above the seaside cliffs at the exclusive Cap d'Antibes near Cannes. When Mrs Cartwright visited Paris she didn't just book the best hotel suite, she took the entire floor. Freddie knew how to show her a good time, and whisked her from one society party and fashionable nightclub to another, introducing his matronly catch to all the bright young things, who immediately praised her for her gown, her hair, her shoes, her looks. She must have felt young again, accepted by the new guard. After all, any friend of Freddie's was a friend of theirs. A fleet of limousines was always waiting to ferry Beatrice and Freddie as well as his partying entourage from restaurant to theatre to nightclub. Freddie's wardrobe grew enormously courtesy of Beatrice's expense account. He liked to look smart. She liked him to look smart. Freddie had landed in clover, and life was good. He had high hopes that his relationship with Beatrice could go much further. Her divorce from Captain Cartwright was due to become official by the end of 1939. And there was the prospect of Beatrice inheriting a vast fortune from her elderly father. Freddie made himself indispensable to Beatrice, playing her like a violin and extending his physical efforts whenever his services were needed. Yes, Freddie had hooked himself a big fish, and he wasn't going to let it escape.

However, as the months rolled on into the summer of 1939, a dark storm cloud gathered over Freddie's best-laid plans. The spectre of the little man with the brush moustache whose piercing dark eyes Freddie had stared into way back in February 1936 at the Winter Olympics as he dipped the British flag was looming ever closer. Hitler's success in marching unopposed into the Rhineland three weeks after the Winter Games had emboldened him to keep pushing further. After all, Britain and France had done nothing to stop him seizing the Rhineland, so who would stop him now?

During the 1936 Summer Olympics in Berlin, while the world watched black American Jesse Owens humiliate Hitler's so-called master race on the track, behind the scenes Hitler was busy solidifying his plans for total war. Summoning top aides and leading industrialists to Berlin, Hitler ordered a secret plan to make Germany self-sufficient within four years, and to invest all its resources in arms and a military build-up. In November 1937 Hitler laid out his plans to his generals for '*Lebensraum*', the expansion of German borders and the German occupation of eastern Europe to provide food and oil for the new *Deutsches Reich*. On 12 March 1938 Hitler ordered German troops to march into his birthland of Austria. He insisted this wasn't an invasion but an *anschluss*, a natural joining of the two Germanic states. Thousands of cheering Austrians welcomed the German army, raising their arms in the Nazi salute. Hitler was hailed a hero, and tens of thousands greeted him enthusiastically. His tour through Austria was a triumph. The round-up of the Jews of Austria began immediately. Once again, Britain and France did nothing.

More than anything, political leaders of both Britain and France feared another European war. France was still on its knees after the devastation of World War I. The death toll had been staggering, leaving the Allied nations exhausted. France lost close to 2 million dead and more than 4 million wounded – that's 4.4 per cent of the entire French population lost, a higher proportion than any other country in the war. Britain lost more than a million dead and 1.6 million wounded. Germany lost 2.8 million dead – 4.3 per cent of the population – and 4.2 million wounded. But rather than reel back in horror from the thought of another war, just two decades later Hitler encouraged Germans to feel they had been robbed of victory and resent the impositions of the Treaty of Versailles. Immediately after his successful seizure of Austria, Hitler threatened to invade Czechoslovakia to 'liberate' the German-speaking population in the Sudetenland border region.

In September 1938 Britain's Neville Chamberlain and France's Édouard Daladier met Hitler in Munich to try to dissuade him from military action. In what became known derisively as the appeasement, they agreed to hand over the Sudetenland to Germany holus-bolus. Czechoslovakia had no choice in the matter. Chamberlain returned to England to utter the now infamous words 'Peace in our time', although many Britons were sceptical. Winston Churchill said: 'We have sustained a total and unmitigated defeat.'[5] The French welcomed the move. There would be no war. At least not in 1938. Sure enough, within months Hitler had marched his troops in and seized the entire nation of Czechoslovakia. Unknown to Chamberlain and the others, Hitler wasn't ready to fight a war in 1938. The German army would have suffered huge losses if they'd had to fight an invasion of Czechoslovakia, and Hitler probably could have been stopped – at least for a while – at this point. But after the Munich Agreement, Hitler was unstoppable. The German war machine was building up to maximum power.

Next on Hitler's menu was Poland. So far, he'd got away with his expansion of German borders and horrific actions against Jews in his own country and the newly occupied lands. Finally, Britain and France realised they had to step in and stop Hitler. In March 1939 Britain and France signed a treaty with Poland to go to war if Poland were invaded by Germany. It was too late. Hitler didn't believe they would act. While Britain and France dithered and didn't include the Soviet Union in their discussions, in August Hitler secured a secret pact with Stalin's Soviet Union to divide Poland between them. The Soviets had watched while the Western Allies gave Hitler everything he asked for. Stalin and his generals thought they would be on their own if Hitler sent his armies east. On 1 September 1939 Hitler launched his *blitzkrieg* and raced into Poland. The invasion of Poland was over within weeks. On 3 September Britain and France declared war on Germany. They then did nothing.

Despite the enormity of declaring war, after a few days the atmosphere in Paris and London calmed down. No German bombs had rained down on French cities. The Germans seemed to be content to stay in Poland executing people. Life returned to normal and people went about their business. Cafes, restaurants and nightclubs remained open and the frolicking crowds returned. Maybe it was all a bluff. Surely Hitler would keep looking to the east. He'd repeatedly said he had no quarrel with Britain or France. Hitler had even bowed and kissed the hand of Wallis Simpson as she and the now abdicated king gleefully accepted his invitation to his Berchtesgaden home. The aristocrats and the wealthy respected Hitler. They were quietly grateful he was there to stamp on the throat of the Bolsheviks. Too bad about the Jews, but what can you do? High-society partying continued unabated, and Freddie kept right on with it. Even though Britain had commenced conscription, Freddie wasn't to be part of that. He was Australian, and Australia had sent only volunteers to serve overseas in the military. Even though Australia had declared war on Germany, the exact moment Britain did, Freddie felt he would be all right in France. In these uncertain times, however, he knew it would be wise to secure himself a ticket out if things turned ugly, so he redoubled his efforts to impress the American matron Beatrice Cartwright. She did seem to be very taken with him. If there were to be a shooting war in Europe, then New York would be the place to be for Freddie. He may have been fearless on the bobsled run or at the motor racetrack, but the idea of fighting to the death over ancient European borders seemed a ridiculous notion to Freddie. Besides, many of his friends thought Hitler was actually doing a good job.

France certainly had no desire to stir up a fighting war. French troops along the quiet German border were asked by a Reuters reporter why they did not shoot at the German guards who were standing in clear sight. They looked shocked at the question. 'If we fire, they will fire back,' one replied.[6] As September dragged into October and November without any military action along the French/German border, the troops lolled about, not under-going training. They started to complain of poor conditions and feeling ill, and some deserted to go home. To keep them entertained, the French High Command arranged for Edith Piaf, Josephine Baker and Maurice Chevalier to put on shows for the border-front troops.

The French generals couldn't believe Hitler would invade France. Despite being poorly equipped and badly trained, the French army was enormous. Many elements in the French government were rabid anti-communists and they feared the strength of communism in France. Some saw the Nazis as a better alternative, even if it meant foreign occupation. On the German side, the Poland campaign had used up more bullets and shells than anticipated. Hitler was furious when his generals told him it would take some time to build up sufficient arms to invade to the west of Germany. Winter fogs hindered air attacks. Better to wait until the spring. Some secretly hoped that by then Hitler would be gone. Several assassination attempts had failed; maybe one would get him. The Germans called it the *Sitzkrieg*, the sitting war. The British dubbed these tense winter months the 'phoney war'. Maybe the whole war would just dissipate without the armies clashing.

Also in September, Beatrice Cartwright was advised via telegram that her father had fallen ill. In October she travelled to New York by ship. She left without Freddie. He was very much a French dalliance, and she wasn't keen on having him with her as the Cartwright clan gathered for the imminent death of their patriarch. She had spent much of the 1920s and 30s in France, and considered her Casa Estella villa at Cap d'Antibes her real home. The outbreak of war in Europe would make it difficult for her to return to the villa – and to Freddie. Correspondence with Mrs Cartwright held by the US Department of State shows that the day after her father died, on 25 February 1940, she asked the head of the passport division to renew her a passport because she needed to return to Europe for a period of six months. Her nine-year-old son, William Aubrey Cartwright, was in England, a ward of the Chancery Court, and the English court refused to allow him to travel to America. She wrote:

> They will however allow him to stay with me in France. He is in poor health and it is of the utmost importance that I be allowed to have him stay with me in the southern part of France. Secondly, I have lived in Europe since 1921 and as a result have accumulated substantial financial interest in both England and France which it is necessary for me to look after.

She also said the Anglo-American Ambulance Corps at Cannes had asked her to contribute and assist them personally. 'I feel also that it might be an excellent plan to set up some knitting machines where socks and scarfs for the soldiers can be made at the house.' She even offered to come to Washington to answer further questions.[7] Upon her father's death, Beatrice Cartwright inherited a staggering US$8 million – around US$591 million in today's money. She wasn't a woman to be denied, and she had powerful friends. The passport division of the State Department agreed to renew her passport so long as she sailed to Italy, not France, because it was in a state of war. She sailed on 16 March 1940, and landed in Italy, then made her way to Paris where Freddie was waiting to greet her. Time was pressing.

On 9 April 1940 Germany invaded Denmark and Norway. Denmark fell quickly with little resistance. Germany wanted to use the Norwegian coast as safe harbours for its navy and shipping to get around a British naval blockade. In Paris, Freddie and the French watched nervously. Still, the Scandinavian fighting didn't affect them. The border of France was lined with massive fortifications called the Maginot Line that, surely, would halt the Germans. Unfortunately, the fortresses stopped at the heavily forested southern border of Belgium. In May the British force standing on the French border ready to help defend France numbered eleven divisions. The Germans had long-held secret plans to invade the neutral and relatively defenceless Netherlands and Belgium to force their way into France without tackling the Maginot Line. Like Poland, the Low Countries were excellent tank country. The German military envisaged turning the *sitzkrieg* into another *blitzkrieg*. It knew that British and French armaments and field equipment were woefully inadequate and outdated, and the troops poorly trained. The Allied generals thought it inconceivable that they would once again be fighting on the Somme where so many soldiers had been ripped apart in the trenches just over 20 years earlier.

The morning of 9 May 1940 dawned as a beautiful spring day. Belgian soldiers planted pansies around their barracks. Soldiers used the sunshine to wash and dry their uniforms. In Paris the street cafes were packed as people enjoyed the warm sun. Many men wore officers' uniforms, granted leave by the High Command. Chestnut trees had burst into green leaf. At 9pm, as Freddie escorted Mrs Cartwright to dinner in Paris, in Berlin the military HQ broadcast just one word to its poised armies and air force: *Danzig*. It was the code word for the invasion of the Netherlands, Belgium, Luxembourg and France to start at dawn.

The sudden attack caught the Western Allies by complete surprise. Luftwaffe bombers and fighters attacked as the first streak of dawn provided just enough light to catch Allied planes on the ground. Across France one airfield after another was quickly destroyed, leaving a huge hole in the French air force. Before the sun was up, paratroopers had already captured strategic points such as bridges, dykes, railways and road junctions. Tanks poured over the border and roared at full speed into the Netherlands and Belgium; within two days they reached the Dutch coast. Panzer tanks pushed through the Ardennes Forest, something the French had thought impossible. On 13 May, General Erwin Rommel led his troops across the border river Meuse from Belgium into France and met only light resistance. He held the bridgehead until engineers built pontoon bridges to allow columns of tanks across. The invasion of France had begun. Shocked French generals warned the government that the Germans could be in Paris in just three days.

Paris was in panic. Anybody who had a vehicle was packing up and heading south, away from the invading Germans. The roads were quickly clogged. Beatrice Cartwright told Freddie she was staying in Paris. The United States was neutral. Thirty thousand Americans lived in France in 1940, most of them in Paris.[8] She thought there would be safety in numbers. Other prominent wealthy Americans weren't leaving Paris either. Peggy Guggenheim refused to halt remodelling her apartment at Place Vendome where Chopin had died. She was busy buying up paintings at bargain prices from artists who were fleeing the city. She later wrote that she watched panicked Parisians teeming past her balcony to the city gates. 'I can't imagine why I didn't go to the aid of these unfortunate people. But I just didn't; instead I drank champagne with Bill [her latest lover].'[9]

The Americans in Paris were convinced Hitler wouldn't harm US citizens and risk a conflict with Washington. Beatrice told Freddie that as an American citizen she had nothing to do with this war and would be treated with respect by the Germans. Despite the chaos of war, she was still hoping her sickly son could be brought over from England to France, where she could look after him at her beautiful Casa Estella. Freddie tried to convince her that would be impossible. All flights out of Paris were gone, none were coming in. The English wouldn't send a sick boy over the Channel to a war in France. Beatrice was beside herself.

'And what about you, Freddie? You are one of Germany's enemies. They can shoot you on sight.' Freddie just nodded, and shrugged, giving her that cheeky grin he knew she loved. This was the moment. If an invading horde of Huns didn't get this multi-millionairess to marry him, nothing would.

'The most important thing is to make sure you are safe, dearest,' he replied. 'I have to get you out of Paris. We can't wait any longer. Please. We can't take everything. Just leave it. I have a car waiting. I know the way to get south off the main roads, a special way. Remember I did it in under ten hours just a few years ago.'

The truth was that Freddie wasn't all that worried about the Germans. He knew a lot of very influential Germans, many of them leading Nazis. But you never knew with invasions. They could be tricky. All it would take would be a scared young kid in a soldier's uniform with a gun, or some officious Gestapo bastard, and the adventure would be over for Freddie McEvoy. Freddie continued:

'My only worry is that if they stop us and take me away because I am Australian it will leave you alone and defenceless. How could you drive down to Cannes through all this chaos and soldiers roving the streets? Worse still, deserters might try to take the car. Look, if we marry and I can say I am married to you, an American, it could get us through roadblocks.'

'Really, dear? You think so? Well, let's do it now. Do you know someone who can marry us and give us the papers so we can get out of here before the Germans arrive?'[10]

Of course, it just so happened that Freddie did know somebody who could marry them right away. On 24 May 1940, Frederick Joseph McEvoy, penniless Aussie Don Juan and lover of all things that went fast – be they machine or woman – married a multi-millionairess. Freddie finally won the prize he had been aiming for all his adult life.

CHAPTER 6

FREDDIE UNDER THE NAZIS

While 378,000 British troops were trapped on the beach of Dunkirk desperately waiting for the fleet of small boats to evacuate them to England, Freddie and his new wife were in Paris furiously packing their bags preparing to escape by driving the tortuous roads south towards Cannes. Freddie hadn't been joking about it being a dangerous trip – not just due to the Germans but also French soldiers escaping the invaders.

Northern France was already teeming with hundreds of thousands of refugees from the Netherlands, Belgium and Luxembourg fleeing ahead of the German invaders. By the start of June, between 6 and 10 million of France's population of 40 million had left their homes out of fear of the Germans. In central Paris, which normally had a population of almost 3 million, two in three had left or were packing to leave the capital before the German army arrived.

Freddie knew he and Beatrice had to get out of Paris quickly and head south before the city was encircled by the rapidly advancing German army. Outside their luxury hotel it was utter chaos. There was no time to pack up everything – just the most valuable jewellery, papers, and large bundles of cash, both French francs and US dollars. In times like this, one never knew the value of cash, but the jewels could always be exchanged for safe passage. Paris was emptying fast. Shops had shut. It wasn't possible to buy food. One Parisian recorded in their diary what they saw in the first days of June:

> The odd passer-by. The Rue de Chateaudun deserted. Same thing around the Opera, the Avenue de l'Opera, and the streets off it. All buildings have their doors closed . . . the grands boulevards . . . as far as the eye could carry, absolutely deserted, all the shops closed. And the silence . . .[1]

A Parisian who stayed wrote:

> The only living thing we could see was a little grey dog which walked interminably round a tree on the pavement beneath us. All day long it walked in circles around the tree. From time to time one of us went down to comfort it, but it ran away, only to come back when we were gone.[2]

Millions of French headed south, hoping the Loire River would form a new border, a trench line as the Somme and Marne rivers had done in World War II. Towns and villages on the way found their streets glutted with refugees, all seeking food and a roof over their head for the night. In Limoges 200,000 people were sleeping rough in the parks and gardens. Many who crammed into cars didn't know how to drive, and blocked the roads with collisions and breakdowns.

Trains were packed. On 10 June a foreign journalist saw 20,000 people trying to board trains at the Gare d'Austerlitz:

> I have now been standing wedged in this seething mass for over three hours. A woman standing near us has fainted. Two agents force their way through the crowd and carry her off over the heads of the crowd. Children are crying all around and many babies in arms look like being crushed to death.[3]

The trains often only went short distances outside Paris before disgorging passengers from their crammed carriages onto country platforms, then returned to the city to get more people away from the dangerously packed Paris railway stations. In the confusion families lost members, children got separated from parents. In the next few months the Red Cross and other agencies reunited some 90,000 children with their families.

Somehow Freddie had to manoeuvre through all this chaos to get himself and his wealthy bride to safety in the south of France. He had one big advantage – he knew all the smaller roads heading south like the back of his hand. He'd taken the most powerful vehicle in the small collection of valuable cars owned by Beatrice Cartwight . . . now Beatrice McEvoy. He figured the mountains would provide the safest route. They would be unlikely to come across tanks or troop carriers on those roads. He aimed to get as far west as he could, then head south via back roads and drive over the mountains, then along the south coast toward Cannes and Casa Estella. If Italy invaded from the east, they would be in trouble, but he'd heard nothing about Italy joining Germany in the invasion of France. Typical for the Italians. That Mussolini was all piss and wind.

It's at about this point that a dark curtain falls over the 1940 activities of Freddie McEvoy. No record of his name can be found in the French or German archives. A search of French police files on foreigners in France in 1940 does not mention him. Meticulously kept German records of the thousands of foreigners who were interned during the 1940 occupation of France do not carry his name. Records in the British Foreign Office provide file numbers for Frederick Joseph McEvoy, but British officials insist the files can't be found. They say they were either lost over the years or destroyed to save space. They say they do not have a Frederick Joseph McEvoy in their files or at the UK National Archives – even though Freddie had a relatively high profile due to his sporting achievements representing Britain. British Intelligence records from the time are still not available to the public.

Freddie never told anybody what happened during this dark period of his life. There were rumours, of course. Some said that Freddie was acting as an undercover agent for the British Secret Service. Others claimed he collaborated with the Nazis, that he became a Nazi agent, that he'd been seen entering the German embassy before the invasion, that he'd mixed with high-powered Nazis in the Parisian nightclubs. British undercover agents in Vichy France were said to be looking for him. Some said that was all a ruse, that he was actually a double agent pretending to be on the Nazi side so that he could feed German Intelligence

THE SCANDALOUS FREDDIE McEVOY

false information from the British. If so, there are no records of it. Besides, it wasn't exactly in Freddie's nature to stick his neck out for somebody unless there was something in it for him. Freddie didn't ever give a sign of being a patriot or a warrior. He was very much an internationalist who thought war was a foolish venture. He liked to be friends with everyone. Sure, he might have expressed some admiration and understanding of Hitler's position and Nazi thinking, but he wasn't alone in having that attitude among the aristocrats and wealthy circles of which he had been part.

However, it is possible to trace through official records and reports that Freddie did eventually get his new wife to relative safety in the south of France. Not only that, but somehow amid all the chaos he got Beatrice on a plane that took her out of Vichy France to neutral Portugal. In Lisbon she was met by friends who put her on a ship to New York. She later learned that her former British husband, Royal Navy Captain Charles Aubrey Cartwright, was killed in action in May 1940 during the evacuation from Dunkirk.

But Freddie was trapped. While Beatrice was a rich American and therefore neutral and untouchable, Freddie was Australian and his country was at war with Germany. If he'd stayed in occupied Paris he would most likely have been rounded up and interned for the duration of the war.

His situation in southern France was different. There was chaos even as Marshal Pétain signed an armistice with the German invaders on 22 June. The armistice allowed the ageing extreme right winger Pétain to nominally sit in power in southern France, and he set up a puppet government in the spa town of

Vichy. The town was chosen simply because it had lots of hotels to accommodate officials and it was closer to Paris than the big cities such as Marseille or Lyon. French Vichy troops sealed the border to Spain and Switzerland – a border Freddie hadn't been able to cross – and southern France was now a supposedly 'Free Zone', unoccupied by German military forces. It certainly wasn't free if you were Jewish. Pétain's regime quickly started to round up Jews across Vichy France. It also wasn't free if you resisted German control of France. In 1940 and 1941 there were no active resistance fighters in France, but anyone who spoke out against Hitler and France's collaboration was quickly imprisoned. Pétain and his followers thought this little bit of false autonomy in southern France was preferable to surrendering completely to German occupying forces and having SS jackboots in the home of every French family. They'd seen what had happened in Czechoslovakia and Poland, and thought collaboration was far better than occupation.

Hitler agreed to the armistice simply because it meant he didn't need to tie up his army occupying the whole of France. In occupied France, Hitler had Paris and the French west coast, two-thirds of the French population, two-thirds of cultivated land and three-quarters of French industry. Why use German troops in southern France when the French would do the dirty work for him? Germany actually encouraged the French to rally around the flag of Marshall Pétain. The old French hero of World War I would do all that Germany wanted. Pétain wasn't quite a fascist; he was more of a feudalist who believed there was a natural order in human society in which lords like himself ruled the country while peasants did all the work. Pétain agreed that nearly all the produce of Vichy France – industrial and agricultural – would go to Germany. Pétain and other French conservatives welcomed the opportunity to overturn the freedoms of the old French republic and establish a police state. In return for obedience and collaboration with Germany, Vichy France would retain control of the French Navy and France's colonial empire. Pétain also agreed that under the terms of the armistice, France would now help Germany in the fight against Britain.

It was that last clause in the armistice that gave Freddie the most problems. He was stranded on the French Riviera. Freddie thought he could have use of Beatrice's 88-ton yacht moored at Cannes, the beautiful *Black Swan*. If he could get aboard and set sail under a neutral American flag he might be able to get away from Vichy France. But the yacht was registered in Beatrice's late husband's name, and flew the British flag. On 20 July 1940 the US State Department received a telegram from the US Embassy in Bern, Switzerland, passing on a request from the US consulate in Nice, France to authorise registration of the *Black Swan* as a US vessel. The telegram stated that ownership of the yacht had already been transferred from the 'British husband to his American wife Beatrice McEvoy – contemplating sending vessel to United States shortly under own steam'.[4] The application had to have been pushed by Freddie trapped on the Riviera. But two days later Washington knocked back the request. The US State Department replied:

> It is contrary to the policy of the Department to approve transfer of vessels from belligerent to American flag. Accordingly, assuming the *Black Swan* is presently registered

in the belligerent country, authorisation to issue provisional certificate of registry cannot, repeat not, be granted.[5]

So, even though the United States was sympathetic to the plight of Britain, it – being neutral – could not accept registration of a vessel from a nation that was at war. Freddie's escape by sea had been blocked by a frustrating diplomatic technicality. The *Black Swan* stayed tied up at Cannes until it was eventually seized by the Germans and used by holidaying officers.

But Freddie still had use of Beatrice's fabulous Casa Estella, and more than enough of his wife's money to keep the wolves at bay. Any troubles with inquisitive Vichy gendarmes were quickly resolved with cash slipped into their hands. Even though Freddie was a man of military age from Australia, a nation at war with Germany, at this stage in 1940 Australia was technically not at war with Vichy France. If Freddie kept his head down and stayed out of trouble tucked away in Beatrice's seaside villa near Cannes, he should be all right. German policy was to leave British nationals in Vichy France alone unless the Gestapo suspected them of subversive activity.[6] Local officials regarded Freddie as a jolly, friendly chap who posed no threat. Bribes paid to Vichy officials kept them focused elsewhere. Many friends and others trapped by the German invasion were hiding in villas and mansions in the hills behind Cannes and on the Cote d'Azur.

Freddie's situation became far more precarious when Britain decided it could not allow the French fleet to fall into German or Italian hands. The French had a considerable navy – three modern battleships, five dreadnought battleships, one aircraft carrier, seven heavy cruisers, 11 light cruisers, 32 heavy destroyers and 80 submarines. Most French warships were moored in the southern port of Toulon and on the north African coast. French naval officers were in a terrible situation. French naval ships had joined Britain's Royal Navy as allies during April's Norway campaign and in May helped evacuate British and French troops from Dunkirk. Britain and General de Gaulle, the Free French leader in London, pleaded with French naval captains to escape and join the Free French forces in Britain to continue the fight against the Germans. Some did, but the bulk of the fleet followed orders and declared themselves to be under the authority of Vichy France and, for the moment, neutral. The fleet moored in Toulon had orders to scuttle the ships if the Germans tried to seize them. The rest of the fleet was scattered in British ports and across north Africa, mainly the Algerian port of Mers El Kébir.

Britain could not allow the French warships to fall into German hands. On 3 July 1940 the Royal Navy launched Operation Catapult, a mission to seize or sink French naval ships that had not joined the Free French. In the early hours, without warning, British sailors stormed aboard French naval ships moored in Plymouth and Portsmouth. The first shots between the Royal Navy and the French Navy were fired in Portsmouth when a French sentry shot at the boarding party, killing a sailor and two officers. The sentry died in a hail of bullets. The Royal Navy captured two old battleships, two destroyers and five submarines in British ports. In Alexandria an old French battleship and heavy cruiser were disarmed. The fleet in Toulon was too well protected by shore batteries for the Royal Navy to move in and seize them. The four French battleships at the Algerian port of Mers El Kébir were vulnerable. A British squadron blockaded the port and presented the French Admiral Marcel-Bruno Gensoul an ultimatum: sail with the squadron to Britain and join the Free French Navy, or offload the crews and take the ships to a British port, where they would be disarmed. The powerful Royal Navy squadron, under Admiral James Somerville, comprised an aircraft carrier, a battlecruiser and two battleships along with cruisers and destroyers. Their firepower far outweighed the French and they could lob shells in from the sea onto the stationary French ships. Somerville's message to Gensoul was clear: if he didn't agree to the British demand, he must scuttle the French ships or they would be sunk by Somerville's waiting squadron.

The deadline for the ultimatum passed, and shortly before 6pm the order came from new Prime Minister Winston Churchill: sink the French ships. The powerful British battleships opened fire from 16 kilometres out to sea, and their huge shells slammed into the French ships. They were sitting ducks. One French battleship blew up, killing 977 crew. The French returned fire, but it was hopeless. Two French battleships and three destroyers were badly damaged. Only one French battleship escaped and made it to Toulon. All told, 1297 French sailors were killed and 350 wounded. Just two Britons were killed. As a military action it was a British success, but many tears were shed on the Royal Navy ships for what had been done to men who had been Allies just a few days earlier.

The attack at Mers El Kébir caused outrage in France. It handed Hitler a huge propaganda coup against the British, and he beat it as hard as he could. Across France, all media were under the control of Goebbels' propaganda department. French radio broadcast stories of the slaughter of innocent French sailors.

Posters went up on street corners depicting the treachery of the British on the 'neutral' French Navy. Newspapers carried stories of the bravery of gallant French sailors who died under the 'treacherous onslaught' of British battleships. Inside the Vichy government, there was increased pressure to join Germany in the fight against Britain. The number of Frenchmen seeking to join de Gaulle's Free French in Britain plummeted. Anger exploded at any Britons still in Vichy France. French planes bombed Gibraltar. Around 13,500 British civilians who had fled from Gibraltar to Casablanca were at risk of being attacked by mobs; for their own safety they were escorted at bayonet point to the wharf, where they were forced onto ships and removed.

The July attack on French ships in Algeria put Freddie and other expats trying to lie low in Vichy France in the summer of 1940 in a terrible position. It got even worse in September. De Gaulle believed that after the demonstration of British determination to prevent the French Navy falling into German hands, a similar show of force at Dakar in the Vichy-controlled west African colony of Senegal would persuade French ships there to come over to the Free French. In the Dakar port were the unfinished battleship *Richelieu*, two cruisers, four destroyers and three submarines. If they came across, they would be a very handy addition to the Allied fleet. If the British could capture Dakar it would not only provide a strong Allied naval base for the southern Atlantic, but locked up in Dakar were the gold reserves of the Banque de France and the exiled Polish government. The prize of warships and gold was too great a temptation, and Churchill agreed that de Gaulle could join the British task force sent to capture Dakar. They envisaged a repeat of the successful

Algerian action. The British force included the aircraft carrier *Ark Royal*, battleships *Resolution* and *Barham,* five cruisers, 10 destroyers and transports carrying 8000 troops. Among them was a small detachment of Free French and African troops. The Royal Australian Navy heavy cruiser HMAS *Australia* also joined the task force near Senegal. With a name like that, Vichy France would have no doubt Australia was also part of the attack on the French Navy.

HMAS *Australia*.

The operation was bungled from the start, and rapidly descended into farce. The sight of the mighty Royal Navy task force assembled off the coast was meant to strike fear into the Vichy French on land. But thick fog ensured the awesome sight remained hidden. Intelligence had assured de Gaulle that the Vichy French at Dakar would defect at his call. Leaflets dropped by plane a day earlier had told the Vichy French that de Gaulle had arrived and his emissaries would fly in the next day. Free French planes flew off *Ark Royal* and landed at Dakar airport expecting to be welcomed as heroes. The Vichy French were indeed waiting for them – and promptly threw them in jail. The British sent launches into the harbour carrying de Gaulle's representative, but machine guns on the shore defences opened fire on the small boats, forcing them back. Vichy French ships tried to leave the harbour but were fired on by HMAS *Australia*. The Australian cruiser badly damaged a French destroyer, which caught fire and was beached. The rest turned back to the harbour. Shore batteries opened fire on the *Australia*, prompting an unsuccessful gunfight between the British fleet and the shore guns. Several British ships were hit and the fleet had to withdraw. HMS *Resolution* had to be towed to Cape Town. It was a humiliation for de Gaulle and a setback for Churchill.

Vichy France hailed Dakar as a great victory. French newspapers and magazines were filled with stories and photos of the brave Vichy French defenders. 'The French were no longer on their knees, they had proved they had something to offer, here was leverage,' wrote historian Colin Smith.[7] The collaborators in the Vichy government were keen to point out to their German masters that France was now fighting Britain and her Dominions. Some in the Vichy regime wanted to go further and become outright allies with Germany against Britain. After all, wasn't Hitler going to win the war? Better to be on the winning side. If that had happened, it would have seen Freddie McEvoy seized from Beatrice's luxury seaside villa and locked up in some dreadful prisoner-of-war camp, or worse. Others in Vichy's puppet regime saw a better advantage for France in keeping things cool, staying neutral; best to just wait and see. Luckily for Freddie, when faced with a difficult choice the Gallic instinct to shrug the shoulders, reach for another cognac and do nothing finally won the day.

Hitler didn't push the Vichy regime. His focus was now on the east. Frustrated by the success of the RAF in the aerial Battle of Britain, Hitler secretly abandoned plans to invade Britain. On 18 December Hitler ordered the Wehrmacht to prepare top-secret plans for a *blitzkrieg* to be launched against the Soviet Union in the spring of 1941. Hitler also had to get his ally Mussolini out of trouble in Italy's failing invasion of Greece. Britain had just delivered massive blows against Italy – three Italian battleships were destroyed in an air raid on the Italian port of Taranto, and British and ANZAC forces had Italy on the run in north Africa. Vichy collaborators who argued that Britain was finished were forced to shut up. In November Pétain privately admitted to the US *charge d'affaires* in Vichy, Robert Murphy, that a British victory would be better for France than if Germany won the war.[8] Pétain recognised that Britain under Churchill would never make any kind of peace with Hitler. If France joined Germany, Pétain saw France once again embroiled in a bloodbath. Hitler would happily fight to the death of the last Frenchman.

Freddie McEvoy was undoubtedly saved by that decision of the Vichy government: to collaborate with the Nazis but keep the collective French head down and take no action against the Western Allies. The winter of 1940–41 on the French Riviera passed with Freddie only bothered by the inconvenience of the daily struggle to find food and the persistent demands for bribes from local officials. The money Freddie had stashed away couldn't last much longer, and as conditions worsened, the mood of the ordinary Frenchman in southern France was getting angry. That anger was being turned against those who seemed to be surviving better than them – the wealthy, the black marketeers, those who had jobs with the Vichy regime. More and more Jews in hiding were being informed on to the gendarmerie. Historian Ian Ousby wrote that 'the Germans were surprised at how ready the French were to betray each other'.[9] By early 1941, Vichy France had more than 30 prison camps holding anti-Nazis, communists and, most of all, Jews, in appalling conditions. Of 17,000 prison inmates held by the Vichy regime, 11,000 were Jews.[10] Freddie had money, and he had a prominent nose. How long before the accusatory fingers would be pointed at him? Would he be safe regardless of how many friends he had in the hierarchy? For Freddie, it was clearly time to get out of France and join his generous, and very rich, new bride in America.

Freddie did whatever he had to do to obtain an exit visa from the Vichy French authorities. Whether it involved paying a huge bribe, pulling in favours he had earned over the years during which he had lived in France, or striking a deal with the German Abwehr, the military Intelligence organisation, isn't known. He was in a nation of collaborators where collaboration was official government policy. It would be surprising if Freddie didn't do a bit of collaborating of his own to secure the exit visa. Freddie certainly never admitted to doing anything treasonous. Regardless of that, whatever he did to get an exit visa from Vichy France, it had him labelled for years as a suspected Nazi spy.

Official records in the US archives reveal that on 4 April 1941 the US consulate in Nice issued Freddie McEvoy an entry visa to the United States because he was married to a US citizen. But consular officials had their reservations and questioned how he was able to gain an exit visa from Vichy France considering that all visas had to be approved by the German officials looking over the collective Vichy shoulder. Freddie left France on 26 April 1941 bound for Lisbon. On 31 May, Freddie sailed on a neutral American ship to New York.

FBI Director J Edgar Hoover heard about the Australian Frederick J McEvoy from the US State Department. On 17 July 1941 Hoover wrote to his regional chiefs an internal letter marked 'Internal Security'. He ordered FBI agents to keep a watch on Freddie McEvoy because he could be a Nazi spy:

Dear Sirs,

Information has been received from the State Department, Washington DC, that Mr Frederick McEvoy was issued an immigration visa at Nice on April 4, 1941. He is an Australian and believed to be the husband of a wealthy American by the name of Beatrice Cartwright McEvoy. She is believed to be many years older than he and is presently residing in the United States.

McEvoy left Nice for Lisbon on approximately April 26, 1941, and then proceeded to the United States. It is reported that in Nice and its environs he had a questionable reputation. An exit visa was issued to him by the French government, and according to the present interpretation of the Armistice Convention, due to the fact that he is of military age and a British subject he is not eligible to receive this exit visa. Because of this it was believed that he obtained the visa with the express authorisation of the German military authorities in Paris.

On May 31, 1941, McEvoy left Lisbon by clipper, giving the Waldorf Palace as his New York address . . . [11]

An internal memo dated 3 April 1942 from the Passport Division of the US Department of State concerning visas for Beatrice McEvoy repeated the comments that Freddie, a man of 'questionable reputation', must have received German military authorisation to obtain the exit visa from France:

> Additional information has been received on Frederick McEvoy to the effect that he has maintained close association with persons who are strongly pro-Nazi in sympathy . . . derogatory information of a personal nature has also been received on McEvoy, but in none of the reports received to date is it stated that Mrs McEvoy is involved in any activities inimical to the best interests of the United States.[12]

Freddie had just leapt out of the frying pan right into the fire.

CHAPTER 7

THE FBI FINGERS FREDDIE AS A NAZI SPY

After the hardships of Vichy France, Freddie landed in the lap of luxury in New York. Beatrice was one of the richest women in the city and she rented an exclusive penthouse in the Waldorf Astoria Towers, the most salubrious address on Park Avenue. The ornate 47-storey hotel was the world's tallest at the time. It was also the most expensive, designed to cater specifically for the very wealthy of New York, and hosted guests such as the Duke and Duchess of Windsor.

Beatrice had a long-term lease on Suite 28A that comprised 10 bedrooms and drawing rooms, for which she paid a monthly rent of US$1200 (US$37,000 in today's money). On top of that came food, liquor, parties, flowers, maids, chauffeurs and butlers, which pushed the monthly bill to more than US$1 million in today's money.

Despite the luxury and opulence surrounding him in New York, Freddie didn't stick around for long with his much older millionaire wife. While he'd been tied up in Vichy France, his good mate from long ago and partner in many glorious romps, Errol Flynn, had become a Hollywood superstar. In 1934 Flynn's good looks had been spotted at an English theatre by a Hollywood talent scout and he'd got his big Hollywood break in the huge 1935 swashbuckler hit, *Captain Blood*. Publicists at Warner Bros studio didn't think Americans would take to an Australian – they were generally regarded as uncouth, untamed, unrefined, uncivilised, uncontrollable and far too ready to strike up a brawl – and so they billed the dashing, swashbuckling and devilishly handsome Aussie as an Irishman.

Regardless, Errol Flynn tried as hard as he could to live up to the wild reputation Australians had in America. He partied hard, he womanised hard, he drank hard and he fought hard with anyone who crossed him. His Hollywood fame grew and grew: in 1936 *The Charge of the Light Brigade* was another massive hit; in 1938 *The Adventures of Robin Hood* filled cinemas around the world; in 1939 came *The Private Lives of Elizabeth and Essex*; in 1940 *The Sea Hawk* was swashbuckling at its very best . . . Errol Flynn was Hollywood gold, and he was living life in the fast lane. As soon as Flynn heard his old mate Freddie McEvoy was in New York, he rang and told him to get over to Los Angeles for the time of his life. Women of all types, abilities and ages were throwing themselves at Errol, and he needed help to meet the demand.

Freddie must have felt as if he were living in a gilded cage in Beatrice's luxury apartment. Beatrice was all very nice and caring, and she provided a generous allowance for her newly reunited playboy husband. But for Freddie, Beatrice's New

York society friends were all so much older, and so goddamn proper. Beatrice was one of the top New York society doyens and expected Freddie to be on his best behaviour. On Freddie's arrival in New York, Beatrice threw a lavish dinner to welcome – and show off – her handsome husband to her friends. Included in the dinner invitation were several Australian military officers and senior embassy officials who happened to be in the city. Their presence must have embarrassed Freddie, as they would have had some awkward questions about what he had been doing in France for the past 12 months, how he managed to get out of the country and whether he intended to join up.

Freddie felt he had to get away from Beatrice, but he needed her money and so couldn't just walk out. The phone call from Errol Flynn came like a lifeline to a drowning man. Just a few weeks after arriving in New York and the reunion with his much older and very rich wife, Freddie took off for LA to meet up with his movie star playmate. Officially, at least to the syndicated gossip pages on 1 June 1941, it was a business trip with Warner Bros, 'not as an actor'. The columnist added that Beatrice was still trying to get her now 12-year-old son brought to America from bomb-blasted England. She was willing to charter 'the finest plane available and make a round trip to England' to bring the boy to New York, but her son by her late husband Captain Cartwright RN was still classified as a 'ward in chancery' and could not be removed from England, war or no war. The columnist quipped: 'Ask Bea if she thinks money is everything, and she will quickly tell you it isn't.'[1]

When Freddie landed in Los Angeles in June 1941, Errol Flynn was taking a break from filming a movie about the famous

General George Custer who was killed fighting Indians at the Battle of the Little Bighorn. It was a fantastic role, just right for Flynn – Custer was a troublemaker who refused to stick to the stiff army rules, wore non-regulation uniforms, conducted pranks on his fellow officers and threw out the rule book to fight from his guts. Of course, recklessness got Custer killed. Flynn loved the character and was proud to be playing a real American war hero.

Flynn quickly whisked Freddie up to the isolated ranch he had just completed building on a mountain high above Hollywood at the top of the steep, precarious, winding Mulholland Drive. The ranch house with swimming pool and enormous entertainment area was designed by Flynn himself as a bachelor's pleasure dome, built specially for wild parties and orgies. A secret door behind the bar in the vast living room led to a small triangular sitting room with a view through a two-way mirror into the women's bathroom. Upstairs he installed a secret panel that looked down into the bedroom below, positioned right above the king-size bed. Lying on the bed, all you could see was a mirror on the ceiling, but from upstairs it was a two-way mirror that Flynn could use to gaze down on the action below without the participants' knowledge. Flynn had other hidden viewing portals to look into the dining and living rooms. A steam room outside was decorated with frescoes of buxom women engaged imaginatively with portly men.[2]

Flynn was keen to explore every conceivable sexual adventure he could dream up. There was luxury on display too. On the walls he had paintings by Van Gogh and Gauguin; tiles hand-glazed by Goya decorated the bar. His den, or home office, was wood panelled with paintings of seascapes and models of sailing ships. Mulholland Farm was Errol Flynn's escape, a place where he could indulge his whims and fantasies far from the prying eyes of the press and the law. The ranch was isolated, and Flynn had only coyotes for neighbours. His parties fast became legendary, and there were plenty of attractive women angling for an invitation. And some uninvited ones. Despite the isolation, some curious young ladies did make their way all the way up the hill and climbed the fence to knock on his front door. Errol Flynn once said he liked his whisky old, and his women young. Flynn's trouble was he liked them too young, even below the legal age of 18. It would soon get him into big trouble with the law.

The details of what Errol Flynn and Freddie McEvoy, and other assorted members of Flynn's entourage of wild men and even wilder women, got up to in those weeks of June 1941 up at Mulholland Ranch were not recorded. However, whatever happened was enough for Freddie when he got back to New York to tell his wife that they were packing up and moving to Hollywood. This would have come as a shock to the matronly Beatrice, who was now nudging 65 and very much a pillar of New York upper-crust society. New Yorkers tended to look down on movie people in Hollywood, and regarded Los Angeles as a crass town of crooks, conmen and dames on the make. Which it largely was. New Yorkers' attitudes to LA haven't changed much since then.

Beatrice was a lady who knew how to make an entrance. On her arrival in Los Angeles, one of her good friends in the disrespectable city's respectable society threw a ball in honour of Beatrice and her mysterious new husband. The society columns recorded that the big names to attend the ball included Errol Flynn, British diplomat Sir Charles Mendl, banker Lawrence Turnure, Gloria and Reginald Vanderbilt, Lady Thelma Furness, Cesar Romero, Mrs Douglas Fairbanks Sr, businessman Huntington Hartford, gay nightclub owner Catherine Baroness d'Erlanger, and two names that would come up later in FBI reports – Daniel Sickles and Hugh Fenwick.[3]

What Freddie didn't know was that the eagle eye of the law was just about to swivel right on him. For weeks FBI agents had been keeping a close watch on Freddie following Director J Edgar Hoover's order on 17 July 1941 to investigate the Australian's background. Hoover demanded regular detailed reports on Freddie's activities: who he met, what they discussed, his financial transactions and his personal relationships, 'to determine whether they are of a subversive nature'.[4]

On 6 August 1941 Hoover received a long report on Freddie compiled by FBI Special Agent HD O'Neill. Marked 'Frederick G [sic] McEvoy – "Internal Security"', its front-page summary said that in May 1940 the subject (Freddie), an internationally known 'automobile driver and possibly in service of British government', married an extremely wealthy granddaughter of a former Standard Oil president.[5] So the FBI identified the mysterious Australian Freddie McEvoy as a possible British secret agent – a veritable James Bond 007 well before Ian Fleming invented the super-spy. Sadly, getting Freddie's middle initial wrong does not inspire much confidence in the FBI agent's sleuthing ability. Oddly, the FBI could not find any record of Freddie arriving in New York at Ellis Island, the processing point for new arrivals from overseas.

Special Agent O'Neill reported that 'subject [Freddie] and wife departed New York on 17 July 1941 and currently residing in Beverly Hills Hotel, Beverly Hills, California'.[6] The FBI agent couldn't find any business connections of Freddie McEvoy. The agent reported that all Freddie's financial expenses were covered by his wife, with no questions asked by Beatrice's accountant, the source of Agent O'Neil's report.

The FBI's Los Angeles office picked up the surveillance on Freddie McEvoy. On 30 August Special Agent Frank Angell filed a 12-page report on the comings and goings of Freddie during the previous five weeks in LA. Angell reported that an FBI informant among the employees of the Beverly Hills Hotel said Mr and Mrs McEvoy 'have very little to do with each other and pride themselves on having separate establishments at the hotel'.[7] They had two separate cabanas near the hotel swimming pool. That came with two separate telephone lines, and the FBI recorded every phone number they called and that came in. Their mail was also monitored.

The official Beverly Hills Hotel hostess, Sally Starr, told Special Agent Angell that she had seen Freddie in Paris in 1928 and again in 1932. 'Even at that time he was considered nothing but a gigolo,' Starr told Angell.[8] She said while Freddie was at the Beverly Hills Hotel he was frequently seen in the company of Prince Artchil Gourielli, who was married to the much older cosmetics self-made multi-millionaire Helena Rubinstein. Gourielli was cousin of a man who went by the name Gogi and owned and operated a nightclub on the strip in Hollywood. It's highly likely that Freddie knew Gourielli from his time in the French millionaire playgrounds of the Riviera. Helena Rubinstein

The Beverly Hills Hotel in the 1940s.

grew up in Australia, where she started her cosmetics business before moving on to London, Paris and New York at the outbreak of World War I. In 1938 she married Prince Gourielli, a penniless aristocrat playboy of dubious royal Georgian connections. They were both staying at the hotel.

Hotel cleaners, barmen, pool attendants, security personnel, receptionists, managers, doormen, maids, switchboard operators, chauffeurs, concierge, waiters and waitresses were all called on to provide snippets of information on whom Freddie saw, where he went, his manner and demeanour, his moods and what he talked about. The pool manager, Hayden Fithian, was a particularly keen snitch. He told Special Agent Angell that he didn't hear what was said when Freddie had his group of friends around, but he 'could not be too good an American because he was always conversing in either French or German or some other foreign language with the foreigners who were with him in his cabana'.[9]

One visitor to Freddie's cabana was of particular interest to the FBI. When one of the informants told Agent Angell that a Captain Daniel Sickles had been seen drinking with Freddie in the hotel bar, the FBI man's ears pricked up. Sickles was on the FBI files as a bit of a suspect character. An Englishman, son of a former British ambassador to Belgium, Sickles told everybody he was the liaison officer at the Douglas Aircraft Company in Santa Monica, California and also at the American Tank Company. Both were key defence industries. Another FBI agent checked with Douglas Aircraft Corporation and could not find any official connection Sickles had with the company. In fact, Sickles wasn't known to any aircraft officials the FBI had managed to contact so far. It was very suspicious.

Sickles had been staying at the Beverly Hills Hotel on and off for some time. He gave an address in New York as his home. Sally Starr, an enthusiastic informant, said she believed that Sickles had spent a lot of his life in Europe because he spoke French, but that he had a wife in New York and had also been having an affair with an American woman called Sandra Rambeau. Thirty years earlier she had been born Dorothy Rambo in Springfield, Missouri, and was working as a telephone switchboard girl when she got a place in the chorus line of the 1933 film *42nd Street* and changed her name to the more exotic Sandra Rambeau. Starr said she'd heard that Rambeau had been following Sickles all over the United States.

Miss Rambeau must have been a busy girl. Apparently, Freddie had been having an affair with her as well. When Sickles wanted to bring Rambeau into the hotel, Beatrice McEvoy reacted angrily. She flew in a rage straight to management, demanding Sandra Rambeau be banned from the Beverly Hills Hotel. The furious Mrs McEvoy said that if Miss Rambeau was admitted to the hotel, then the entire McEvoy entourage would leave.[10] It was quite a scene. Beatrice was paying all the very extensive bills, so management had no choice. Sickles left and moved to the nearby Beverly Wilshire Hotel where Rambeau was staying. In the past Beatrice had been prepared to overlook Freddie's extra-marital dalliances, but obviously that was in Europe, not in America in front of all her society friends. Freddie had overstepped the mark.

Agent Angell checked out this Sandra Rambeau. He found she had an FBI file entitled 'Sandra Rambeau – Espionage G'. A national defence informant had told the FBI in July 1941 that Rambeau was regarded as a Nazi agent. She was an American citizen who had lived in Germany and France for many years before war broke out in Europe. On her return to the United States, she denied press reports she had been married for a time to 72-year-old Nazi General Franz Ritter von Epp, a confidant of Hitler, senior member of the Reichstag and Reichskommissar for the state of Bavaria. She was in Paris when the Germans invaded and was 'reportedly very friendly with many high-ranking German officials'.[11] She was a female version of Freddie McEvoy, using her charms in and out of the bedroom to beguile one wealthy and powerful man after another. She was known as the queen of occupied France, moving around with impunity until 1941, when she left France and returned to America. She conceded she had no trouble leaving occupied France and that 'influential friends may have interceded on her behalf'.[12] She told a reporter America should stay out of active participation in the European war. She lived at the Hotel Pierre in New York, very expensive digs for a single woman of no visible means. The espionage report described her as 'an internationally known play-girl, has often voiced anti-Semitic sentiments, and is in contact with the French Vichy Embassy in Mexico City'.[13] It concluded: 'Subject [Rambeau] is thought to be a German agent and may be in California on a mission of espionage.'[14]

Shortly after the blow-up with Mrs McEvoy at the Beverly Hills Hotel, Rambeau left the Beverly Wilshire Hotel on 10 August and gave her forwarding address as the Hotel Ritz, Mexico City. Agent Angell said he learned from Los Angeles Police that Rambeau was being 'kept' by Freddie McEvoy. It is quite possible that Freddie knew her in France before and during the German occupation, because they would have mixed in the same partying society. She was a leading figure among the stage entertainers at the Monte Carlo Casino, Freddie's main hunting ground. He certainly met up with her in Hollywood. The social pages had a photo of a beaming Freddie in a tuxedo dancing closely with the very attractive Sandra Rambeau at the El Morocco nightclub, the latter bare-shouldered in a body-hugging dress highlighting an expensive-looking jewel necklace and earrings. She is also beaming, looking very happy in Freddie's arms. Perhaps it was this photo that set off Beatrice McEvoy.

News that Freddie was cavorting with a suspected Nazi agent intensified the FBI's interest in him. It began looking deeply into everyone with whom Freddie came into contact.

Among the circle in which he is travelling at the present time there is a great deal of talk about his having refused to have any part whatsoever in the present war. He is said to be very intensively pro-war and not to care about whether Germany or England succeeds in winning this present conflict. He is a close friend of Fred Engels who is said to be a very pro-Nazi American.[15]

Agent Angell reported that at a dinner party held at an estate in Santa Barbara, Engels very publicly announced that 'there was only one dominant figure in the world today, namely Adolf Hitler.'[16] Engels went on to declare that America was being driven into the European war by Jews close to President Roosevelt. Agent Angell said Engels' remarks were relayed by several distinguished people at the dinner, including two members of the British nobility. If these two nobles were the Duke and Duchess of Windsor it would be quite a turnaround for them, because they had delighted in meeting Hitler themselves shortly after the abdication, and were known to have Nazi sympathies.

Engels was not present at a Hollywood nightclub on 22 August when Freddie was reported to have made remarks to a group of high-society figures that included Lady Thelma Furness, who had been the mistress of Edward, the Prince of Wales, before he took up with Wallis Simpson. One of those present told someone who told Agent Angell that Freddie had made several 'pro-Nazi, anti-American, and anti-Roosevelt statements'. No mention is made of how many drinks had been imbibed or what the circumstances were, but it was the first indication for the FBI that Freddie had pro-Nazi sentiments. That, plus his

```
This case originated at:  NEW YORK CITY, N.Y.              File No. 100-6441
Report Made At:        Date        Period    Report Made By:
Los Angeles, Calif.    9/18/41    9/4,8,9,12,  H. FRANK ANGELL        IST
                                  16,17/41
Title:                                 Character of Case:
FREDERICH G. McEVOY                     INTERNAL SECURITY - G

    Synopsis of Facts:

                    Subject left the Beverly Hills Hotel, Beverly Hills,
                    California, September 15, 1941 for New York City.
                    Forwarding address Waldorf Astoria Towers.  Rumor he
                    and present wife contemplating divorce.  Information
                    re the activities of SANDRA RAMBEAU previously set
                    forth in Los Angeles report instant case, and she is
                    identical with the Subject in the case of New York
                    origin entitled:  "IDA HEDIN, SANDRA RAMBEAU, also
                    known as DOROTHY RAMBO, Internal Security".  RAMBEAU
                    last reported in Mexico City, D.F.  McEVOY reportedly
                    a close friend of FRED ENGELS, allegedly pro-Nazi.

                                        P.

    REFERENCE:

                    Report of Special Agent H. FRANK ANGELL, Los Angeles,
                    California, dated August 30, 1941.
                    Report of Special Agent W. FORBES WEBBER, Kansas City,
                    Missouri, dated August 23, 1941, in case entitled
                    "IDA HEDIN, SANDRA RAMBEAU, also known as DOROTHY
                    RAMBO, Internal Security".
                    Telegram to New York City, September 17, 1941.

    DETAILS:

                    At the time of the dictation of writer's reference report,
                 it will be recalled that Mr. and Mrs. McEVOY had left the Beverly

    Approved & Forwarded:                     Do Not Write In These Spaces
                            S.A.C.
    Copies:
     5/Bureau        4 New York
     2 Kansas City   2 San Antonio
        (Inf.)           (Inf.)
     (1-KC 100-2091)4 Los Angeles
                    (1 LA 100-6538)
```

Confidential FBI report on Freddie's movements.

connection to Sandra Rambeau and mixing with men who had
suspicious connections to the armaments industry, put Freddie
right in the spotlight as a suspected Nazi spy.

An actor called Edward Ashley-Cooper came forward to tell
the FBI of his suspicions about Sandra Rambeau. Ashley was

actually an Australian, born Edward Montague Hussey Cooper
in Sydney in 1906, who had dropped the Cooper part of his
name in Hollywood to prevent confusion with another actor
of a similar name. Like Errol Flynn, Ashley played down his
Australian background when he got to Hollywood after a reasonably successful run in Britain. He'd won the key role of the
dastardly George Wickham in the 1940 Hollywood movie *Pride
and Prejudice*, and he continued the dastardly character when
he sat down with the FBI. Ashley didn't have nice things to say
about his fellow Aussie Freddie McEvoy, describing him as a 'a
big time gigolo, well known on the Riviera in France, and all told
a very undesirable person'.[17] Ashley didn't know whether Freddie
was a secret Nazi, but he thought Sandra Rambeau probably was.
He said Sandra Rambeau had been Freddie's mistress in France
while she was engaged to marry Indian Maharaja Bishnu, nephew
of the King of Nepal. Ashley also said that Rambeau had had an
affair with Prince George, the Duke of Kent, younger brother
of King George VI. (She wouldn't be alone there; the Duke had
numerous affairs with both men and women including romance
writer Barbara Cartland, playwright and performer Noël Coward
and Soviet spy Anthony Blunt. Prince George, who, like his eldest
brother, the abdicated King Edward VIII, reportedly had Nazi
sympathies, died in a mysterious plane crash in 1942.) Ashley,
who seemed to relish his role as FBI informant, said as soon as
the Germans occupied Paris, Rambeau struck up an affair with a
high-ranking German army officer. Ashley said he was surprised
when he saw her pop up in America. She must have been sent
to the United States by German Intelligence, Ashley said, and
he urged the FBI to keep a close eye on her.

Sandra Rambeau – Freddie's lover and Nazi spy.

Another Australian to talk to the FBI in connection with the Freddie McEvoy investigation was movie actress Carmel Myers, then the wife of LA attorney Ralph Blum. Daughter of an Australian rabbi and Austrian mother, she made her Hollywood name playing an Egyptian seductress in the silent screen version of *Ben Hur*. At a dinner she hosted at her Sunset Boulevard mansion formerly owned by Gloria Swanson, Myers saw Freddie's friend Fred Engels once again spout off against Jews and President Roosevelt. Myers told the FBI her husband, a Jew, almost came to blows with Engels after he told the gathering that aviator Charles Lindbergh was right to oppose American entry into a war against Germany. Myers said movie actress Ruth Moody, wife of American tennis star Lester Stoefen, was the only one at the dinner to support Engels. When the subject of German U-boat attacks on US ships carrying weapons and supplies to beleaguered Britain came up, Myers said Moody remarked: 'I'd sink the ships too.'[18] The FBI spoke to Ralph Blum, who said Engels was a gigolo living off his wife's money and became anti-American when he realised how much the US Treasury was taxing them. Agent Angell concluded this report saying he only included Engels because he was reportedly close to Freddie McEvoy.

Vice president of the Vultee Aircraft Corporation, Hugh Fenwick, also had gossip on Freddie that interested the FBI. Fenwick said he had a casual acquaintance with Freddie in France in the mid-1930s and described him as 'nothing but an international pimp'.[19] Fenwick, who must have been one of the few not charmed by Freddie, said Freddie's wife only married him because she was tired of giving him money, and that if she was going to continue funding his lifestyle he'd have to make an honest woman of her.

Bearing in mind that they'd married just days before the Germans occupied Paris, this is hardly likely to have been the ultimatum that passed between them. But Fenwick did have some good words for Freddie, in a backhanded sort of way. He told the FBI he doubted Freddie would be engaged in espionage or anything like acting as a German agent in the United States, because he was nothing but a self-centred playboy.

However, Fenwick had plenty to say about Sandra Rambeau. Fenwick reported he was at a Hollywood nightclub and heard

Rambeau loudly declare: 'The English are no god damn good, the Germans have the greatest system in the world and the English have been dominating world affairs long enough.'[20] She only stopped her tirade when an English actor who was with her, Reginald Gardiner, told her to shut up because she was embarrassing herself and the other people at the table. Fenwick said he knew Rambeau in Europe before the war and she was known as an 'international society prostitute'. He confirmed earlier reports to the FBI that Rambeau shacked up with a high-ranking German army officer in Paris even before the invasion. He said Prince Edward (later to abdicate as king) had forced his younger brother Prince George to break up his embarrassing affair with Rambeau, but only after she had got away with some of the crown jewels. Rambeau was, Fenwick said, 'the typical female espionage agent'.[21]

Maybe she wasn't a particularly smart one if she was sounding off at the top of her voice in a Hollywood nightclub about how wonderful Nazi Germany was. But Fenwick's account was music to the ears of the FBI, which now believed it had uncovered a nest of Nazi vipers complete with sultry seductresses and movie stars, and saw Freddie as very much part of it. J Edgar Hoover ordered his agents to intensify their investigation.

In a new report in September, Special Agent Angell noted that while there may have been strains between Mr and Mrs McEvoy, they left the Beverly Hills Hotel together with assorted maids and butlers on 27 August in three luxury Cadillacs bound for Santa Barbara. Reading between the lines of the FBI report, Freddie then left his chagrined wife kicking her heels in the Biltmore Santa Barbara Hotel while he took off with his mate

Errol Flynn and a bevy of beauties 'fishing' around Catalina Island, 35 kilometres off the coast. Catalina was the secluded playground of movie stars and starlets, the rich and the corrupted. As the days ticked over, Beatrice grew more and more annoyed at Freddie taking off. After all, it had been only a few months since his return after being trapped for a year in Vichy France, and she'd crossed the nation to be with him in California. Now he'd disappeared out to sea to 'fish'. She knew that fish weren't what Freddie was catching out on that yacht with sex fiends like Errol Flynn on board.

The FBI got the switchboard operator at the Biltmore Hotel to monitor all the calls to and from the McEvoy group's rooms. Freddie called his wife four times from Catalina Island, during which, the operator reported, Mrs McEvoy tried to persuade her husband to return from his fishing trip and join her at the hotel because it was becoming 'embarrassing' for her to keep on having to explain his absence. 'She also wanted to know what interests he had on Catalina Island, and he had steadily maintained that she would not understand.'[22]

Beatrice understood only too well what Freddie was up to. The switchboard operator said a lot of their conversation was conducted in French, which the operator couldn't follow, but you can bet she said, '*Tu es un minable, un moins que rien!*' Maybe she even sent the harsh unladylike words *connard*, *abruti*, *salaud*, *débile* or *obsédé* blistering down the phone line. After more than a week of this, Beatrice suddenly upped and returned by plane to New York City. The FBI recorded that Freddie followed her a couple of weeks later. She did, after all, pay Freddie's bills.

Meanwhile the FBI went through a log of all the phone calls Freddie made from the hotels he had used in California. Many were to women in Beverly Hills, often the wives of wealthy Californians. One number he called frequently was the Los Angeles home of Mrs Stephen Raphael, wife of one of Britain's richest men, who was known to the British consul in LA as an international playboy. Many calls were also made to mob-connected movie producer Pasquale 'Pat' DiCicco, who at the time was courting 17-year-old Gloria Vanderbilt, heiress to a railway fortune. Young Gloria, who was worth about US$70 million in today's money, was being fawned over in Hollywood nightclubs such as Ciro's and Mocambo by movie stars Bruce Cabot, Errol Flynn and Van Heflin. Freddie must have been cursing the fact that he was already married when he saw how keen the young heiress was to escape her overbearing minders, as well as her unstable mother and a grandmother who wanted her to become a nun. Oddly it was DiCicco, film-star handsome and always snappily dressed in white, who beat the movie stars and snared the rich girl. DiCicco married the barely legal Vanderbilt in late 1941. They divorced in 1945.[23] (Gloria Vanderbilt's aunt Thelma, twin sister of her mother, was another mistress to Prince Edward, the Prince of Wales, until she was supplanted by her best friend Wallis Simpson. Gloria had three more husbands and four children, including CNN journalist Anderson Cooper.)

Strangely, Hugh Fenwick, who had dismissed FBI suggestions that Freddie could be a secret agent for the Germans, didn't mention during his FBI interview that he had been in phone contact with Freddie several times since he arrived in California. That's something the FBI discovered only when it examined the phone calls Freddie had made from his hotel room. It is possible Fenwick's put-down of Freddie as nothing but a pimp was an arranged attempt to diminish FBI interest in Freddie.

Freddie also frequently called the LA home of actor Bruce Cabot, who was a close friend of Errol Flynn. The three amigos operated as a team as they partied hard through Hollywood nightclubs and bedded willing women across a string of Beverly Hills mansions. Freddie and Bruce would become even closer in the months ahead, but first Freddie had to find out whether Beatrice was going to tolerate his gross infidelities and keep him on the matrimonial payroll. The answer came quickly. Returning to New York from carousing in LA, Freddie found himself barred from his wife's apartment complex in the luxury Waldorf Astoria building. He took up digs in the equally luxurious Savoy Plaza Hotel overlooking Central Park before finding an apartment at ritzy 1 East End Avenue, looking over the East River at East 79th Street. It was no coincidence that Sandra Rambeau should then appear in New York, managing to be seen by gossip columnist Jimmy Starr at the 21 Club where celebrities went to be seen by gossip columnists. Drinking cocktails with Rambeau were society queen Countess Dorothy Dentice Di Frasso – who had her own FBI file for her suspected links to fascists and Nazis – and movie-star networker Doris Stein, wife of Hollywood powerbroker Jules Stein. The Countess could very well have been singing the praises of Freddie McEvoy to her fellow networking cock-tail-sipping gossips. Di Frasso held enormous influence among Hollywood and American high society; to be excluded from one of her famous society parties meant an end to membership of the social elite. Di Frasso had inherited US$17 million (in today's money) and married an Italian count, spending a million dollars fixing up his 16th-century Villa Madama in Rome. It was there that she met Mussolini and entertained Goebbels and Göring. Divorced and back in the United States when war threatened, Di Frasso enjoyed the company of good-looking younger men, and became particularly enamoured with Freddie. She was one of his most generous patrons and spread his fame among her influential and wealthy friends by proclaiming that Freddie's ardour and performance in the bedroom were worth all the money she gave him.[24]

Freddie's time wasn't wasted in New York. He used his pals in the millionaire fraternity to gain membership of New York City's very, very exclusive River Club, a health and fitness centre running across the end of 52nd and 53rd Streets. It included a place to moor one's yacht on the East River. A sparkling ball-room, swimming pool, tennis courts, dining room and luxury apartments on the top floors were just a few of the perks of membership, the aim of which, the club said in its promotion, was 'social intercourse'. Membership was strictly limited to 400 blue-chip upper-crust society folk with names such as Astor, Roosevelt, Vanderbilt, Morgan, Pulitzer, Rockefeller and Grace. Freddie, ever the charming upper-class social networker, was mixing it with New York's richest. Even if Beatrice turned off the cash tap, the opportunities for a skilled operator in this new world were boundless.

As winter closed in, Freddie did what many New Yorkers did: he headed south to the hot new playground of Miami, Florida, and on to Cuba. The FBI was still hot on his trail, and the Miami bureau reported that Freddie 'played around' with the British consul in Havana, Cuba, Rodney Sauer, and other British friends.[25] Freddie must have felt right at home. Havana in the early 1940s was a swinging city devoted to excess and pleasures to cater for all tastes. Casinos ran 24 hours with guests dressed to the nines. Opulent nightclubs drummed late into the night with Cuban music. Some held live sex shows that would have made Emperor Caligula blush. The bordellos of Havana were notorious, offering every kind of sexual adventure that even the most deviant client could dream up, many of which would be illegal in the United States and Europe. As 1941 drew to a close, Freddie was on the edge of divorce from his wealthy wife, but he was having a ball. He saw no reason for that to change.

CHAPTER 8

AMERICA GOES TO WAR, FREDDIE
GOES TO HOLLYWOOD

Japan bombed Pearl Harbor on 7 December 1941. Four days later, Germany declared war against the United States. This was a mere blip on the horizon for Freddie McEvoy. The FBI recorded him saying the war was 'a jolly nuisance' because it prevented his return to France and the playgrounds of Cannes and Monte Carlo, where he wanted to pursue his pleasures.[1] The FBI's informants reported that at one point Freddie did proclaim his wish to be able to join the Royal Australian Air Force and aid his country in the war – but he did nothing about it. Freddie, aged 34 and very fit, could easily have turned up at an Australian or British consulate and volunteered for active service. He didn't. But as far as the FBI was concerned, Freddie was off the high-priority list as a suspected secret agent for Nazi Germany, at least for the time being. Informants in Florida and Cuba said they had never heard Freddie express sympathy for the Germans. As the

United States joined the war, the FBI had bigger fish to fry than a frivolous Australian playboy whose only action seemed to be in the bedrooms of wealthy women.

America in the late 1930s did have a very active Nazi movement, and American Nazis didn't bother hiding. Soon after Hitler took power in Germany in 1933, Nazi party ideologues reached out to the Americans of German heritage to unite with them in the great cause of German national socialism. Nazi propagandists believed America had more 'German blood' than any other nation, and that if those Aryans united they could exert considerable influence in Washington. Hitler, on the other hand, saw the United States as a nation riddled with Jews, 'a nation of millionaires, beauty queens, stupid [music] records and Hollywood'.[2] Nevertheless, in 1933 Deputy Führer Rudolf Hess gave Heinz Spanknöbel, a German migrant in the United States, authority to form an American Nazi organisation. Based in New York, members of the Friends of New Germany wore a uniform of white shirt and black trousers with a badge showing a red iron cross and swastika in the centre. By the mid-1930s they had several thousand members who harassed German-language newspapers to print Nazi material. But the organisation wasn't united, and the United States deported Spanknöbel as a foreign agent.

In 1936 the Friends of New Germany was succeeded by the German American Bund (union) led by Fritz Julius Kuhn, a veteran of the German army in World War I. Kuhn couldn't be deported because he was an American citizen, and under his stewardship the Bund quickly grew from several hundred to tens of thousands. The hard-core Bund members dressed in brown shirts, black ties and khaki pants, and declared themselves to be true patriotic Americans; they proclaimed George Washington the world's 'first fascist' who knew democracy could not work.[3] They held Hitler Youth-style camps across the country, attracting thousands of children, teenagers, young men and women of German descent to join night-time torch rallies along with para-military exercises in forests and fields. This was accompanied by lengthy studies of Nazi ideology and haranguing speeches by Kuhn. In New York on 20 February 1939, at a packed Madison Square Garden, the Bund held a Hitler-style rally that attracted 22,000 American Nazis. Dressed in crisp brown Nazi uniforms, they cheered and gave the Nazi salute as Kuhn, who liked to call himself the American Führer, spoke from the stage ridiculing President Roosevelt as 'Rosenfeld' and his New Deal as the 'Jew Deal'. Kuhn, dressed in paramilitary uniform, demanded a 'socially just, white, Gentile-ruled United States'.[4] A massive banner of George Washington covered the back of the stage, and thousands of men and women in SA-style uniforms marched into the stadium bearing the US flag side by side with swastika banners led by military drums. One protestor managed to reach the stage and was grabbed; to the cheers of the crowd, he was beaten up by stormtroopers. They then dragged the protestor off stage, where he was forcibly taken away by New York City police. Instead of monitoring these American Nazis, police on horseback outside the stadium battled with protestors who were trying to disrupt the self-declared 'pro-American rally'.

German military Intelligence, the Abwehr, had a massive oper-ation underway in the United States well before the war. They placed dozens of secret agents – most of whom were German migrants who had fought for the Kaiser in World War I – in key jobs across the United States to obtain information that could be used in the event of war. Leader of the operation was Fritz Duquesne, a South African who spied for Germany in World War I. He went on to become a US citizen, and in 1934 joined an American pro-Nazi group. He led a coterie of spies in New York, supplying valuable information to the Abwehr of ships' sailing times and tonnage, as well as US arms developments including details of new bombs, gas masks and munitions factories. For two years the FBI gathered evidence on the spy ring, with several double agents infiltrating the group. When the FBI finally swooped on the Duquesne spy ring in 1941, 32 men and one woman were arrested and convicted. Duquesne was jailed and released in 1954 because of poor health. He died two years later.

In June 1942 the Abwehr tried again: German submarines dropped four agents at Amagansett on Long Island, 180 kilometres north of New York City, and another four agents on a beach in Florida. They were to act as terrorists, blowing up factories, power plants and railways. They were promptly betrayed by two of their number who turned themselves in to the FBI and then dobbed in the teams. Six were executed, and the two who went to the FBI received lengthy jail terms.

After Germany declared war on the United States, the self-proclaimed American Führer, Kuhn, was arrested, convicted and sentenced to two-and-a-half years' jail – not for being a Nazi, but for tax evasion. With Germany at war with the United States, leaders of the Bund fled to neutral Mexico, where they became part of Nazi Germany's large network of spies, agents, sympathisers and financiers. Operating under a sympathetic totalitarian

Mexican government, the German embassy in Mexico City was running a large and deeply enmeshed spy ring that stretched into the United States and down through South America.

One of those the FBI suspected of being a major Mata Hari-type Nazi spy operating out of Mexico was vivacious blonde German actress Hilde Krüger. Perky and bubbly, 28-year-old Hilde had been the poster girl for the uniformed female version of the Hitler Youth – the Bund Deutscher Mädel. She first appeared in Mexico shortly after war broke out in Europe, and soon came to the attention of the FBI when informants in Mexico City overheard her in hotel bars praising Hitler. She was particularly enamoured with Propaganda Minister Joseph Goebbels, and hinted to anyone who would listen that she had been his lover in the years before the war. Goebbels met her when she was just 19 and playing small parts in German films. Within months of their meeting in 1934, she was being cast in a string of Nazi propaganda anti-Semitic films.

Hilde Krüger, Freddie's lover and Mata Hari Nazi spy.

Hilde Krüger's claims to have been Goebbels' lover do stand up to scrutiny. Despite the Propaganda Minister's rat-like looks, club foot and a body weakened by childhood polio, Goebbels scored a string of lovers, earning him nicknames such as the Bock (ram) of Babelsberg. Goebbels even enjoyed the services of the notorious Berlin brothel Salon Kitty, run by the Gestapo to eavesdrop on the brothel's clients. Around 20 women were recruited from high-ranking Nazi families – both wives and daughters – and given special training to elicit revealing pillow talk from their targets.[5] Goebbels particularly liked women to perform lesbian acts for him.[6] He wrote about Hilde Krüger in his personal diary, describing her in April 1937 as '*schön, aber dumm und schimmerlos*', meaning 'beautiful, but silly and clueless'.[7] Goebbels took her to top-level Nazi garden parties where Hitler was present. Also present were several of Goebbels' other lovers – all budding actresses he'd promised to get into movies. One of his favourites was Czech actress Lída Baarová. It was an open affair that risked his marriage until Hitler ordered him to break it off.[8]

Nothing happened in German movies without Goebbels' approval. The Propaganda Minister had the biggest casting couch in movie-making history, and he made full use of it. Goebbels' diary states that in May 1937 he took Hilde Krüger and two other young pretty actresses on a boat cruise on a lake near his Berlin home. Also along for the cruise were Goebbels' wife and mother – and Adolf Hitler. '*Sehr nett und gemütlich*,' (very nice and cosy) Goebbels wrote.[9] He added that during the cruise he and Hitler had a pleasant talk about when it was right to be merciful. They agreed mercy could be granted for crimes of passion, but 'heads must be chopped off for real crimes'.

According to Goebbels' diary and propaganda ministry files held today in German archives, by the summer of 1939 Goebbels had tired of Hilde Krüger. He black-balled her from any further roles as an actress; she could only find work as a costume seamstress. Some sources say the head of the German military Secret Service, Admiral Wilhelm Canaris, personally selected Hilde for special undercover work in the United States and Latin America. She was exactly the Mata Hari type of agent who would have been sent to Salon Kitty for special training in the art of seduction, and to learn how to satisfy the sexual needs of even the most perverted of targets.[10] Hilde left Germany for the United States in August 1939, one month before Hitler invaded Poland. Did Canaris dispatch her with a special spying mission to the United States? The German archives don't say.

In January 1940 Hilde checked into the Beverly Wilshire Hotel. Money seemed to be no problem. But Hollywood wasn't interested in the Teutonic blonde – her English wasn't good, and she was an awful actress. But she had other talents, skills she had perfected keeping Goebbels happy between 1934 and 1937 and possibly at Salon Kitty. Such talent was welcomed among the party set in Hollywood. The German consul introduced Hilde to Gert von Gontard, an heir to America's Anheuser-Busch brewing company. Hilde spent 1940 chasing von Gontard around America, but his family warned him against this Nazi-connected D-grade actress, and she couldn't elicit a wedding proposal out of him.

However, Hilde did win the financial backing of the richest man in America, oil billionaire J Paul Getty. He was a notorious miser, but it was he who picked up all of Hilde's hotel bills and travel expenses. Getty was a friend and admirer of Adolf Hitler; even after the European war began in 1939, Getty was at the centre of a secret cabal of American industrialists and financiers who provided support to Nazi Germany. Getty still sold a million barrels of oil to Hitler, delivering it to Germany through Russia, which was not yet at war with Germany. Getty didn't care what people thought about him. He was rich – filthy rich – and could afford to be mean, cruel and vindictive to those around him. He thought a waiter at New York's Pierre Hotel was rude to him so he bought the entire hotel in order to fire him. Many dodgy characters with Nazi connections got free accommodation and jobs at the ritzy hotel.[11] One of them was Hilde Krüger. She was mixing with Getty and other top American industrialists who were secretly backing Nazi Germany or were sympathetic to the Nazi cause – mainly because they were vehemently anti-communist and thought Hitler was doing a good job crushing communists in western Europe.

Some of the biggest names in American industry actively assisted Nazi Germany before the United States joined the war at the end of 1941. The Rockefeller-controlled oil giant Standard Oil smuggled oil past the British naval blockade to Germany in tankers displaying the neutral flag of Panama. Telephone giant ITT manufactured telephone equipment in its Spanish factory and sold it to Germany. General Electric had a deal with German steel giant Krupps to monopolise the world trade of tungsten carbide, necessary to harden machine tools; it made phenomenal wartime profits. Hitler kept an anti-Semitic book written by Henry Ford on his desk, and the car manufacturer helped finance Hitler's rise to power. Vehicles made by Ford and General Motors were used by both sides in the war. Coca-Cola's German subsidiary pumped out soft drink that was drunk by German troops. (After the war, the German subsidiary returned all wartime profits to the US parent company.)

In the Holocaust Museum in Washington, DC stands a tabulating machine bearing the insignia IBM. Thousands of such punch-card machines were sold to the Nazi regime to catalogue every citizen in Germany. They were used to identify Jews and record the fate of every inmate of the concentration camps.[12] In May 1941, Joseph Kennedy, former US ambassador to the United Kingdom and father of John F Kennedy, and Wall Street bosses met Hermann Göring in Vichy France and afterwards donated money to the Nazi cause.[13]

But the FBI didn't keep a watch on these horrific treasonous activities of America's powerful industrial giants. J Edgar Hoover and his Special Agents were much more intent on colourful characters such as Freddie McEvoy, Errol Flynn, Hilde Krüger and Sandra Rambeau. Hoover loved gossip and tittle-tattle with which he could amuse his friends and hold political sway. By 1941 the FBI concluded Hilde Krüger was a top German spy in America. Her file in the US National Archives reveals that the FBI labelled her a Mata Hari seductress in early 1941 when it searched her luggage at a border crossing into Mexico and found a dog-eared copy of a book called *Mata Hari: Courtesan and spy*. 'Pertinent passages had been scored,' the FBI noted, incontrovertible proof for them that she was a spy who specialised in seduction.[14] German defector and Hollywood star Marlene Dietrich told the FBI she had heard that Hilde was a German secret agent. When

Hilde crossed the border into Mexico, FBI agents based there were ordered to keep a close eye on her. Reports quickly came back that Hilde Krüger was 'the female lure for the German government in this area, being a very promiscuous woman and also very beautiful'.[15]

It just so happened that Freddie McEvoy was in Mexico City at the same time as Hilde Krüger. He'd gone down to join Sandra Rambeau for a naughty weekend, far from the increasingly prying eyes of his wife Beatrice. Errol Flynn was also going to join the fun. Freddie had got tickets to the bullfights for them. It was inevitable the four lust birds would find each other. FBI informants were all ears as the four chatted and laughed in a Mexico City bar. Freddie was obviously entranced by the blonde German newcomer to their little play group. He had a good friend in the US consulate in Mexico City, Robert McGregor. Freddie asked McGregor what he knew about Hilde Krüger. McGregor was in charge of the US embassy's citizenship section, so he had access to the files on people who travelled between Mexico and the United States. On 16 June 1941 McGregor wrote a chatty letter:

Dear Freddie,

Quite by chance I ran into a discussion of your friend Hilde Krüger the other day . . . the German actress has been investigated for more than a year as she flitted across the US claiming to be on the run from Nazi Germany, but she's known to be a close friend of Goebbels and one of the party girls around Hitler and top Nazi figures in the late 1930s. New York socialite

Alice Curtis said she had run into Hilde in St Moritz in 1939 and she was one of a bevy of gals that were called upon occasionally to furnish a little 'joy through strength' to the Hitler Goebbels combinations by night frolicking a la Nero. She was often in Hitler's company . . . she is an apparition in this part of the world . . . she certainly must be a fascinating vixen to judge by the stories that go the rounds. This is the gist of her story I have heard and I send it to you for whatever purposes it may serve.[16]

This raises the possibility that Freddie had already crossed paths with Hilde during her time in St Moritz in early 1939. By that time Hilde was being pushed out of the Goebbels party scene thanks to the fury of Frau Magda Goebbels, who had had enough of Joseph flaunting his many movie floozies in her face. Even so, it was very indiscreet of McGregor to pass on to Freddie that Hilde was regarded as a German spy by US Intelligence. Maybe McGregor didn't know of the FBI's suspicion that Freddie was a German agent. Either way, the rendezvous with Hilde in Mexico put Freddie back on the FBI's watch list. The FBI's interest was further aroused when Hilde gave the names of Errol Flynn and Freddie McEvoy as references for a visa when she planned to cross the border into California. Despite the FBI's reservations about Hilde, she was allowed to travel up to Los Angeles in the late summer of 1941 to attend a party hosted by German consul general Fritz Weidemann – a skilled diplomat for Nazi Germany. Freddie and Errol were at the party, and informants told US military Intelligence that Hilde – dressed 'very provocatively' – got quite drunk and, along with German-born actress

Luli Deste, was 'Heil Hitlering all over the place'.[17] Maybe it was done with a German sense of irony, but it wasn't the smartest move for an undercover Nazi agent. Hilde spent the war in Mexico marrying a string of very rich Latin men, and playing small parts in forgettable Mexican films.

Hilde and Luli weren't the only ones shouting 'Heil Hitler' in California in the summer of 1941, six months before the United States joined the war. American Nazi groups were well funded through the German consulate and German ships that docked in California, each carrying a Gestapo officer. The first open Nazi rallies in Los Angeles were held just seven months after Hitler took power in Germany. Swastika flags and brownshirted thugs lined Broadway Street in the centre of the city. Goebbels understood the power of movies to influence the masses, so the Gestapo dispatched a score of Nazi agents to work behind the scenes in Hollywood to try to combat the use of American movies to attack Hitler. The German consulate pressured movie moguls to remove anti-Nazi rhetoric in their films by declaring they would not be allowed to be shown in Germany. Money talks in Hollywood, and during the late 1930s most of the studio bosses agreed to make the cuts. However, several Jewish movie moguls hired undercover operators to infiltrate the Nazi groups. They uncovered plots to assassinate Jewish movie makers and actors, and plans to build up a supply of weapons for the time they could launch anti-Semitic riots.[18] But LA police were not interested in taking action against the Nazi groups. Los Angeles Police Chief Jim 'Two-Gun' Davis said Hitler was only doing what was best for Germany – that the real problem wasn't the Nazis but the communists.[19] The moguls' private undercover agents discovered Nazi plots to murder Jewish film producers Louis B Mayer and Samuel Goldwyn. Charlie Chaplin was also to be assassinated out of revenge for mocking Der Führer in his 1940 film *The Great Dictator*.

The FBI was concerned that those who opposed fascism might go too far and give aid to communists. Between 1936 and 1941 the FBI kept a close watch on the Hollywood League for Democratic Action, a group that actively opposed the spread of Nazism. An FBI report said that in its fight against Nazis the group was 'over zealous in working for the anti-fascist cause' and that funds sent to fight fascists 'have become diverted to communist channels'. FBI file No. 65-796 lists about 20 members of the League – all of them blacked out except for one: Errol Flynn.[20]

Some movie makers, most of them Jewish and some exiles from persecution in Germany, were intent on using the powerful medium of movies to awaken America to the dangers of Nazism. English film producer Victor Saville told author Charles Higham that he struggled for years to make the film *Keeper of the Flame* about a charismatic national hero who succumbs to fame and fortune and becomes a secret fascist. 'Every effort was made to stop this picture,' Saville said.[21] The national hero, backed by sinister industrial billionaires, plans to use racism, union bashing and anti-Semitism to divide the country and then mount a coup to take over the United States. It was based on a book by Australian author Ida Wylie, who wrote under the non-gendered initials IAR Wylie. Even though Spencer Tracy and Katharine Hepburn played the leads, the film wasn't released until March 1943. It was slammed by MGM head Louis B Mayer and Republican leaders, who said it equated wealth with fascism and was far too left wing. Curiously, the film came incredibly close to a real 1934 plot hatched by right-wing industrialists who poured millions of dollars into the Liberty League, a right-wing group that intended to mount a coup against President Roosevelt using popular retired General Smedley Butler as a figurehead.[22]

Shortly before Japan's attack on Pearl Harbor, Freddie was enjoying himself at Palm Beach, Florida. On 7 December 1941, the US fleet was treacherously bombed at Pearl Harbor and the United States was embroiled in the Allied fight against Nazi Germany and Imperial Japan. Freddie saw no reason to involve himself in this world war. He was engrossed in trying to carve out a new source of funding for his costly lifestyle. Beatrice had had enough of his shenanigans and told Freddie she was divorcing him. Freddie was stunned. He'd understood their marriage was based on an agreement – he was to play the dutiful husband for nine months of the year, with most weekends off. Apart from that, he believed he was free to do whatever he wished for the remaining three months of the year. Freddie later explained to a friend: 'Don't get the idea that this was a cold business deal. With all that loot hanging from her I loved her with a mad passion.'[23]

In Florida Freddie met a woman he described as a 'luscious blonde'. He turned on the usual Freddie charm, and the lady showed the usual female interest in the studly Aussie. But the blonde had a girlfriend with her who was becoming a bit of a roadblock to Freddie's efforts to get the blonde to his hotel room. A young man sitting next to their table looked rather lonely and Freddie invited him to join the three of them for a drink. 'I bought him a couple of drinks and we became good friends, such good friends that I fixed him up with the blonde's girlfriend, Freddie later told a friend.'[24] Freddie's liaison with the blonde lasted several days, during which he graphically demonstrated in the bedroom his medal-winning technique of sideways bobsledding – sliding up and down the curves, grinding humps and all. Freddie later recalled that one night during their sporty exertions a violent electrical storm had lit up the bedroom as clear as daylight.

When Freddie returned to New York, Beatrice and her lawyers were waiting for him.

'There was a terrific scene in their office,' Freddie recounted to a friend. 'I've heard of people being compromised by photographs but they had me in talking pictures. The little bastard I was buying drinks for was a private detective hired to keep an eye on me. I've got to give him credit though. He did a helluva good job. He didn't miss a pose and his recording machine didn't miss a syllable of my conversation.'[25]

What Beatrice heard shocked her to the core. There on the tape was Freddie saying to his blonde lover, who may well have also been in on the act as a private eye: 'Compared to making love to Bee this is the difference between a vacation in the Bahamas and drilling a road.'[26] Freddie was mortified. 'Beatrice, poor soul, suffered a stroke and has been confined to a wheel chair.'[27]

Freddie was out. Beatrice had the evidence she needed to get the divorce. The FBI knew all about the escapade; America had been at war for months but the FBI was still following Freddie's every move and tapping his phone. Special Agent WW Cochrane wrote in a report dated 9 September 1942 that on 9 April Freddie was in his room at the Savoy Plaza Hotel in New York when he received a phone call from a Colette Labardonnie. She was calling from the Plaza Hotel in Buenes Aires, Argentina.

> Miss Labardonnie stated that she had arrived on the afternoon of the same date, is not yet married but expects to be married within a few days. Subject [Freddie] stated that he was in love with her and that he would be granted a divorce from his current wife within six weeks. Subject further advised Miss Labardonnie that he would arrange for her to obtain a visa so that she could come to New York where he would marry her the day his divorce was granted. Miss Labardonnie stated that she was not convinced about his intentions, but that she would think the matter over and write him on the following day.[28]

Freddie was obviously already lining up the next meal ticket before the old one expired. Smart girl, that Collette from Argentina. Despite Freddie's declarations of eternal love, she didn't reappear in any records relating to Freddie. One thing was certain, though: she must have had money.

Despite FBI director J Edgar Hoover's reported penchant for wearing women's clothing in private and his long-lasting intimate friendship with his assistant Clyde Tolson, those in the FBI were a moralistic lot. Special Agent Cochrane wrote in the comment section of his report on Freddie: 'Subject unsavoury.' But Agent Cochrane had some good news for Freddie, at least as far as the FBI interest in him went. He concluded:

A review of the investigation to date fails to indicate that subject is pro-Nazi in his sympathies, or that he is engaged in any subversive activities. The only allegation that subject may be pro-Nazi is found in the report of Special Agent Frank Angell of Los Angeles dated 30 August 1941, where it is recorded that Los Angeles Confidential National Defence informant no. 541 reported that Alex Baglass in Los Angeles has said that McEvoy made pro-Nazi, anti-American and anti-Roosevelt statements. These allegations were not confirmed.[29]

Agent Cochrane wrote that Freddie had friends who were probably Nazis – probably even Mata Hari-type spies. Certainly, the FBI and the military Intelligence service had pinged Hilde Krüger as a Nazi spy. In July 1942 a US secret agent slipped into the room of known Nazi agent Werner Barke in Mexico City and copied a notebook. From it he compiled a list of 150 names of German agents operating in Mexico. Hilde was number 80. The comment from the American agent about Hilde read: 'Nazi spy of the worst kind. She has friendships with the highest officials of the [Mexican] government.'[30]

They were both being watched, but Freddie seemed to be in the clear. Agent Cochrane recorded that Freddie left New York's Savoy Plaza Hotel in May 1942, bound for 1337 Schuyler Road, Beverley Hills, the home of Hollywood movie star Bruce Cabot. On 11 December 1942 FBI Director J Edgar Hoover wrote to Adolf Berle, Assistant Secretary of State, on a matter of internal security concerning Frederick McEvoy. Hoover attached the report of Special Agent Cochrane and wrote: 'This is a closing report and is in further reference to information concerning this individual which has been submitted to you in the past . . .'[31]

Freddie, unaware that for the past two years the FBI had had every waiter, pool cleaner and barman within earshot reporting what he said and tapping his phone, had finally been cleared. The heat was off.

But could Freddie secretly have been an important Nazi spy without the FBI spotting it? Charles Higham, an English journalist who wrote an in-depth book on Allied industrialists who traded with Nazi Germany, also wrote a controversial book on Errol Flynn. His 1980 book *Errol Flynn: The untold story*, caused a huge storm that was met with shock and outrage. In it, Higham claimed both Flynn and Freddie McEvoy were key agents for the Abwehr, the German military spy organisation.

Higham claimed he had uncovered enough evidence to prove the swashbuckling star Errol Flynn was secretly a Nazi sympathiser who worked undercover for Hitler. Higham based much of his account on Flynn's long friendship with a mysterious Austrian, Dr Hermann Friedrich Erben. In 1929 Erben conducted anthropological field studies in Australia's isolated Cape York, and then went on to meet Flynn while the latter was adventuring around New Guinea in 1933. Erben travelled the world as a ship's doctor, and he took the young Flynn around Asia's seediest dens of iniquity. Erben, a member of the Nazi Party, introduced Flynn to a circle of rich and influential fascists. When Flynn struck fame in Hollywood with *Captain Blood*, Erben turned up and persuaded Flynn to join him to witness the Spanish Civil War at first hand. Higham claimed it was really an undercover mission on behalf of the Gestapo to gather names of Germans fighting against General Franco. Higham also claimed, without producing any evidence, that Flynn secretly met Hitler in Bavaria in 1938. This is highly unlikely. There is nothing in German records about such a meeting, and the German propaganda machine would have made much of a big Hollywood star shaking hands with Der Führer. It is true that when the FBI was going to deport Erben from the United States as a spy, Flynn lobbied hard, even writing to the President's wife, Eleanor Roosevelt, pleading to allow Erben to stay in the country. Higham claimed Flynn smuggled Erben out of the United States on his yacht *Sirocco* and got him down to Mexico.

While there are massive doubts about Higham's claims of Errol Flynn being a Nazi agent, it is true that Flynn had friends who were Nazi agents. He certainly made anti-Semitic statements, writing to Erben in 1934 describing a business associate as a 'slimy Jew', adding: 'I do wish we could bring Hitler over here to teach these Isaacs a thing or two. The bastards have absolutely no business probity or honour whatsoever.'[32] But that attitude was fairly common at the time, and such prejudices wouldn't necessarily make someone a Nazi.

Higham was even stronger in his accusations against Errol Flynn's best friend Freddie McEvoy. Higham claimed Freddie had gone over to the Nazi cause at the 1936 Winter Olympics and spent the late 1930s bringing rich socialites into Hitler's orbit, and that after the German invasion of France Freddie escaped internment because he was having an affair with a high-ranking Gestapo official (Higham doesn't say whether this was a man or woman) and spying on the socialites of the French Riviera. Higham incorrectly states that Beatrice stayed with Freddie in

France for a year after the German invasion. But he wrote that Freddie was ordered by the Gestapo to go to America to work as a German agent. This would explain how Freddie got the exit visa from Vichy France, and would confirm the suspicions of the US consul in Nice who gave him a US entry visa. But Higham offers no evidence that the Gestapo signed up Freddie as its agent. Extensive searches in German military, Gestapo and French occupation records found nothing on Frederick McEvoy.

Higham then makes an even more extraordinary claim about Freddie's activities during his visits to Mexico and his sailing jaunts around the Caribbean:

> Through codes and secret ink contacts with German diplomat and secret agent Theodore Herstlet, who had been living in Mexico . . . Freddie arranged to set up U-boat refuelling bases on the east coast of Mexico and Central America.[33]

Higham gave no source for this explosive claim in his book. He wrote that after the war Herstlet told historian Ladislas Farago that Freddie 'did begin to set up these bases before he was stopped by [US] naval intelligence'.[34] Farago died in 1980 just before Higham's book came out. The claim was hearsay, with no evidence. In 1972 Farago had been discredited when he incorrectly claimed he had a photo of Hitler's deputy Martin Bormann alive and well in Argentina. The photo turned out to be of a local teacher. Bormann had died in Berlin in May 1945, and his body was identified through DNA tests in 1998.

American naval Intelligence had indeed suspected that refuelling and resupplying German submarines operating along the

US east coast was happening in isolated coves and bays in the Caribbean. It was believed local Nazi sympathisers were supplying fuel and supplies for ideological or financial reasons. 'The principal suspects were the Gough Brothers network in British Honduras [now Belize] and several suspected sites in eastern Columbia and Venezuela,' wrote historian Thomas Schoonover.[35] US surveillance planes picked up modestly sized vessels carrying barrels on their decks. British and US military police arrested the Goughs and 18 others in July 1942, but they were released in April 1943 for lack of evidence. It is possible that Freddie sailed around the Caribbean searching for refuelling spots for German submarines. It would be in his character to accept money for such information. He needed money and would have had no ideological scruples against making useful comments to German agents about secluded inlets and bays he had come across.

Before Higham died in 2012, he gave all his research papers and accumulated files to the Cinematic Arts Library at the University of Southern California, Los Angeles. I spent weeks poring through Higham's boxes and boxes full of files, notes and documents gleaned from the CIA, FBI and US military Intelligence, and I found no evidence to support his claim that Freddie scouted refuelling bases for German submarines. Further searches in FBI and US State Department files on Freddie McEvoy held at the US National Archives in Maryland did not even hint at Freddie's involvement in such a U-Boat spying operation.

On the contrary, in October 1944 the US Naval attaché in Mexico City, Captain AS Hickey, wrote a friendly letter to Freddie in Los Angeles saying he was sending 200 feet of undeveloped film footage taken by Freddie of underwater fighting techniques using a spear gun. The film being made by Freddie was aimed at teaching Allied forces the use of underwater masks and spears in underwater fighting. Captain Hickey told Freddie he would help him get the film through Customs and the censoring process. 'Trusting that I will have the pleasure of seeing you again in this area [Mexico City], I am with best wishes, sincerely yours.'[36] In Warner Bros' archive of historical papers is a 1945 documentary film listed: *Underwater Spear Fishing*. The producer is F McEvoy.[37]

There is no way the US Navy would have been working with Freddie on an instructional film if it even suspected he might secretly be working for the enemy.

CHAPTER 9

FREDDIE AND ERROL HIT THE HEADLINES

J Edgar Hoover had evidence Errol Flynn and his friend Freddie McEvoy were moral degenerates. Not only were they playing the field with women across America, both married and unmarried, they were getting away with it. Even though Hoover had his own secret hidden behind the closet door, he was outraged that nobody seemed to care about what Errol and Freddie were doing, even worshipping them for their debauched sexual behaviour. Cuckolded husbands hadn't challenged them to a duel. Women weren't outraged that they had been discarded. The two Aussies had plenty of brawls in nightclubs and bars, yet they always came out on top. Plus, they were mixing with highly suspect people who were most likely secret agents of Nazi Germany, maybe even doing a bit of spy work themselves. After all, they were foreigners.

After the United States joined the war, many movie stars rushed to join the military. Sure, for some it was more for show than to actually fight, but they were out in public in uniform, doing their bit for the country. Jimmy Stewart was in the reserves and already had his pilot's licence when the Japanese bombed Pearl Harbor; he flew combat missions over Germany and eventually reached the rank of US Air Force Colonel. Henry Fonda said he didn't want to fight the war in a studio, and joined the navy to serve on a destroyer. Douglas Fairbanks Jr and Kirk Douglas also joined the US Navy. Clark Gable, even at age 43, flew bombing raids over Germany. David Niven, one of Errol's partying pals, joined the British Army and took part in D Day. Alec Guinness joined the Royal Navy. Others, such as Ronald Reagan, were put in uniform and served in propaganda movies.

Hoover was furious that the greatest swashbuckling, sword-swinging, action man of pre-war movies, the dashing hero of *Captain Blood*, *The Charge of the Light Brigade*, *The Adventures of Robin Hood* and *The Sea Hawk* was sitting on the sidelines enjoying himself. A nasty jibe in a newspaper column could have been prompted by Hoover. The 'Charming People' column by Igor Cassini in June 1942 mocked Flynn for saying he had got a deferment from the Draft Board because of a heart condition. Heck, Cassini wrote, Errol Flynn was the 'hero of the greatest screen battles, tennis champion of the movie colony, an ex-boxer and the greatest athlete of Hollywood'. The columnist sneered at Errol's friends who said the actor was 'burning up at the criticism', and claiming that he wanted to get into the army at all costs. 'Errol looks healthier to us than many men they take every day. If it's his heart that is weak, Flynn should have been buried long ago.'[1]

Errol Flynn, swashbuckling movie star, rake, and
best friend of Freddie McEvoy.

Hoover sent a copy of the column to the chief FBI agent in California and ordered him to find out on what medical grounds Flynn had been knocked back for military service. 'This inquiry should be conducted in a very discreet manner so that the fact it is being made will not be publicised,' Hoover wrote.[2] Hoover got the reply two weeks later: it said Errol Flynn was disqualified for military service – a 4-F official disqualification – by a US Army examining physician because of 'tuberculosis, pulmonary chronic reinfection type in the right apex'.[3] Despite his glowing good looks and athletic performances on screen and in bed, Errol Flynn was a sick man. Freddie knew it, and as a good friend he kept a close eye on Errol. Not that Freddie held Errol back in any way from his sexual exploits and philandering. After all, both men were rakes, rogues, rascally rapscallions, cads and bounders of the most extreme variety. Besides, Errol had a bad reputation to uphold, and Freddie was there to assist him.

Freddie had practically moved into Errol's Mulholland Ranch while his divorce from Beatrice was working its way through the legal system. The multi-millionairess still had a soft spot for the Aussie charmer, and she hadn't cut him off entirely. Freddie still received a generous allowance from her – around US$4000 a month in today's money – and she'd given him the yacht *Black Swan,* still moored in German-occupied Cannes. Even though Freddie was sharing the large Bel Air mansion with Bruce Cabot and assorted other Hollywood actors, he spent a lot of his time with Errol Flynn. Mulholland Ranch had become a virtual drop-in centre for every scoundrel in Hollywood who could make their way up the long winding mountain road far above Hollywood. One day Freddie brought with him one of his gambling buddies, Alexandre (no surname was ever given), supposedly a former manservant to Russian nobility who was a mad keen gambler on the horses. Errol made him the house butler, a job that included trying to control the endless conga line of pimps, wanton hussies, gamblers, down-at-heel actors, over-the-hill sporting heroes, tourists, fans, conmen, salesmen, wannabe starlets and gangsters who rocked up to the door. Errol and Freddie both relished being around colourful characters and they weren't particularly choosy about whom they drank with, nor fussy about who ended up in their bed.

'Of course there were pretty girls. The more the merrier. Pals like Freddie McEvoy, Bud Ernst, Johnnie Meyers and Bruce

Cabot brought them up. I always like men about me, roisterers, fun guys, rompers . . .' Errol Flynn later wrote in his memoirs:[4]

> For some kinds of fun, the friendship that two men can have or
> a gang of fellows can have simply can't be beat. It is a different
> feeling than what you get from being with a woman, and no
> woman can replace the gambling-sporting-handicapping air
> that men together can establish.[5]

Errol, Freddie and their entourage indulged in endless sunny days of tennis, lounging around the huge swimming pool, and of course the constant stream of parties that late in the night developed into bacchanalian orgies. Errol never had much trouble attracting beautiful women, but he admitted he stood in awe of the seduction technique of Freddie McEvoy. 'Freddie's case histories showed that if you step up to the dame and just stare at her, then walk away, she's a cinch to meet you later,' Errol told one reporter.[6]

In August 1942 Errol received his naturalisation papers, making him a citizen of the United States. To celebrate he threw a huge party on his yacht *Sirocco* off Catalina Island. Chief guests were Freddie McEvoy, Bruce Cabot and Stephen Raphael, the very wealthy English playboy who had left his socialite wife to move in with his buddies Freddie and Bruce at the Bel Air mansion. Errol told the terrible trio to bring as much 'fanny' of both sexes as they could muster.[7] The party raged on for four days. An exhausted Freddie then flew to Mexico, where he had quickly become a key member of the swinging society of wealthy expats. Errol had just finalised his divorce from his first wife Lili

Damita, a stunning firebrand French-born actress he'd married in 1935. It was a tempestuous, sometimes violent coupling that in 1941 resulted in a son, Sean. Lili now vowed to take Errol for every cent he had.

Errol thought it a good idea to get away, and asked Freddie if there was a girl in Mexico City he could have fun with. Freddie told Errol he had just the girl in mind. When Errol met 18-year-old Blanca Rose Welter, daughter of a Dutch oilman, he was simply awestruck. Raised in Venezuela and Mexico, she was stunning with chestnut hair, exotic green eyes and a spectacular figure. For Errol it was lust at first sight. But Blanca, wise for her years, played it very cool when she met the Hollywood megastar. Freddie was amused as he watched Errol tell her she was so beautiful he could get her a starring role in one of his movies – then observed Blanca knock back this usually successful seduction ploy. She'd been beating off Latin lotharios since she was 15, and even though Errol was very handsome and dashing, she wasn't particularly impressed. Errol started floundering. He presented Blanca with a topaz, a ruby, then a diamond ring that cost a small fortune. Still, no go with Blanca. Errol flew with her to Acapulco – with her mother as chaperone – but even luxury hotels drew a blank with Blanca.

This called for desperate measures. Errol and Freddie, the two greatest lovers of their time, put their heads together and decided to go with classic Mexican wooing. They borrowed guitars and practised till they could reasonably perform a Mexican love song. The two men appeared under Blanca's balcony at the Ritz Hotel dressed in Mexican costumes and serenaded the teenager from below. Freddie made a strategic retreat when at 3am Blanca finally appeared on the balcony in her nightgown. Errol re-enacted his *Robin Hood* climbing skills and ascended the drainpipe and a difficult trellis to her balcony. Blanca was so struck by Errol's romantic athleticism that, laughing her head off, she succumbed to Errol's charms and they embraced.

The next morning Errol admitted to Freddie that he still had not managed to bed Blanca. Freddie suggested that if old-fashioned serenading didn't succeed, he should try blood in the sand. Freddie reasoned some women were excited by the sight of blood and death. Errol took Blanca to the bullring in Mexico City to see the great Manolete perform. Blanca was awestruck when Manolete flung his scarlet cloak at her feet – well played, Freddie. Blanca threw Manolete a yellow rose, and the whole stadium applauded the traditional act of chivalry. Blanca was thrilled by the attention, and when Manolete joined Errol and Blanca, Freddie and friends for dinner that night, Blanca was absolutely dazzled. If this was life with Errol, she wanted it. As Errol discussed with Blanca her steps to becoming a movie star, he suggested a change of name. He and Freddie came up with Linda Christian – a reference to Errol's long-held claim to be a descendant of *Bounty* mutineer Fletcher Christian.

The wooing of Linda Christian only ended when Jack Warner, owner of Warner Bros studio, summoned Errol back to start work on a new film. It was Errol's first wartime propaganda film – *The Edge of Darkness* – in which Errol played a heroic Norwegian resistance fighter. Filming was suspended due to bad weather, and Errol spent the time in bed with his co-star Ann Sheridan. They were discovered by her husband, Irish-born actor George Brent, who was badly beaten up in the ensuing fistfight with Errol. They divorced months later. Linda Christian arrived in Hollywood and she and Errol were lovers for a year, only breaking up when Errol found someone else who was a bit younger. She went on to a Hollywood career, including being the very first Bond Girl in a 1954 television film of *Casino Royale*.

Blanca Rose Welter, later known as Linda Christian.

Errol usually didn't have to try so hard to find willing women. He recounts a story in his memoir that after a busy day on the movie set he decided to turn in early and was surprised to find sitting on the edge of his bed 'the most adorable girl twins; one blonde, the other brunette. I stared. In the vague light it was like seeing double. What a pleasant intoxication.'[8] The girls were giggling, and the swashbuckling actor wondered who they were and how they had got into his bed. He called for Alexandre the butler, and demanded an explanation. 'Who let them in and what are they doing here? What are you doing? What kind of house do you think this is anyway?' Errol Flynn took a second look at them – my goodness they were both beautiful girls. He turned back to Alexandre. 'Now look, if you know what's good for you, and you don't want to be fired, you get ONE of them out of here.'[9]

At least that's the line Errol chose to put in his memoirs. If there were twins waiting in Errol's bed it is doubtful he would turn one of them out. By all accounts, from both Errol's friends and his detractors, wild times were had at Mulholland Ranch. Errol made full use of the network of two-way mirrors and secret panels to spy on his house guests. He particularly liked to go upstairs and look down through the ceiling's two way-mirror positioned right over the downstairs guest king-size bed. Voyeurism was just one of Errol's many kinks. Freddie knew about the hidden peephole above the downstairs bed, and declined Errol's offer to join in the peep sessions he held up there. The truth was, Freddie didn't give a hoot whether Errol was watching. Freddie could have performed sexual virtuosos on the stage of any opera house in front of a packed audience without it affecting his tempo. Errol once joked to Freddie about the Kama Sutra positions he'd seen him get through the previous night with a lady in the downstairs bedroom. Unperturbed, Freddie shot back: 'Well, pay close attention, Flynn, and you just may learn something.'[10]

Flynn biographer Charles Higham said Flynn and his blokey entourage started a betting school using the two-way mirror. They got Los Angeles' top madam Lee Francis to send up a string of girls to occupy the bedroom under the mirror, then placed bets on who could last the longest with the skilled professionals. Stopping for a rest would lose a competitor the bet. Higham says Bruce Cabot, 'proud of his powerful physique and sexual staying power', was the first to volunteer. The hidden observers clapped and cheered at the moment of orgasm.

> Then Errol would perform. Despite, or perhaps because of, his constant drug taking, he was remarkably virile in his thirties. His male friends recall that he enjoyed showing off exceedingly hard and sustained erections, and could hold back from an orgasm for more than an hour. He was a practised master of oral sex.[11]

According to several sources, Errol indulged in some sexual antics in which Freddie had no interest – namely, with athletic young males. Jane Chesis, Errol's personal secretary and friend, told American broadcast network ABC's *20/20* program in 1980 that she seldom found Errol alone in bed. 'He rarely slept alone and I never knew what I would find him with – a young girl, a young boy, or a bicycle.'[12] Chesis says she once asked Errol why he slept with men when he could have any woman he wanted. 'He said: "Just because half the population is male, is there any reason why I should deprive myself of half the pleasure?"'[13]

When women went to the downstairs ladies' bathroom at Mulholland Ranch they had no idea that Errol Flynn and his male buddies were listening in to their chatter. Errol, who had bugged the bathroom and could see them through a two-way mirror, later wrote in his memoirs:

The things I learned about myself and my friends were astonishing. These lovely ladies came out with the frankest talk. I learned more about myself in ten seconds – the time it took to put a toilet seat down – than in a year any other way. And such language! Any notion that a woman's mind is nobler, purer, higher, more decent, cleaner, or anything else gentler, or superior, to a man's is pure delusion.[14]

Apart from the perpetual pursuit of women and adventure, both Freddie and Errol were earning a fearsome reputation as nightclub brawlers. Gossip columnist Jack Lait reported that Freddie got into a fistfight with Hollywood producer Robert Hakim at the exclusive West Side Tennis Club. Hakim was an Egyptian-born French filmmaker who, like Freddie, was spending the war in Hollywood. Lait wrote that, according to Hakim, Freddie said something that offended Mrs Hakim, prompting him to defend his wife's honour. Freddie said that was bull. He told the columnist that, on the contrary, it was Hakim who 'flipped a crack' about his mate Errol Flynn and Freddie simply bopped him in the face. Lait reported: 'Anyway, they sewed Hakim's face up like a baseball and McEvoy was no prettier for a gash from a tumbler smashed on his jaw.'[15] Witnesses to Freddie's pugilistic skills at the tennis club included none other than Hollywood stars Hedy Lamarr, David O Selznick, Mickey Rooney, William Powell and Harold Lloyd.

One headline stemming from a nightclub brawl had everyone in stitches: 'Flynn laid low with Spanish omelette'. It began with Errol and Freddie knocking on at the Hollywood nightclub Mocambo on Sunset Boulevard. This Mexican-themed club with live cockatoos, macaws and parrots behind glass walls was the place where all Hollywood stars went to be seen – Clark Gable, Humphrey Bogart, Lauren Bacall, Charlie Chaplin, Carole Lombard, Myrna Loy and Marlene Dietrich were all frequently there after it opened in 1941. Freddie and Errol and their lady friends had seats next to the dance floor when suddenly a brawl broke out at a table nearby. It wasn't the usual fight between drunken movie stars; this was a slap-down, hair-pulling, scratching, screeching, kicking catfight between two attractive women – a blonde and a brunette. Freddie and Errol watched enthralled as the tumbling catfight rolled onto the dance floor in front of them. First the blonde was on top, pounding the brunette below, ripping at her tight silk dress. Then the brunette gained the ascendancy, wrestling the blonde to the ground and ripping at her dress. Skin-hugging silk dresses were the height of fashion in those war years, and it was customary to wear them without underwear so as not to reveal visible panty lines. Well, naturally in the course of the confrontation, as legs waved in the air, the dresses on the ladies rose up to the hips, prompting much mirth from Freddie and Errol who were watching intently.

'Wonderful isn't it, Freddie?' chimed Errol.

'Excellent,' replied Freddie, their eyes glued to the female fracas.[16]

In due course, club bouncers separated the duelling dames and the Mocambo resumed its festivities. A gossip columnist raced over to Errol and Freddie and asked whether they knew what the fight was all about. Were they fighting over Errol?

'Damned if I know,' replied Errol. He didn't know either of the brawlers. But, he added helpfully, when they were on the floor with their legs in the air he could tell which was the blonde and which the brunette.

At that point the brunette, who had been standing behind Errol without him knowing she was there, grabbed two raw eggs from a passing waiter and crashed them on Errol's head. Errol later recalled: 'I put my hands to my hair. A lot of yellow came down with them. At last I've had it, I thought . . . my brains!'[17]

Waiters rushed to clean up the egg running down Errol's face, and the gossip columnist had his omelette headline. The bodacious brawlers were later identified as rich mob-connected society gal Virginia Hill and 'entertainer' Toby Tuttle – providing *The Los Angeles Evening Herald-Express* with the headline 'Egg bops Errol Flynn in Battle of Beauties'.[18]

Another fight night in the Mocambo drew Errol's blood. His beloved dog Arno had fallen off his yacht *Sirocco* trying to catch flying fish, and was lost at sea. The Schnauzer's body washed up on a beach several days later. Errol was rarely seen without Arno by his side, a few times even at nightclubs. He was with him on movie sets, barking and jumping around whenever the director yelled 'Cut!' because he knew his master was now free to play with him. When the Coast Guard called to say they had found Arno's body and asked whether Errol would like to claim the body, Errol was so upset he couldn't bear to see the dog's lifeless remains. Errol said no, just send him the collar, which he later buried in a small animal cemetery he had on his ranch.

Movie columnist Jimmie Fidler put a nasty spin on it, writing: 'Errol Flynn, whose love for his dog Arno has been much heralded, didn't even bother to go get his body when it was washed up on shore. That's how much he cared for him.'[19] It was unfair. Every person grieves in their own way. Errol simply couldn't bear to see the remains of his faithful dog with the life gone from him. The vicious column hurt Errol to the core. A short time later Errol was at Mocambo with Freddie and Bruce Cabot when he saw Jimmie Fidler sitting at a table with his wife. Errol made a bee-line through the dancers straight for the columnist. Fidler got up, his hand extended to shake. Errol didn't close his fist, just slapped Fidler so hard he flew across the table.

At that moment Errol felt a sharp pain in his ear: Fidler's wife had picked up a fork and jabbed him with it, leaving blood flowing down Errol's neck. Fidler had Errol charged with assault. As the court hearing started, Errol wisecracked: 'The lady obviously has good table manners – she used the right fork.'[20] Fidler and Errol later became good friends – not so his wife.

Errol Flynn had also copped some malicious press for his military deferment, but reporters generally loved Errol and Freddie. They were such damn good copy: the worse they were, the better the story, and the more newspapers and fan magazines they sold. On one occasion Errol and Freddie decided to play a bit of a trick on the gentlemen of the press. Errol invited a select group of newspapermen – and they were all men – up to the Mulholland Ranch for a chat. The talk was on the record, with Errol relaxing in an arm chair holding court about life and making movies while Freddie hovered in the background. Suddenly, to the amazement of the newspapermen, two women, stark naked apart from high heels, strolled into the room from a door behind Errol, chatting to each other. Without a glance at the stunned newsmen, they strolled nonchalantly past the reporters to another door, continuing their conversation as though nothing untoward were afoot. The reporters were aghast, watching open mouthed. When the reporters asked Errol what was going on, he turned around just in time to see two shapely bottoms disappear through the door. 'Oh that,' Errol said with a dismissive wave, keeping a straight face. 'Just a couple of my girls, ready at a moment's notice.'[21] Not a word about the prank appeared in the newspapers, but the walk of Errol's naked ladies became the stuff of Hollywood reporter legend. Years later Errol told the story in his autobiography *My Wicked, Wicked Ways*.

J Edgar Hoover got wind of the episode and ordered yet another investigation into the sexual antics of Errol Flynn and his philandering friends. A heavily censored FBI report was released under Freedom of Information 70 years later, and what wasn't blacked out reveals the shock of the investigators at the antics:

Flynn is described as a highly sexed individual who is frustrated in his normal desires, and very attractive to women. He has an active case of tuberculosis at present and is classified by the Draft Board for this reason. He is regarded as a person of low moral character with absolutely no regard for women, who has affairs with every woman with which he has been associated in motion pictures. The statement was made to [name deleted] that Flynn has had an affair with every woman who he has ever worked with 'from grandmothers on down'. He has been known to entertain women in his dressing room while on set. He has frequently boasted of his powers of conquest and has openly made bets that he would seduce women who have appeared difficult.[22]

The FBI report on the sexual proclivities of Errol Flynn and his cronies, including Freddie McEvoy, came around the same time as a special FBI report on prostitution in Los Angeles. It said thousands of girls were lured to LA every year with the hope of breaking into movies. Around 500 went missing, later to be found in 'subterranean recesses of commercialised vice'.[23] The FBI report added that a talent agency sponsored private modelling shows at the Hotel Knickerbocker favoured by the movie industry or at private functions 'where stars like Errol Flynn attend'. It said the girls and young women were wined, dined and promised movie careers until they gradually became demoralised. 'When ripe they are developed into obscure models and from there to "party girls" and down the slope into prostitution and immorality to finally "skid row"'.[24]

The report claimed a well-known female Hollywood columnist, a former madam (whose name was deleted from the report), used girls to spy on Hollywood stars to gather material both for her gossip columns and to blackmail the actors and other Californian personalities. The report also stated that in 1939 Errol Flynn hired a man to procure young women for him and had him put on the Warner Bros payroll so Flynn could have the girls waiting in his dressing room. That ended when studio boss Jack Warner got wind of it, sacked the procurer and ordered Errol to stop those antics on studio property or he would be fired.

Errol Flynn had been getting away with this sort of behaviour for years. He publicly joked about his penchant for young females, frequently declaring: 'I like my whisky old, and my women young.' Not for one moment did he even consider looking at birth certificates to ensure the girls were over the legal age of 18. So, when a couple of plain-clothed LA detectives turned up late at night at his Mulholland Ranch door in September 1942, Errol wasn't particularly concerned. He had just got back from filming the war propaganda film *Edge of Darkness* and was relaxing alone in his home. He told the butler Alexandre to let the police officers in and greeted them in his lounge room, all signs of the two-way mirrors and the past fun and games hidden. Errol thought the detectives were pleasant enough, and he was curious. He offered them a drink. They agreed to coffee, and Alexandre went to fetch it for them.

Had Errol been a little wiser to the ways of LA police he probably wouldn't have agreed to see two detectives when he was alone. It's far better to have a witness of your own present so there aren't two persons' words against one. After pleasantries over coffee, the senior detective put his cup down and pulled out a notepad. Alarm bells should have rung for Errol, but he was still curious rather than wary.

'Mr Flynn, we have a very serious charge against you,' the detective said. Errol sat back, surprised. He asked what it was.

'Well, your accuser is in Juvenile Hall and we've come to take a statement from you.'[25]

'What for, what's going on, what charge?'

The detective paused. Both stared at the movie star to gauge his reaction to the next words.

'Statutory rape.'

Errol fell back in his chair, stunned. He later claimed he didn't even know what statutory rape was. Rape he knew – it was not something he ever had to do; his problem with women was beating them off – but he wondered what 'statutory' meant.

'I don't know what you are talking about,' Errol said, bewildered.

'It concerns a Miss Betty Hansen – and we are holding you . . .'

'I've never heard of her. Who is this Betty . . . Hansen you say?'[26]

The detective said Betty Hansen was a 17-year-old girl LA police had picked up for vagrancy. In her possession was Errol Flynn's phone number, and she told police that the movie star had had sexual intercourse with her on 27 September 1942 at a party held at a Los Angeles mansion. Police said they checked, and the swank mansion at 345 St Pierre Road, Bel Air was the rented residence of Freddie McEvoy, Bruce Cabot and Stephen Raphael, and there had indeed been a party held there that night.

Errol had had many women at parties held at Freddie's place. The bedrooms upstairs in the rambling Bel Air mansion were frequent scenes of debauchery of all types enacted by both Errol and Freddie. For Errol, sex was a good escape from the card table where Freddie held court, winning money from Errol and rich playboys such as Stephen Raphael. But Errol couldn't remember bedding a partner called Betty, and he'd certainly not raped anyone.

The detective told Errol they'd like him to come down to Juvenile Hall – the police division that handled under-age offenders – and identify the girl.

'But I don't know any such girl,' Errol protested.

The detective smiled to assure the actor all was going to be okay; they just wanted to clear the matter up. The girl had made this claim, and under regulations they had to go through the motions. Would he please just come down to the station to see if he knew the girl? She had given an accurate description of the inside of the mansion and the bedroom upstairs, and of many of the people who attended the party.

'She said she could describe you. She said you were sitting downstairs in an arm chair, she was sitting on the arm of the chair. You then took her upstairs, where you got undressed. She said you kept your shoes on . . .'

A shock ran through Errol. He remembered a young woman – an overfriendly young woman – sitting on the arm of his chair.

'You don't mean that frowsy little blonde – is she a frowsy little blonde?'

'Yes, that's the one.'[27]

The detective had what he had come for: Errol had just admitted he knew the girl. If Errol had had a lawyer or even a reasonably aware friend like Freddie present they would have told him not to say a word, never admit he knew the girl. But now Errol had put his foot firmly in it. And, slowly, he realised it.

'Look, fellas, I need to call my lawyer right away.'

'Now Mr Flynn, you don't need a lawyer. This is just a formality.'

Whenever cops tell you that you don't need a lawyer, it is precisely the time you do need a lawyer. Errol told the detectives to relax, have another coffee, while he made a phone call. He rang young lawyer Robert Ford, the son of a lawyer who had handled his interests for years. Ford told him not to say another word, and said he would meet him at Juvenile Hall. It was now very late at night. The detectives drove Errol down Mulholland Drive and through Los Angeles to Juvenile Hall in the city. Not a word was said for the entire drive. The cops already had what they wanted. It was common cop practice to call in on a suspect late at night when they were tired or drunk. They wouldn't be thinking clearly and might say things they shouldn't. It had worked a dream. Just wait until they told the teenager that Errol had called her a frowsy little blonde. That would certainly get her to go ahead with the prosecution.

Ford was furious when he met the detectives. Why do this so late at night? His client didn't have to identify a person who had accused him. The detectives were unperturbed. Under the law, they said, the accuser and the accused must confront each other. They brought out a rumpled, unattractive-looking girl, hair dishevelled, dressed in the shapeless smock they put on prisoners. Errol reeled back. Had he had sex with *that*? But then he recognised her from the armchair. She had looked very different at the party dressed in a bright silk shirt and tight pants, hair glossy and face made up. Errol knew she was young – but at the time didn't even consider whether she might be under the legal age of 18. Then again, Errol hadn't asked.

'Will you repeat the accusation you made to police,' the detective asked Betty.

She answered in a soft, monotone voice, devoid of emotion as she confirmed that this was the man who took her upstairs. She described the afternoon, playing tennis, then cards in the evening.

'He took me upstairs, undressed me, then he, he, he . . . he did what I told you he did.'

Errol's lawyer stepped in and asked: 'Did you put up a fight?'

'No, no. Why should I?'

At least she wasn't claiming to have been forcibly raped.

The detective turned to Errol. 'Well, Mr Flynn. What do you say about this?'

'Utterly untrue,' declared Errol. 'Certainly, I met her. True she was at the house. I don't know how she got there.'[28]

The lawyer beside him seemed relieved at Errol's answer. His legal advice had been followed. Betty was taken back inside the detention centre and the detective told Errol he could go home.

The Los Angeles District Attorney must have known it was a weak case with Betty Hansen – she faced other charges, and was hardly reliable or likely to impress a jury. They decided to add a second charge against Errol Flynn. Peggy Satterlee was a dancer at the Florentine Gardens nightclub. She'd bragged to friends and police informants that she knew Errol Flynn and had spent a wild weekend on his yacht *Sirocco*. Afterwards she got a couple of days' work as an extra in Errol's film about General George Custer, *They Died With Their Boots On*. The cops took her downtown for questioning and she told them she was only 16 when Errol got her drunk and had his wicked way with her on the yacht. Peggy was a very attractive girl who looked and acted much older than the young teenage years she claimed to be. It was later established that Peggy was at least 18 at the time of the weekend on the yacht, but again Errol had done nothing to find out whether she was of legal age.

Errol now faced four charges of statutory rape – two counts against each teenager. Bail was set at US$1000 and he was ordered to stand before a Grand Jury[29] on 15 October. The sensational news of the swashbuckling movie star charged with rape pushed World War II off the front pages of newspapers across the country. *ROBIN HOOD ACCUSED OF RAPE, THE DIRTY DEEDS OF CAPTAIN BLOOD, ERROL FLYNN CHARGED WITH RAPE* the newspapers screamed.[30] Reporters had a field day writing up all the sexual capers of the hero of the silver screen. They were the biggest headlines Errol Flynn ever got – and Freddie McEvoy was caught up right in the middle of it.

Freddie was to be a prime witness. The party had been held at his rented Bel Air mansion, and as host he was responsible for the conduct of his guests. Freddie was usually the one who arranged to have girls decorating the parties. Did he know some of them might be under age? As a Freddie McEvoy party went, this one had been pretty standard: loads of attractive freewheeling girls, wannabe young starlets, C-grade actresses desperate to move up to B-grade – and oodles of goggle-eyed older men lusting after them. But among the girls present at this particular party was a 17-year-old runaway from Nebraska who dreamed of acting in movies: Betty Hansen. Under Californian law, Errol's dalliances with under 18s Betty and Peggy, regardless of whether they were enthusiastic volunteers, could cost him up to 10 years in jail.

If Errol went to the slammer over this, would Freddie go too? Freddie wasn't worried about his reputation. He didn't have one. Without hesitation he decided to do everything he could to help his best friend Errol Flynn. First the Grand Jury would have to rule whether the case against Errol was strong enough to go to trial. Errol's lawyer was confident the police case was flimsy. Don't admit anything more, and it would be hard for the District Attorney to prove Errol had actually had sexual intercourse with the under-age girls. On top of that, Errol's lawyers were confident the jury would be unlikely to take the word of a couple of young hustlers over that of a glamorous and charming movie star who had women of all types and ages chasing him. Errol's legal team would seek to give the jury the impression that irresistible Errol Flynn simply wouldn't have needed to resort to rape of any sort to bed a woman.

But there were other forces at work seeking to nail Errol Flynn, and his mate Freddie McEvoy could very well go down with him.

CHAPTER 10

FREDDIE PROVIDES THE FALSE ALIBI

For weeks leading up to the Grand Jury hearing, police officers had to be stationed at the gates of Errol Flynn's Mulholland Ranch to make sure the property wasn't breached by women of all ages, including some who were certainly under age, trying to break in to see the star, calling out to him over the fence to do to them what he had done to Betty and Peggy. As this was happening, women from around the nation sent Errol parcels containing their underwear and notes with their addresses and phone numbers. He received many proposals of marriage through the mail, some from women declaring they would be waiting for him when he came out of jail.[1]

A bewildered Errol later wrote of the episode in his memoir:

If you meet a young lady who invites herself on to your yacht knowing in advance full well what the risks are, who the hell asks her for her birth certificate, especially when she is built like Venus? And if afterwards she tells you she has had the most wonderful time in her life, who has been hurt? What is all the fuss about? Why international headlines? Who approaches a prospective sweetheart by asking her to whip out her birth certificate, or driver's licence, or show a letter from her mother?[2]

Errol's appearance at the Los Angeles Courthouse for the Grand Jury hearing was the biggest showbiz event of 1942. Reporters from around the world scrambled to be at the front of the massive crowd to try to get a few precious words from the movie star who could soon be a felon. Some mistook Freddie McEvoy for Errol because they looked so alike. When Freddie was asked whether he was guilty, he could say with all honesty that he was innocent of these charges. It may well have been the only honest thing that Freddie said during the entire trial. The comment was reported as coming from Errol. In reality, Errol obeyed his lawyer and didn't say anything to the crowd.

'I just wanted to sink into the ground. The mere idea of force or rape was unthinkable,'[3] Errol later wrote of his reaction to the crowds swarming around the courthouse. Some cheered, others cried out support, while several booed and jeered. Errol was determined to keep his dignity, using all his acting skills to appear above it all. He played a man of stature and pride who was bemused by the whole thing, a man who could not possibly have committed these crimes. Errol held his head high, squared his shoulders, and made eye contact with all those around him, even smiling at some while maintaining a dignity he didn't feel.

Betty Hansen told the Grand Jury she had crashed the party at Freddie McEvoy's house with another girl. Since the encounter with Errol in Juvenile Hall she had beefed up her initial police statement, saying she had tried to fight off Errol. But under questioning she conceded she didn't struggle very hard. Peggy Satterlee told her story of the wild weekend on *Sirocco*. Freddie then gave his evidence. He swore Errol never left the lounge room the whole evening. Freddie also contradicted Betty's claim that Errol had locked the bedroom door, saying the lock on that bedroom door had been broken for a long time and it was impossible to lock. Freddie swore he was also on *Sirocco* that weekend and nothing untoward happened. He said Peggy had slept in a cabin provided for her, and Errol slept in his. Freddie said he could produce others who were on board and they could testify to the same thing.

The Grand Jury accepted Freddie's alibi for Errol, and very quickly returned a verdict of 'No True Bill', meaning the police case wasn't sufficiently strong to continue to a trial. Errol, Freddie, his friends and the lawyer were jubilant. They were out celebrating the victory when Errol got a phone call. A mysterious voice said that if Errol and Jack Warner, the studio boss, knew what was good for them they would deliver a package containing US$10,000 (US$150,000 in today's money) to a certain spot in Hollywood. Errol told the caller to perform an anatomically impossible act upon himself.

It was a bad move. Two days later the District Attorney told Errol's lawyer he was going to bypass the Grand Jury decision and press the case further. Errol would have to stand trial after all. For a DA to overrule the Grand Jury is rare, but not unheard of. It was within the law. Errol was taken to LA police headquarters where he was fingerprinted, mug shots were taken of his famous face and he was measured for a prison uniform. His bail was continued, but the experience shocked Errol. Now he was really scared. Jack Warner sat Errol down and told him he would stand by him. Ford agreed they should bring in Hollywood's top defence attorney, Jerry Geisler. If anyone could get Errol off the charges it would be Geisler. He'd got Murder Inc gangster Bugsy Siegel off for the murder of mobster Harry Greenberg, and movie director Busby Berkeley off for a drink-driving manslaughter charge when he killed two people. Geisler would cost a fortune, but Warner said the studio would cover it.

Warner, Geisler and Ford did some digging and figured out what was behind the charges brought against Errol Flynn. It had nothing to do with Betty or Peggy. For more than a decade the studios had been paying off crooked LA district attorney Buron Fitts to keep their movie stars out of the police arrest records and the resulting bad publicity. Among them had been Cary Grant and Randolph Scott, whose close relationship could have been declared illegal under Californian law. Scandals involving Barbara Stanwyck, Robert Taylor, Tyrone Power and Charlie Chaplin had been buried by payoffs to crooked cops, corrupt politicians and DA Fitts. After three terms, Fitts had finally been defeated by 'Honest' John Dockweiler. The new DA wasn't as honest as his nickname, and was intent on revenge for being locked out of the job for so long by Hollywood heavyweights. Errol Flynn was simply the first cab off the rank for Dockweiler to strike back at the domineering studios that ran Hollywood. The failure to pay up the $10,000 could have sparked the prosecution. It's also likely FBI Director J Edgar Hoover whispered to Dockweiler to take action against the sex monster Errol Flynn to strike against the sins of Hollywood.

Errol was determined to keep up the pretence of the cheerful bon vivant to his adoring fans. They only seemed to worship him more now that he might go to jail. Errol waved and smiled to the crowds, but inside he was as scared as hell. He was 34 and in his prime, with a massive reputation as a womaniser. He knew he'd cop it tough inside a Los Angeles prison, from both inmates and warders. He and Freddie worked out a secret escape plan if the case started to go bad: Freddie had quietly arranged to have a small, fast plane waiting night and day at nearby Burbank Airport, ready to whisk Errol down to Mexico for a connecting flight to Venezuela – which did not have an extradition treaty with the United States – at a moment's notice. Freddie would be waiting with a fast car outside the courthouse to get Errol to the airport. Freddie's racing-car skills had never left him, and he was confident he could outpace any pursuing cop cars.

The preliminary hearing opened on 2 November with Deputy District Attorney Thomas Cochrane representing Betty Hansen and Peggy Satterlee. It was a short affair, with Betty saying her piece. Cochrane told her to admit that since she arrived in Los Angeles she had told everyone she was 18, but Betty said it was only so she could get a job in a drugstore. Peggy didn't take the stand. When Errol was asked how he pleaded, he said simply, 'Not guilty'. The case was adjourned to 23 November, then further delayed to 14 January. The delay was agonising. Errol was only half-joking when he hung a sign on his bedroom door: 'Ladies, you are respectfully requested to provide your birth certificate or appropriate identification before entering this sanctuary.'[4]

In order to take Errol's mind off the interminable wait, Jack Warner told his star he was needed to perform a song-and-dance number in a wartime morale-boosting musical comedy whose profits would go to the Hollywood Canteen charity that assisted servicemen. The film, *Thank Your Lucky Stars*, was an ensemble flick including Eddie Cantor, Bette Davis, Olivia de Havilland, Humphrey Bogart, Ann Sheridan and Spike Jones. It was Errol's first song-and-dance movie performance, and bearing in mind what was going on in his life at the time, he pulled it off remarkably well. Errol insisted his pal Freddie McEvoy have a part as an extra in the scene with him. It turned out to be quite a crucial part.

In the film, Errol enters a Cockney pub full of bluster trying to sneak a free beer, and sings 'That's what you jolly well get', a comical ditty on his boastful daring deeds in the war. Errol was certainly poking fun at himself and all the derision about him copping out from the fighting. Freddie is seated at a table in sailor's cap and coat, puffing on a pipe. The men in the bar, with Freddie at the back because he was taller than all the rest, egg Errol on to greater bragging of his achievements in the war. The men in the bar, including Freddie, join the chorus while Errol does a commendable jig. Suddenly Errol is hoisted on to the shoulders of two huge men, one of whom is Freddie. Freddie and the other man parade Errol around the bar while everyone sings until suddenly they stop and hurl him out through a window.[5] Largely forgotten today, it was a popular film when it came out.

Critic James Agee called it the 'loudest and most vulgar of the current musicals', but also 'the most fun'.[6]

Freddie didn't get a film credit for his efforts in hurling Errol out a window, but it did lead to a bit-part in another film. Bruce Cabot was playing Vichy French Colonel Fontaine in a rather poor propaganda film set in North Africa called *The Desert Song*. Fontaine was trying to hunt down desert resistance leader El Khobar, leader of the Riff tribal rebels, attacking a railway being built across the desert. Interestingly, Hollywood censors insisted the studio make changes to the original script. Set in 1939 before the Germans invaded France, the real baddies in the film are Germans who secretly plan to use the railway across north Africa to carry troops and munitions in their future war. El Khobar, who by day is carefree American nightclub singer Paul Hudson – hence the song – is on to the plot, and is secretly leading the local Riff tribesmen to stop the dastardly German plan. Wartime censors in the US Office of War Information insisted the French be depicted in the film as unwitting dupes rather than baddies. The Allies had just invaded North Africa, and censors did not want to antagonise the Vichy French in the hope they would join the Allies, or at least not fight. So, in the end Colonel Fontaine discovers the German plot and he joins El Khobar and the Riff to destroy the railway.[7]

The Moroccan street scene created on Warner Bros' backlot for this movie was used several months later for another film set in Morocco. This film followed a similar wartime censor's requirement of being nice to the French. *Casablanca* did much better at the box office and won an Oscar for Best Picture, and is still popular today. However, *The Desert Song* is forgotten, along with

Freddie's minuscule part. Cabot had persuaded Freddie to come along for a day to play his military adjutant. Freddie appears in just one scene, standing on a hilltop in French uniform beside Colonel Fontaine as they lay a trap for El Khobar, played by Dennis Morgan. Freddie must have felt a little odd dressed in the uniform of the Vichy French after he'd spent a year under their heel before he managed to get out of occupied France. He stood stoically, looking every bit the rigid French officer. This time he didn't get to sing or speak any lines. Freddie decided movie acting was not his thing, and declined further invitations to step into scenes with Errol and Cabot. For Freddie, making movies involved too much standing around waiting for others to tell you what to do.

Bit parts in movies with his friends provided a pleasant distraction for Freddie, but now the trial was upon them. Freddie had the escape ready – even driving the 16 miles from downtown LA to Burbank Airport several times via different routes so he knew the roads for a quick getaway. On the morning of 14 January 1943, 2000 fans jostled outside the Los Angeles Courthouse hoping to secure a seat for the best show of the year; some had camped out for two days to increase their chances. Most were women, but there was a banner-waving contingent from the new group ABCDEF, the recently formed American Boys Club for the Defence of Errol Flynn.[8] The man of the moment put on a superstar performance as he alighted from the limousine in an immaculate grey suit. He gave his most dashing smile to the cheering crowd, stopped to pose for photographs from the huge press pack and signed a few autographs for adoring fans.

He waved and gave a cheeky grin before turning and entering the courthouse.

Geisler had worked hard to ensure the jury was made up mainly of women – nine out of 12. The attorney knew from long experience that female jurors would be much tougher on young women who tried to present themselves as innocent and gullible when they clearly weren't. Geisler once said, 'a woman can see things in another woman within minutes, things it would take a man five years to work out'.[9] Errol took his seat at the defence table between his lawyers Geisler and Ford. The courtroom was absolutely packed to the rafters. Reporters from around the

Peggy Satterlee in pigtails behind Errol Flynn and
lawyer Jerry Geisler at the trial in Los Angeles.

world had grabbed almost every seat. Photographers positioned themselves to capture shots of Errol when his accusers Betty and Peggy would have to pass by the defence table.

When prosecutor Cochran called Peggy Satterlee to the stand, Errol almost fell off his chair in surprise. Instead of the glamorous curvaceous nightclub dancer he had agreed to have on board the *Sirocco* for the weekend 18 months earlier, there was Peggy looking like a wide-eyed innocent teenager. The prosecution was claiming Peggy was a mere sweet 16 when Errol had his illegal way with her on the yacht, and the DA's team had dressed Peggy accordingly: flat black shoes with white bobby socks, a full black skirt, and flowered suspenders over a prim white shirt. It made her look as flat chested and childlike as possible, and to top off the juvenile look, her shiny hair was platted in long pigtails. Errol thought she looked like his kid sister, if he had one. His heart sank. If the jury bought this little-girl-lost look, he was done for.

Peggy told the court that on the first night at sea Errol had kissed her on the yacht's companionway and followed her into the stateroom below deck. She said about 10 minutes after she went into her cabin, there was a knock at the door. She said 'Mr Flynn' walked in dressed in pyjamas and asked if he could talk to her for a while.

'I said it was not very nice for a gentleman to be in a lady's bedroom, especially if she was in bed.'

Cochrane prompted: 'What did he say?'

'If you let me get into bed with you I won't bother you. I just want to talk with you.'[10]

Her testimony prompted laughter from fans in the courtroom audience. Just weeks earlier Warner Bros had released the film

Gentleman Jim in which boxer Errol says to the romantic interest Alexis Smith: 'How could I marry you? You are a lady.' She replies, 'I am no lady.' To which Errol grabs her then kisses her, saying: 'And I am no gentleman.'

Peggy told the court that on the second night 'Mr Flynn' entered her cabin, pulled down her underwear and pushed up her skirt. 'I resisted at first . . . I didn't fight or nothing. I just told him he shouldn't have been doing that.' He then 'completed an act of sexual intercourse'. She told the court she had kicked and fought against 'Mr Flynn'.

Geisler tried to break the image of innocence projected by the girl in pigtails sitting in the witness box. He produced glamorous photos of Peggy taken on the yacht and at the nightclub, and showed them to Peggy. She agreed she sometimes dressed like that. Geisler made a show for the jury of clucking and shaking his head in shock at what he saw in the pictures. For a while he didn't show the photos to the jury, leaving the source of his shock to their imagination. Her innocent façade was taking a battering. Under cross-examination Peggy conceded she had not fought as hard as she could against 'Mr Flynn' because she was trying to fight and think at the same time. Geisler then went in for the hard punches. His private investigators had done their job well. Geisler got Peggy to admit the District Attorney had promised to get her a good job if she testified against Errol Flynn, that she was being put up in a good hotel and had been given show tickets, and finally, that she had undergone an 'illegal medical operation'. Everyone in the court knew this meant an abortion. Geisler saw women in the jury frown their disapproval. Peggy also conceded that the prosecutor had promised her they wouldn't prosecute the man involved if she testified against Flynn. She also admitted she had had relationships with two older men, one of whom took her several times to a local mortuary where they had 'fooled around playing hide and seek among the stiffs'.[11] The court was in uproar. Peggy said the man, a 43-year-old Canadian Air Force officer, loved her so much he called her 'his little strumpet . . . that's some kind of English muffin'. She probably meant crumpet, and the judge had to bang his gavel for order to end the laughter. Finally, Peggy Satterlee was destroyed as a viable accuser of statutory rape when Geisler confronted her with a record of her driver's licence: it showed she had been 18 years old at the time of her voyage on *Sirocco*.

Things were looking good for Errol. Freddie relaxed somewhat. So far there was no need for a speedy escape to Burbank Airport. Errol felt so cocky he started to chat to the assembled fans during breaks in the court procedure. He wandered down to the foyer of the courthouse where he was struck by a beautiful red-headed slender young woman serving behind the counter of the cloak room. From then on the girl was on his mind every time he entered the building. As the days dragged on he smiled and nodded to her as he passed. With everyone watching him, he dared not approach her directly, but he asked Freddie to find out her name. Freddie made discreet inquiries. Her name was Nora Eddington, and best of all, she was 18. The downside was that her father worked as assistant to a senior Los Angeles police officer.

Now came the case of Betty and the party at Freddie's Bel Air mansion. This would be harder. Betty Hansen really was 17 at the time of the party, and therefore if it could be proved Errol

Flynn had sex with her, he probably would be found guilty of sex with an under-age girl. It was Geisler's task to destroy her credibility in the stand as he had with Peggy.

Betty wore no make-up and was dressed demurely in a shapeless drab dress and flat shoes. Betty told her story again, but this time she added something important. She said that when 'Mr Flynn' got her in the upstairs bedroom she told him she felt uncomfortable and wanted to go back downstairs. She said 'Mr Flynn' laughed at her and said, 'You don't think I would really let you go downstairs do you?'[12] She said he then locked the door so she was trapped. Betty said 'Mr Flynn' started undressing her. She didn't protest, because she thought he was just putting her to bed because 'of her indisposition'. She said 'Mr Flynn' then started taking off his own clothes.

'He took everything off but his shoes,' she proclaimed, sounding somewhat offended. The courtroom erupted in laughter. Eighteen months earlier Errol Flynn had starred in the smash hit film of General Custer's last stand called *They Died With Their Boots On*. It took some time for the judge to restore order.

Betty Hansen makes a gesture at the trial.

Cochrane then asked Betty whether they had had sexual intercourse. She seemed confused. Cochrane asked if she understood what the words 'sexual intercourse' meant. Betty said she didn't. Cochrane helpfully explained it was when a man inserts his private parts into a woman's private parts. It was all a show for the jury to demonstrate her innocence, but the effect was ruined when an audience member in the court blurted out: 'Just how many private parts does this guy have?'[13]

Geisler took off the gloves, getting Betty to admit she had kissed 'Mr Flynn' after they had sexual intercourse. She said the act took about 30 minutes and that no, it didn't hurt much. 'He said I had nice breasts . . . and he also said I had a nice fanny.'[14] Then Geisler closed in for the kill. Once again Geisler's private detectives had done their work well. Betty admitted that before the party at Freddie McEvoy's house she had been arrested for committing 'oral perversion' on a man in a motel, and on another man at her residence. The courtroom gasped. How come this girl didn't know what the term sexual intercourse was when she clearly knew what oral perversion was? Oral sex was illegal in California at the time, the penalty 10 years' jail – even if the couple were married to each other.

Geisler said: 'You say that Flynn removed your slacks. Didn't you want him to take them off?'

'I didn't have no objections,' she replied, prompting another outburst of laughter.

The courtroom carnival atmosphere continued and reached a fever pitch when nightclub singer Lynn Boyer was called as a witness for the prosecution. She had told police she'd overheard Errol and Betty talking in the bedroom, but once in the stand she gave the impression she was so concerned that her testimony might put the wonderful Errol Flynn in prison that she made a show of bursting out sobbing. She acted out her hysteria in the witness stand, making sure the photographers were ready, then made a grand dramatic gesture of trying to fling herself out the courtroom window before swooning into the arms of Cochrane's deputy attorney John Hopkins.[15] Flashbulbs popped and newspapers all over the country ran the dramatic courtroom collapse. It pushed the war back to page two. The nightclub singer had what she wanted – instant fame.

While the Flynn trial dragged on into its third week and dominated the front pages, the war raged in Europe and the Pacific. Churchill and Roosevelt met in Casablanca to discuss campaign plans and announced that their aim was the unconditional surrender of the Axis powers. Ferocious battles were fought in New Guinea, Tripoli and Tunisia. The US Air Force began heavy bombing of Germany. In the east, Soviet forces tried to retake Stalingrad, and the greatest tank battle of the war was raging between Soviet and German forces around the city of Kursk.

The outrageous spectacle of the Flynn trial was a much-needed distraction from these momentous events. It wasn't only civilians who were glad to have something else to read about apart from the war. In the South Pacific US Air Force ace Greg 'Pappy' Boyington recalled listening intently with his homesick Air Force crews to coverage of Flynn's trial on the radio. Boyington later wrote that the airmen sitting under coconut trees at base waiting for the next deadly mission would cry out: 'Get that goddam war news off the speaker – we want to hear about Flynn!'[16] The blow-by-blow accounts of Errol Flynn's adventures on his yacht and in the bedroom, witnesses trying to jump out the window, and Peggy's romp in the mortuary were a great distraction from the horrible reality of war around them. It was among the servicemen that the admiring moniker 'In Like Flynn' first appeared, and it became the stuff of legend.

Often after the day's testimony Flynn, Freddie, his friends and lawyers took their dinner at Duco's restaurant over the street from the courthouse. Reporters crowded around and Flynn calmly and with great style answered their questions, saying he harboured no ill-will towards the girls. He said they were simply pawns in a plot by the city powermongers against him and the studio.

'I feel sorry for them – they can't really hurt me. I'm sure I'll be acquitted, but their lives are ruined ... I wish I could do something to help them,' he told reporters, who were hanging off every word.[17]

Now it was the time for the defence. First into the witness box was Freddie McEvoy. He told the court he had no idea how Betty Hansen had got into the party at his residence. Certainly, she had not been invited. He conceded many people came and went from his parties, but there was no way he could tell whether a guest had brought Betty with them. Freddie said he certainly would not have allowed her to stay if she had indicated she was under 18. But she had been dressed up to look older. Then came the crucial testimony that was crafted to knock down Betty's credibility. Freddie provided the crucial alibi. He might have been lying his head off in the witness stand committing perjury, but Freddie would do anything to save his mate Errol from the clink. Freddie testified that Errol Flynn was in the downstairs lounge the whole night apart from four minutes, and that Freddie didn't see him go upstairs at any point in the evening.

'I was with Flynn every bit of the time after dinner in the sunroom where we were talking and mixing drinks,'[18] Freddie

McEvoy testified, reported United Press correspondent Frederick C Othman from the courtroom. Othman described Freddie as a tall, broad-shouldered Englishman with a blond moustache. Freddie told the court his business was oil, and his occupation was part-time acting. Very part-time, given his brief appearances in the recent filming with Errol and Bruce Cabot. But then, Freddie always liked to spin a good yarn.

Freddie also said Miss Hansen had to be lying when she testified that Mr Flynn locked the upstairs bedroom door to trap her, because the lock on the bedroom door had been broken ever since he'd moved in to the mansion. It was simply impossible to lock the door. (Flynn later wrote in his memoirs that someone found metal filings on the carpet beneath the door's lock, making him wonder whether the lock had been tampered with to help make Freddie's testimony come true.)

Geisler had attendants bring the door in question into the courtroom as evidence. Sure enough, the lock clearly didn't work. Errol Flynn took the stand. He denied locking Betty Hansen in the bedroom – how could he when the lock didn't work? – and he strenuously denied having sexual intercourse with her. He also denied having sex with Peggy Satterlee on the *Sirocco*. He said that trip was a horror for him because he had lost his precious dog Arno overboard. He said he spent the trip in mourning for the loss of his faithful hound. Crew members testified that Flynn spent nearly the entire voyage at the helm or on deck hoping to catch sight of his missing dog.

Summing up, prosecutor Thomas Cochrane described Flynn as a 'ravisher of young women'[19] who presented to the world a false face of charm and impeccable manners. Cochrane said the only question under law was whether Flynn had sex with under-age girls, not whether they resisted. 'A man who preyed on young girls must be sent to prison where he belongs,'[20] thundered Cochrane.

Geisler was earning every cent of his US$100,000 fee (US$1.5 million in today's money). He'd pretty well destroyed the testimony of Peggy Satterlee, and caused sufficient doubt about the word of Betty Hansen. He reminded the jury of how immoral the two young women were – one had had an abortion and danced among corpses in the city morgue, the other had been arrested for 'oral perversion'. Both acts were illegal. He said both had been given immunity from prosecution if they testified against Mr Flynn. How could they be believed? Sworn testimony from eyewitness Freddie McEvoy put Flynn in the downstairs lounge almost the entire evening. 'Mr Flynn must not be sent to prison because of these girls' lies. It is your duty to return him to his proper place as one of filmdom's brightest stars, and I know in my heart that you will set him free.'[21]

Justice Leslie Stills instructed the jury to ignore Errol Flynn's celebrity status and concentrate on the evidence presented during the trial. He added that the jury should regard the varying testimonies of the two women with extreme caution. Freddie had organised several heavies to march Errol Flynn out of the court if things went bad, and he was waiting outside in the fast car just in case the getaway was needed. However, it was looking good for Errol Flynn. Geisler and Ford were confident. Doubts began when the jury came back after four hours saying they could not reach a unanimous decision. The jury was held overnight in a hotel and would be brought back in the morning. It was an incredibly tense night for Errol and his friends. Freddie assured him everything was ready to get him out of the courthouse if the jury decision went the wrong way.

In the morning the jury signalled it had reached a decision and the court was convened. Justice Stills was handed the piece of paper with the verdict. Four times the forewoman of the jury called out, 'Not guilty'. Errol Flynn couldn't control his glee, jumping to his feet and yelling 'Yippee!' The entire courtroom cheered and broke out in applause. Errol rushed to the front of the courtroom and kissed forewoman Ruby Anderson on both cheeks, shook hands with the rest, signed autographs for them, and was embraced by his supporters in the court. Over the hubbub, Justice Stills thanked the jury, adding: 'I have enjoyed the case, and I think you have.'[22] Jury member Nellie Minear told reporters outside the court: 'We knew Flynn wasn't guilty the whole time, but we didn't want to come out too soon because we wondered what the public might think if we did.'[23] On the steps of the courthouse Errol told the cheering crowd: 'This just goes to show that there is justice in the United States.'[24] *Newsweek* asked Betty Hansen's mother back home in Lincoln, Nebraska, what she thought of the verdict. 'Oh well, nobody got hurt. I have no hard feelings toward Mr Flynn. Betty is the cutest little thing you ever saw, a clean little Christian girl.'[25] Peggy Satterlee, always ready with a good showbiz quote, told *Newsweek* she was going home to her mother in the small town of Applegate, 128 miles north of San Francisco. 'I don't know what I'm going to do. Here I am, just two days less than 17 years old, and I feel like a broken old woman.'[26] She was getting younger every day,

The trial had been great for newspaper circulation. The city editor of the *Los Angeles Herald-Express*, Agnes Underwood, threw a party for Flynn and his team at her home. It was a riotous evening. A photographer dressed up as Peggy Satterlee in bobby socks and pigtails begged Errol to seduce her. They staged a hilarious mock trial with half the witnesses trying to jump out the window rather than testify against 'wonderful Mr Flynn', and the women in the jury kept on swooning. Errol was found guilty and sentenced to a life sentence on a yacht with 12 beautiful girls – each of them 18 years old.[27]

Not laughing was New York politician Edward J Flynn, who was campaigning to be appointed US ambassador to Australia. He lost the job because he got so much hate mail from people who said he should have been found guilty of what he did to those nice girls Betty and Peggy.

Errol Flynn and his pals, along with the lawyers and private detectives who had dug up the dirt used against the girls in the trial, continued celebrating hard in a city nightclub. Amid the frenetic partying, Freddie spied a pretty young woman who looked very much alone. He talked to her late into the night, first establishing that she was definitely 18 years old. Her name was Irene Margaret Wrightsman. At first Freddie thought she might be an entertaining joust for the evening, but what she told him made him think this could be something more. Irene told Freddie she had managed to slip away from her very overbearing family for the night with a girlfriend. They'd managed to talk their way into the nightclub where Errol's party was raging. Freddie was interested in this attractive recently-turned-legal young woman, and he turned on the charm. She seemed enthusiastic and intent on enjoying herself. But when Freddie discovered her daddy was rich – very rich – his interest went stratospheric. His divorce from

Beatrice had been finalised the previous November, and he was on the lookout for another rich wife to support his extravagant lifestyle. This pretty young lady had walked right into his path.

A week later the two walked into the Los Angeles Courthouse and applied for a marriage licence. For Irene, marriage was an escape from her bullying, overbearing oil-millionaire father. For Freddie, Irene was the portal to wealth and a return to the extravagant lifestyle he craved. After all, Errol was back on his feet and perhaps it was time for Freddie to move on from Hollywood. Freddie had had to move quickly, though – 18-year-old Irene would have been a prime target for lusty Errol. News of the marriage application hit papers around the United States. In Pennsylvania *The Wilkes-Barre Record* carried the Associated Press bulletin:

Bobsled Racer to Wed

Fred J McEvoy, former Olympic Games bobsled racer, and Irene Margaret Wrightsman, member of a wealthy Texas oil family, today applied for a marriage licence. McEvoy, 35, previously was married to Beatrice Cartwright McEvoy, Standard Oil heiress. They were divorced in New York last November. It will be the first marriage for Miss Wrightsman, 18, who lives in Santa Monica.[28]

CHAPTER 11

FREDDIE MARRIES OIL THAT FAILS TO GUSH

Love would have to come later in the faster-than-lightning wedding between Freddie McEvoy and Irene Wrightsman. There was simply no time for romance. As soon as Freddie learned Irene was an heiress to an oil fortune, he had the naïve 18-year-old down the aisle as quickly as he could, with Errol Flynn roped in as best man to add glamour for the awe-struck teenager. Freddie knew he had to get the marriage certificate signed, sealed and delivered before the girl's outraged parents could stop the wedding.

Irene's father, Charles Wrightsman, made his fortune in Texas oil. A hard, ruthless, domineering, intolerant tycoon driven by money, Wrightsman was as overbearing and bullying with his family as he was with his employees. Wrightsman moved in the late 1930s to Santa Monica, where his money could buy as many attractive starlets and showbiz girls as he desired, often publicly humiliating his long-suffering wife Irene Stafford. Wrightsman had designs on advancing into high society and was using his oil money to do it. He bought up art and property, and became a skilled polo rider, paying his way into California's upper crust where money counted far more than breeding. In 1942 he divorced his wife, the mother of Irene and her sister Charlene. Wrightsman had driven his wife to alcoholism through his emotional and verbal abuse, often in public.[1] Teenager Irene knew she had to escape her father or her life would repeat the cycle of misery.

Charles Wrightsman was furious when he discovered his teenage daughter had disobeyed him and married Freddie McEvoy. He regarded Freddie as a professional con man, a penniless no-good playboy with no social standing – he wasn't even American – who would not advance the family name one iota. In fact, it could be the ruin of them. So he did what he did to anyone he thought had crossed him: he used money as punishment. He cut his daughter off from the family fortune. The newlyweds would not get a cent from him.[2] As for Freddie, Wrightsman was determined to destroy him too. He had private detectives watch Freddie night and day, trying to dig up something that would destroy the new marriage.

Wrightsman needn't have bothered. As soon as Freddie learned he'd just married an heiress to an oil fortune that wouldn't gush forth a single cent, the marriage was on the rocks. He was still in his prime at 35, and he should be able to lure a wealthy widow, divorcee or heiress who would have enough money to support his lifestyle. The world war was still raging, which stopped a frustrated Freddie from heading back to his favourite hunting ground, the French Riviera. Still, there was plenty of fun and games to be had in the United States, on yachts up and down the Californian coast and around the Caribbean, and most of all, down Mexico way.

Despite his constant pursuit of money, Freddie was a gentleman who didn't set out to harm anyone. He made sure his young wife was ensconced in a pleasant enough home in Los Angeles, but he didn't regard himself as bound to her. He considered the marriage deal broken when she couldn't produce the money supply he expected. Just weeks after the wedding, Freddie was off to Mexico. He could live more cheaply there, and make a living playing cards in the casinos and hotels. He had good connections inside the expat community, and many among the idle rich were happy to 'lend' Freddie money, never expecting it to be repaid. That circle of rich friends included several people who were classified by US Intelligence as German agents. It's not clear whether the German spy network demanded Freddie do certain things for them in return for money, or whether Freddie simply opened doors to rich Americans visiting Mexico for a good time. But questions remain: Was Freddie on the payroll of the German Embassy to help infiltrate Nazi agents in Hollywood? Did he take money to spy for Germany as he sailed around the Caribbean? US Intelligence certainly wanted to know. It kept a watch on him and once again tapped his phone.

On 26 March 1943 the US Secret Service tapped Freddie's phone in Mexico as he called Errol Flynn at his home on Mulholland Drive. This is the FBI summary of the intercepted conversation:

Mr McEvoy asked Mr Flynn if he was going to Mexico definitely. Mr Flynn said he would go via Pan American Airlines. Mr McEvoy asked about the case. Mr Flynn said that a warrant had been issued for Mr McEvoy's arrest, but he, Mr Flynn, had succeeded to have it withdrawn and a 500 dollar bond was necessary.

Mr McEvoy said he had received a telegram from Mr Lane dated March 5th on March 11th in which Mr Lane asked him to be in Los Angeles by March 12th. Mr McEvoy said he would wait to see what the repercussions of the case would be and then would decide whether to sue the hotel or not for the late delivery of the telegram. Mr Flynn asked Mr McEvoy not to worry about it as it would be fixed one way or the other.

Mr McEvoy said he would reserve four seats for the bullfight on Sunday and asked how long he would stay. Mr Flynn said he had plenty of time and the only thing that would prevent his going would be the draft board but he believed he had the matter under control.

Mr McEvoy asked Mr Flynn to bring two guns and his painting. Mr Flynn asked Mr McEvoy if he knew where his (Mr Flynn's) naturalisation papers were. Mr McEvoy said he had them. Mr Flynn asked him to send them by air mail at once because he could not leave the country without them. Mr McEvoy said he would send them tonight. Mr McEvoy said he was anxious to hear what the repercussions of his case would be, and added he could not leave for another month.

Mr McEvoy asked Mr Flynn to wire advising him of his arrival in Mexico so he could meet him at the airport.[3]

The telephone intercept raises several questions. What was Freddie due to be arrested for? How was Errol able to prevent the arrest and have charges withdrawn? What was the $500 bond for? Why did Freddie want Errol to bring two guns down to Mexico? What was the painting he mentioned?

FBI and US State Department files don't answer these questions. Records of the US Secret Service – called the Office of Strategic Services during World War II – are still classified. However, research indicates that Freddie had been trying to extort or exert pressure to get more money from Beatrice Cartwright and her lawyers had taken legal action against him.

The FBI was excited at Freddie's request for Errol to bring two guns and a painting to Mexico. But something didn't add up. Despite the nightclub brawls, Freddie had never appeared prone to gun violence. Besides, guns were easily obtained in Mexico, so why would Errol Flynn risk getting on a plane with them? What did Freddie plan to do with two guns?

Perhaps someone in the FBI eventually realised what it was, because there were no arrests. Freddie and Errol were very keen spearfishermen, and they used newly developed air-powered spear guns for their sport. Freddie and Errol hunted underwater as a team, signalling to each other as they stalked big fish, including sharks. Errol recounted how he once put a spear into a hammerhead shark and Freddie immediately followed by firing a second spear into the beast. The shark was stronger than two grown men; it towed them along through the water at breakneck speed until they had to let it go. On another dive, Freddie signalled Errol to turn around and look behind him. Errol turned, and there, passing over him, was a mass expanse of white belly and huge gaping mouth of a giant manta ray. Errol rose spluttering to the surface to see Freddie laughing his head off. What the FBI didn't know was that Freddie planned to make an instructional film for the US Navy on how to fight underwater using spear guns. However, the mention of two guns in the luggage was just another piece that didn't fit in the jigsaw puzzle that was the man of mystery, Freddie McEvoy.

Errol and Freddie hired a boat and spent an adventurous time diving around the coral reefs of Mexico. Errol told Freddie he was obsessed with young Nora Eddington, the girl working at the courthouse, but she had so far resisted his smooth-talking advances. Freddie suggested Errol bring her down to Mexico so he could woo the 18-year-old just as he had successfully wooed the wary Blanca a year earlier. They laid their plans, and in August 1943 Errol invited Nora down to Acapulco, and even managed to secure her mother's permission. Despite the war raging and enormous demands on the FBI to track spies and enemy agents inside the United States, J Edgar Hoover ordered agents to follow Errol Flynn's every move. They were watching as Errol checked into beachside Cottage 7 at the Hotel La Riviera. A few days later Nora arrived and was given Cottage 14. The FBI had the entire staff of the hotel keeping tabs on Errol.[4]

Hoover was convinced, probably correctly, that Errol Flynn should have been found guilty of the statutory rape of Betty and Peggy in January. Hoover now thought he could drum up charges against Flynn of white slave trafficking – a law designed to prevent cross-border prostitution, which involved paying for the passage of a woman across a state border for the purpose of 'immoral intercourse'. Nora was 18 and above the age of consent, but Hoover desperately wanted his agents to find something immoral he could hang on Flynn. FBI files reveal they had an agent sitting right behind Nora on the plane to Mexico hoping to overhear her conversation.[5]

FBI agents diligently recorded every moment of Errol and Nora's daily adventures. They sailed, swam, fished and shared dinner, often accompanied by Freddie and his wife Irene, who joined them for several days at the Acapulco hotel. Freddie was undoubtedly looking for any excuse to get away from Irene. Gossip columnist Whitney Bolton wrote that he saw Freddie with his new bride sitting in a gloomy corner of a restaurant in Mexico City shortly after they were married, and wrote: 'I never saw two more miserable persons.'[6] It was reported years later that the couple had a baby born in Mexico but sadly the baby died from a tropical ailment.[7]

Freddie and Errol snorkelled using the new spear guns, something of a novelty at the time. They chased sharks under-water, seeking to perfect their hunting technique. They introduced excited teenagers Nora and Irene to snorkelling and the wonders to be found under the surface at the reefs. Waiters and hotel staff told the FBI that Mr Flynn and Miss Eddington appeared attentive and affectionate to each other, but no funny business was witnessed. No sneaking from Cottage 7 to Cottage 14 in the middle of the night. No trying to get the young woman drunk. After a lovely week-long holiday, Nora flew back to Los Angeles. Errol Flynn followed a few days later. The FBI agent's report said: 'It has been ascertained they spent considerable time in each other's company at Acapulco enjoying mutual pleasure in the various facilities offered. No specific information has been developed to date indicating immoral relationship.'[8]

Hoover was frustrated with the report. He wanted dirt, and was determined to get it. He wrote back to the FBI agent demanding more specific details concerning 'possible intimacies between the subject and Miss Eddington at Acapulco'.[9] Hoover ordered his agents to 'thoroughly interview' the cabin boy on the boat to determine 'his knowledge of any possible illicit relationship between Flynn and Eddington', and to check who paid her hotel bill, and whether there were any breakfasts for two in his or her cottage.

Of course, it was possible Errol was behaving like the perfect gentleman in love with a gentle young soul. But Freddie had plenty of friends in high places in Mexico and it's highly likely he got a tip-off about the FBI surveillance, and warned Errol to be on his best behaviour. It wouldn't be out of Freddie's normal modus operandi to pay off the hotel staff. Mexican officials certainly resented the FBI intrusion on their territory, and they were keen to look after well-paying American guests to keep them coming.

Or it might be that the FBI agents were fed up with the vindictive Hoover having them chase tittle-tattle gossip rather than real gangsters and enemy spies who threatened the nation's security in wartime. After all, Nora was a legal adult. The reply Hoover got from the FBI agent in charge of this sordid Peeping Tom operation must have disappointed him. The agent said the boat's cabin boy saw nothing untoward. Both targets stayed in their own cabins all night. To pad out the report the agent listed long details of bus, yacht, shopping and dining arrangements, even recording times the lovebirds retired to their separate cottages in the hotel. Maids didn't find the remains of break-fasts for two, or other tell-tale signs of romantic romping in the bedrooms such as what might be found on the sheets. Finally, the agent reported Nora Eddington paid her own hotel bill.[10] Hoover had been foiled. Or fooled. Either way, Errol was off the FBI Director's hook, at least for the time being.

Errol did marry Nora Eddington a year later in Mexico. Freddie was best man. Nora was pregnant and Errol was ill from diseases he'd caught while wading in Los Angeles swamps filming the war movie *Objective, Burma!* The film infuriated British audiences because it suggested American troops did the fighting in Burma, whereas the operation was almost entirely British. It caused such a stink it was withdrawn from release in the United Kingdom. Flynn became so sick during filming he didn't even try to put on an American accent, slipping back into his Australian drawl. After filming finished in late summer 1944, Errol flew down to Mexico to recuperate and join Nora, who had been staying with Freddie and Irene. It was during this time that Errol became addicted to morphine and other drugs. While Freddie tried to help his friend, Nora kept up a façade for the Hollywood press. She told Louella Parsons for *Photoplay* magazine that Errol was a free spirit who must not be trapped or restrained. 'A wife who demanded a conventional life would become like an iron chain to him. I couldn't bear that. I cannot think of any other man. I can't believe I will love like this again.'[11]

The marriage of Errol and Nora was stormy to say the least. In January 1945, Nora had a baby girl. They named her Deirdre, and Errol set them up in a Los Angeles apartment with Nora's mother living in to help. Errol stayed up at the Mulholland Ranch where his descent into drugs and alcohol worsened. Freddie was one of the very few friends who stuck with Errol as his drug-induced mood swings and rages escalated out of control. Errol later wrote in his memoir that he tried opium for fun, and loved it. But he grew sicker by the day, slipping into incoherence, barely able to move. Freddie stood by Errol, trying to keep track of what he was taking. Errol would tell Freddie he was going to the studio for the day, but he would then rush back to take an opium hit from the syrettes he left on a window sill over the bathroom sink.

'One night I came home, reached into my cache for the daily dose and found nothing. I scrambled frantically wondering if I had, in some stupor, misplaced it.'[12]

Freddie opened the door and asked Errol what he was searching for. When Errol replied, 'Nothing', Freddie hit the roof.

'You stupid sonofabitch – have you seen yourself lately?' Freddie said furiously. Errol was a mess. His skin was pallid, his eyes bloodshot, his hands shaking, his speech slurred. Errol snapped back at Freddie, saying he didn't know what he was talking about, at which point Freddie grabbed him by the arm and dragged him into the living room and up to a fire burning in the fireplace.

'There, that's where your dope is,' Freddie said pointing at the fire. 'Now what are you going to do about it?'

'You bastard! You're a guest in my house. How dare you! Do you mean to say . . .'

'Sure, I burned them. All of them!'[13]

Errol flew into a rage, letting fly with his best punch and catching Freddie right on his prominent aquiline nose. Freddie grabbed Errol and shook him vigorously, shouting he was being a fool. Errol fought, trying to get Freddie off him, but Freddie had a grip of steel, and kept shaking Errol. They rolled around the study exchanging blows, wrestling as each tried to get in a knockout punch. Furniture smashed as they churned around the room looking like a bar-room brawl in a western movie.

'You sonofabitch!' screamed Errol. 'Come outside. I'm not going to soil my place with your blood.'

Freddie obliged his best friend, and they moved outside. Errol knew Freddie wasn't a skilled boxer but he hit with enormous power and had a grip that could crush. Errol tried to keep his distance, moving around and flying in boxing jabs he'd learned while filming *Gentleman Jim*. Errol knew that if Freddie got his arms around him, that would be it, Freddie would destroy him. For a good 45 minutes each tried to lay out the other. Eventually they fought to a standstill, both men exhausted, kneeling on the ground gasping for breath.

'I'm not going to get up again,' Freddie puffed. 'Why should I be knocked down by you? If you are stupid enough to go on with this, nobody can stop you.'[14]

In that moment it hit Errol like a lightning bolt: he was being a complete fool. Freddie McEvoy, his best friend, was trying to save his life. Errol shook his head, then reached out and shook Freddie's hand. Errol retreated to his den, and didn't leave for several days. While Errol went through withdrawal, Freddie waited patiently outside Errol's room, sending in food and water. Freddie fended off studio demands for Errol's presence with excuses that he was ill. Finally, after days of purging his body of the drug, Errol emerged.

He later wrote: 'The only real thing that came of it was my realisation of what a good friend Freddie really was.'[15]

Once Errol shed the drugs, he was back working on films. Movies released before his trial had gained a new lease of life thanks to the publicity, and were raking in the dollars. Fans wanted to see Errol in action. The phrase 'In Like Flynn' had become the catch cry for anything relating to success with ladies. Warner Bros was keen to cash in on his popularity and get Errol Flynn into as many movies as possible. In quick succession came French resistance movie *Uncertain Glory*, the battle film *Objective, Burma!* and a western, *San Antonio*. Errol was in huge demand for interviews, and on one publicity round he took Freddie with him to New York. As usual, there were scores of women waiting when he emerged from a radio interview. Freddie and Errol noticed a very attractive redhead waiting in the crowd. Errol signed autographs, and then was surprised when he saw the redhead waiting outside his hotel room. Errol looked at Freddie, and Freddie gave a big wink. Freddie was a fast worker. Errol invited her in. Errol later said in his memoir he hired the young lady to play a prank on the press. He got her to dress in a nurse's uniform and then come in during interviews to take his pulse and place her ear next to his heart, make notes on a clipboard, then leave, all the time keeping a straight face.

'This was absolutely platonic and she had no duties outside of upsetting my friends,' Errol wrote.[16] Oh, sure. Errol added that the redhead provided 'services' to Freddie while he soaked in a bath. 'He [Freddie] loved a bubble bath and always had a small rubber toy duck floating in it.'[17] The arrangement ended suddenly when the redhead's fiancé stormed into the hotel demanding she immediately leave the devilish clutches of the two Australian rogues.

In 1944 Freddie's young wife Irene gave birth to a girl they named Stephanie. At the age of 37, after a lifetime of bedroom adventures, Freddie McEvoy was a father. However, Freddie didn't feel committed to the notion of the three of them as a family. The decision of whether he should stick around was pretty well solved for him when Charles Wrightsman, upon discovering he had a granddaughter, imposed his presence. The tyrannical oilman and his new, much younger wife seized control of both Irene and his baby granddaughter. He barred Freddie from seeing his wife and daughter. Irene was back in the cage she had grown up in and, like her mother, she resorted to drink and her mental health suffered. The disaster of the marriage with Irene left Freddie to regard himself as free to chase fortune and pleasure wherever he could find it. Divorce was only a matter of time.

With time on his hands, Freddie persuaded Errol to lend him his boat *Sirocco* to make periodic runs between Los Angeles and Mexico. Freddie wanted to beef up something he had been doing on a small scale in yachts for years – smuggling. Four years of wartime restrictions and shortages meant there was a huge demand from the wealthy of LA and Hollywood for the luxuries of life, such as alcohol (in particular tequila), cigars and drugs, and a cross-border trade in jewels, guns and humans. It is not clear from what can be gleaned from research in US archives just how heavily involved Freddie became in smuggling desired goods between Mexico and California, but it seems it was enough to keep him in considerable cash during a hard time.

US Customs became suspicious of the activities of the *Sirocco*, and stepped in to try to curtail the boat's movements. Customs agents seized a radio transmitter that had been ordered for Flynn's yacht, declaring it was a breach of export controls and could not be taken down to Mexico. Such a transmitter would have been very useful to signal enemy ships or submarines or to tell shore boats when to come out to sea to collect contraband.

Meanwhile, Errol Flynn had been slipping further and further into depression. He knew his performances in his latest films had been mediocre at best. He was virtually an automaton, going through the motions. He withdrew from his wife Nora and his two children, locking himself up for days on end in his Mulholland hilltop ranch. It was only when Freddie returned from one of his smuggling excursions with the *Sirocco* that Errol would emerge from his self-enforced isolation and go down to the dock to see his beloved boat and sit with his best friend. They'd relax for hours on board, Freddie telling tall tales of his derring-do on the high seas in an attempt to jolt Errol out of his melancholy. The war in Europe was finally drawing to a close, and Freddie told of his plans to return to the French Riviera. Part of his divorce settlement with Beatrice was the yacht *Black Swan*, which had been sitting in Cannes harbour throughout the war, used by Vichy French and holidaying German officers. Freddie could only guess what condition it was in and told Errol he was keen to get over to France as soon as possible to grab ownership of the yacht before someone else sailed off in it. He suggested

Errol join him in France as soon as things settled down and the boat was seaworthy so they could have some fun.

Talking with the ever-optimistic Freddie perked Errol up no end. He looked around the *Sirocco* and thought the best way he could cheer himself up would be to get a bigger boat. He'd seen a beautiful ocean-going yacht called the *Zaca* in a sailing magazine. It had sailed around the world twice, but had been commandeered and painted grey for naval war service. When Errol saw the *Zaca* was up for sale he knew he had to have it. He bought it and had it fitted out for luxury cruising. *Zaca* was Errol's dream boat. He had a special flag made to fly on the mast – a crowing scarlet rooster. Errol thought it a fitting emblem for a man of his disreputable reputation. 'A rampant cock sport, that's what I am to the world today, a goddam sex symbol,' Errol explained to his old pal, actor David Niven.[18]

Sex was to get Errol and Freddie into trouble again, this time in Miami. According to author Charles Higham, Errol and Freddie shared a hotel room with a woman they had hired for the night. 'In the morning, after they checked out, the girl was found dead. The police questioned them closely but a bribe silenced an investigating officer,' wrote Higham in his controversial book on Errol Flynn.[19] According to Higham, Errol gave a deposition to the inquest into the woman's death, which concluded she died of a heart attack. Strangely this incident wasn't reported anywhere else. Newspapers would have been all over it if they got a whiff of such a sensational story. Also odd was that Higham made little of it, mentioning it only in passing. There were no documents or evidence of the incident in the dozens of boxes of research papers Higham left to the University of Southern California. Many other claims concerning Errol and Freddie made by Higham lacked evidence, and his claims often conflicted with FBI documents and other sources. Perhaps this story of a fatal threesome was just a tall story Higham repeated. Still, immediately after this supposed incident Freddie skedaddled quick smart out of Florida.

While Errol went cruising with his beloved new *Zaca*, Freddie managed to get to France within months of the war ending in Europe. He headed straight for Cannes, and was delighted to find that his old playground had got through the terrible war relatively unscathed. The US-led Allied force had landed on the Riviera just south-east of Cannes in August 1944 and met relatively weak resistance. German forces were scattered and diminished by divisions that had been pulled out to fight on other fronts, so the Allies didn't have to bomb or shell Riviera cities from the sea. The Germans retreated from the coast, harassed by French resistance forces and Allied paratrooper attacks. The Allies liberated Marseilles and Toulon within weeks of the landing. This meant nearly all the coastal mansions and elegant villas dotted along the Riviera escaped the destruction wreaked upon the rest of Europe. Freddie was overjoyed to find the *Black Swan* intact, and only a little worse for wear. He lived on board and got to work restoring the yacht to her former graceful beauty.

The millionaires who had pulled out of France when the Germans invaded started to trickle back to reclaim their estates on the Riviera. The British aristocracy, however, weren't so quick to return to France. Many of them had been hard hit by the war, both financially and through the loss of human life. Nevertheless, money was starting to flow back to the playgrounds of Europe on the Riviera, the Alpine resorts and Paris. Americans, especially those who'd made money from the war, along with aspiring eastern-bloc emigres, were keen to see the Riviera return to the pursuit of pleasure and opulence they'd missed during the war.

One of the first to return to the Riviera was the Aga Khan, popular society figure and multi-millionaire titular leader of a section of Muslims called the Nizari Ismailis, who paid him a tithe of 10 per cent. It kept him in palaces, racehorses, fast cars, high fashion and glamorous friends in return for spiritual leadership of a people of northern India and what later became Pakistan. Once word spread that the fabulously wealthy Aga Khan, royalty of the international social set, was back on the Riviera, others flocked back to the beautiful sun-drenched coast to recapture the decadent life as it had been before the war.

Freddie, ever with an eye for the main chance, saw that there were opportunities to be had as Europe brushed off the debris and emerged from the devastation of war. Freddie was busy working on *Black Swan* on the Cannes dock when a short portly chap strolled up to watch him scrape and paint. With a thick Cockney accent the fellow asked Freddie whether he fixed up boats for a living. Freddie said no, it was just a hobby and he was fixing up his yacht from the ravages of war. Freddie would never admit he worked for a living. Everything he did had to be only a hobby. Money had to appear to come to him naturally from nowhere. It was all part of the image. The Cockney certainly wasn't the usual upper-class Brit who frequented the Riviera. They got talking about yachts, and Freddie quickly realised this odd little man knew nothing about boats. Here's a chance, thought Freddie. The Cockney introduced himself – George Dawson. Freddie had never heard of him – he wasn't part of the society he mixed in – but when Dawson pointed out the villa on top of the hill that he'd just bought, Freddie was suddenly interested. This bloke didn't have airs and graces, but he must have money. It was a fortuitous meeting of two grifters. Dawson was pleased to meet a down-to-earth Australian on the French Riviera, especially one who seemed to have time on his hands. He didn't ask what Freddie did for a living, and Freddie didn't say. Best appear to be one of the idle rich than a penniless opportunist.

Dawson said he wanted to buy a yacht to keep on the Riviera; a nice big luxury yacht on which he could take guests out, and to have fun with his friends. Could Freddie recommend such a yacht that might be for sale? Well, come in spinner, thought Freddie. It just so happened that he had heard of a good yacht that could be for sale. For the right price, of course. It would probably need a bit of work to make it shipshape. Freddie said he knew the owner, but he was fussy and would be reluctant to sell to someone he didn't know. He loved the boat, see, and didn't want to sell it to just anyone.

Dawson had grown up in the tough working-class streets of London making his fortune buying and selling trucks, and he knew a con when he saw it. He was quite a conman himself, and he liked this charming Aussie. They shook hands on a deal: Freddie would find him a yacht, negotiate the purchase, then fix it up for him. Freddie kept a straight face, but inside he was cheering with joy. Play this right and he could skim a huge chunk off the top.

Freddie fulfilled his part of the deal. He found a rather dilapidated 250-ton vessel, the *Momosan,* one of the largest pleasure vessels on the Riviera. It was owned by Argentinian shipping magnate Alberto Dodero, a party-loving tycoon Freddie had met through Beatrice at one of her pre-war shindigs held for the Duke and Duchess of Windsor. The official price was US$125,000 – US$1.5 million in today's money. Dawson was unperturbed at the price and agreed. Freddie had his commission and the work of the transforming the vessel to luxury yacht. Freddie cleaned up on the deal.

He continued to do work for Dawson that wasn't quite so above board. Dawson was making a fortune as a military stores dealer, buying and selling war material – tens of thousands of trucks, bulldozers, jeeps, Quonset huts, tents, blankets and other assorted items – left in Europe by the Americans. For the US Treasury it was cheaper to sell them in Europe than to bring them back to the United States. Dawson had got in early, flying himself to war-torn western Germany even before peace had been declared. He literally bribed his way into US storage depots to see the quartermasters. Money exchanged hands and Dawson had a deal. Dawson later said he paid five to ten pounds cash for American trucks that were worth £2000.[20]

A consummate wheeler-dealer, Dawson struck secret deals with eastern bloc and north African countries desperate for transport and building machinery to reconstruct their war-torn nations. US equipment wasn't supposed to go to communist states, and certainly not to China or North Korea where war with the United States appeared to be imminent. Dawson worked a network of dummy sales slips to hide the true destination of his shipments – Marshall Tito of Yugoslavia reportedly got more war surplus equipment from Dawson than he did from the Soviet Union – and Dawson made a fortune from the racket – US$100 million (US$983 million in today's money) according to a US congressional committee inquiry.[21] It didn't necessarily arrive in cash. The Soviets liked to pay in gold, which Dawson laundered through Tangier where he converted it to diamonds. He would then sell these diamonds in France, Belgium and England.

This is where Freddie proved useful. Once his yacht *Black Swan* was seaworthy, he would slip from the French Riviera to Tangier, pick up the diamonds, then smuggle them into France. Freddie also had good connections to sell the diamonds, acting as the middleman on many deals, presenting the diamonds with a whisper to prospective buyers that they were being sold by wealthy clients in a spot of financial trouble who wished to remain anonymous. And Freddie knew who might be interested in buying – people such as the Aga Khan, wealthy American socialites, tycoons and movie moguls frolicking on the Riviera who could present the diamonds to their trophy girlfriends.

According to journalist Michael Stern, Freddie even got to pull a few crooked sales deals for Dawson. One of the biggest involved 1800 trucks Dawson was trying to offload. Freddie got in touch with his friend Alberto Dodero, from whom he'd bought the *Momosan* for Dawson. Freddie successfully arranged a provisional sale of the trucks to Dodero, who was then going to sell them on to Evita Peron, who planned to convert them to buses for Argentina. However, during the negotiations, Dodero died. The deal fell through, and Freddie missed out on a US$2.5 million commission.[22]

But there were other deals, and Freddie was in business. Apart from his *Black Swan* on the Riviera, within a few years he had a beautiful apartment in Paris that overlooked the racetrack in Auteuil, and an office on the Champs Elysees.

The only thing missing in Freddie's life now was a rich wife, and maybe – just maybe – this time he could afford to marry for love.

CHAPTER 12

FREDDIE FINDS LOVE, FREDDIE STYLE

Freddie was enjoying his first Christmas in Paris since the war. The city of light was filled with music and dance and joy as Parisians shook off the horrors of the German occupation. Freddie found many of his old friends still there, trying to put the war behind them. Nobody asked questions about what happened during those dark years. There were too many secrets, too many horrible memories, too many terrible things they'd had to do to survive. Some collaborated with the German occupiers, did business with them, informed on those in hiding. Some profited from the German occupation, taking property and possessions from Jews who disappeared into the Nazi camps. It just wasn't done to ask. For many the shame ran deep.

Freddie reluctantly confided to some of his Riviera friends that he'd been interned for a while, but he'd managed to escape to America. He was far too modest to admit to heroic deeds. At least that's the impression he gave. Others heard rumours that Freddie had been a British secret agent, that he gave the Germans false information to help others escape. It was a rumour that could very well have been started by Freddie himself, but Freddie, along with most in the high-society milieu, chose discreet silence as the best policy.

Repercussions for the common men and women of France who had survived by collaborating with the Germans had been swift and brutal. Many French women who'd fed their families by sleeping with German soldiers were beaten and had their heads shaved. Around 10,000 people believed to be collaborators were executed, many in kangaroo courts carried out by the Resistance. Marshal Pétain, who ran Vichy France like a medieval fiefdom, was convicted for treason. He was sentenced to death, but his sentence was commuted to life in prison for his heroic deeds in World War I.

France's high society was intent on putting all that ugliness behind them. The colourful bunting was up, chandeliers lit, cocktails served, dancing resumed, and the best frocks brought out. Freddie was still married to Irene, who was back in the United States, but the Aussie playboy was in full swing, back on the prowl for a wealthy widow or heiress. Freddie was delighted when who should walk into the Parisian gala ball he was attending but the lovely and very, very, rich Barbara Hutton, the lady who in 1936 had bet him $10,000 he couldn't drive from Paris to Cannes in under 10 hours. She was now by far the richest woman in the world – worth more than US$1 billion in today's money – having inherited the Woolworths emporium empire. In 1942 she had married the most debonair, handsome and respectable movie actor of the day – English-born Archie Leach, better known as Cary Grant. Errol Flynn hadn't been on Barbara's radar; he didn't have the respectable bit. Besides, Barbara was 30 years old when she married Cary Grant, far too old to interest Errol Flynn.

Barbara had already gone through two marriages when she wed Cary Grant. The first was at age 20 to a rather suspect Georgian princeling called Alexis Mdivani. The playboy received a US$1 million dowry and was intent on getting much more when they divorced after two years. It left her with the title 'Princess'. Next was domineering Count Kurt von Haugwitz-Reventlow, an abusive Dane who once beat her so savagely she ended up in hospital. She divorced this nasty piece of work after two-and-a-half years, gaining custody of their son Lance. Barbara lacked personal confidence before she married the count, and afterwards she was a mess, racked by insecurity and fear. The experience left her scarred, anorexic, a frequent drunk and a drug addict. Done with lesser money-grabbing European aristocrats, she married the prince of the silver screen, Cary Grant. The press dubbed the couple 'Cash and Cary'. However, by all accounts Grant wasn't interested in her money. Cary Grant had plenty of his own money, and he was the first of Barbara's husbands who had genuine affection for the woman who, after her two previous marital disasters, had become known as the 'poor little rich girl'. Freddie appeared at an opportune time. Grant, a closet bisexual, had other interests to pursue, and the ever-restless Barbara was looking for her next handsome escort. When Freddie bumped into Barbara in late 1945, he was a more mature 38-year-old, and even though Barbara was now 33, Freddie could see she was in trouble.

Freddie was quick to renew his friendship with Barbara over that Parisian Christmas. Barbara was pretty well separated from Cary Grant by this stage, and though Freddie was still married to Irene he hardly saw her. According to several biographies, Barbara was at the time a troubled soul, hitting the bottle hard and fearful of anyone getting too close to her. Her portrait artist and close friend Savely Sorine said she constantly made herself the heroine in her own make-believe life, and any man she liked was instantly the hero.

'She is like an actress, her life is a book. It is not real but she lives it . . . when the dream is over the hero dies and he is just a friend,' Sorine told author Dean Jennings for his book on Barbara Hutton. 'She comes to see me and she is wonderful. An hour later she has changed. She is Jekyll and Hyde within the body of a woman.'[1]

Today it could be classified as depression. But Barbara trusted Freddie. For her he was a friend from swinging Paris of the 1930s who had been tragically separated from her by the outbreak of war before their relationship had a chance to bloom. He was fun to be around, and she didn't see him as a threat. Freddie was playing his cards very carefully. He understood quite a bit about this affliction of the black dog, as Winston Churchill dubbed depression. Freddie had done his best to pull his friend Errol Flynn out of the depths of the dark places a mind can go, and the drugs they seek to accompany them. Freddie took Barbara to the clean mountains of St Moritz – she paid for the best suites, of course – hoping the gleaming white snow and bright blue skies would help cleanse her.

Freddie and Barbara were often seen in close company in Paris's fashionable restaurants and nightclubs. They certainly weren't a couple who would go unnoticed by the gossip columnists and celebrity-hunting photographers. Columnist Igor Cassini knew of Freddie's penchant for rich women, and dubbed Freddie 'The Big Dame Hunter'.[2] The unwanted title stuck, much to Freddie's annoyance. He believed he had much more class than that, and saw himself as more of a service provider than a gold digger. Freddie allowed Barbara to unburden herself of her insecurity, and the pain of her previous marriages. He was playing for high stakes. He knew that to succeed in wedding the richest woman in the world he would need to play his cards very carefully, and with consummate patience. When Barbara returned to the United States for the winter of 1946, Freddie accompanied her. They settled into a luxury mansion in the picturesque village of Franconia in the White Mountains of New Hampshire. It was idyllic – skiing, sleigh riding and tobogganing all day, cosy nights by the huge log fire. It should have been a sure-fire hit for Freddie. Barbara's divorce from Cary Grant had come through. She was a free woman. Unfortunately, Freddie was still technically married to Irene, even though they had been separated for more than a year. But divorce in those days required a reason, such as infidelity or cruelty. Freddie couldn't very well deny the first, but he'd be damned if he would be publicly shamed by the accusation of the second. He would have to get Barbara to agree to wait for his divorce to come through the complex legal process.

Freddie didn't know it, but behind the scenes forces were at work against him. Despite bestowing all his considerable charms of seduction on the financially blessed Barbara Hutton, Freddie was failing to reel in the greatest fish he'd ever had on his considerable hook. Freddie was mystified. For sure he'd got Barbara into bed where he had, as usual, been spectacular. Chroniclers of the times said Barbara confided to friends that Freddie was the only man who could bring her to orgasm.[3] But for the first time in his long successful career of seducing wealthy women, Freddie wasn't completing his mission. Hutton's biographer Dean Jennings says Barbara was warned off Freddie by one of her confidantes – Savely Sorine's new Russian-born wife Anya. Jennings says Anya was very much in love with Barbara, and she was determined to protect what she thought were Barbara's best interests.

'I stopped it,' Anya Sorine told Jennings. 'I was the one who kept her from him, but it was a near thing. I am glad I did so. It would have been a terrible mistake, and Barbara knew I was right.'[4]

It's just as well Freddie never found out about Anya's stab in the back; he could fly into a fury if anyone got between him and a pot of gold. In the spring of 1946 Barbara returned to New York. She bought the Franconia mansion they had stayed in because it held many happy memories for her and him – and she gave it to Freddie. Perhaps Freddie should have realised it was a farewell present. Nevertheless, Freddie boarded a ship bound for France with a large cash payment from Barbara, and 40 of her trunks. Barbara told friends she now thought of France as home, and later flew to Paris. Reporters were hot on her trail, filing stories of an imminent wedding between the richest woman in the world and the Australian sportsman playboy. 'Woolworth Heiress may marry Australian' reported Brisbane's *Courier-Mail* on its front page on 13 April 1946. 'Relatives are trying to do everything to prevent her marriage to McEvoy, whom newspapers describe as a popular handsome heiress hunter,' the paper reported. 'The family insist the relationship is purely platonic. But friends say "It's love".'[5]

Staff at The Ritz Hotel were delighted to see the return of Barbara Hutton. Paris was once again becoming the playground of rich Americans. She gave one of her rare interviews to a Paris newspaper, in which she said that for the first time in her life she felt independent, with no one to tell her what to do:

> All my life I've been bullied by men – first by my father, then by my husbands because unfortunately I am the sort of person who can't stand scenes. When people start yelling I say 'yes' as quickly as I can to keep them quiet.[6]

Freddie and Barbara moved together into the best suite at The Ritz. A few weeks later Cary Grant arrived in Paris for a movie and was heading to The Ritz when he suddenly remembered reading in the gossip pages that Barbara was staying there with Freddie. He realised the papers would undoubtedly report the excitement of an awkward love triangle at The Ritz, and he told the driver to take him to another hotel. Grant, ever the gentleman, stayed out of sight until it was time to leave Paris.

Society gossips were hungry for a Barbara/Freddie love story. Photographer Paul Renauden of *France Soir* was ordered to get a picture of them together. He hung around The Ritz until he saw them slip out the back door and hop into a limousine. He followed them with a fellow paparazzo as they drove to an isolated villa outside Paris. Renauden told author Dean Jennings he climbed a tree from where he could look into the grounds and waited patiently in case they came out into the garden. Hours later Barbara came outside with Freddie, and Renauden snapped their picture from the tree. Freddie heard the camera click and leaped over the fence to race after the photographer. He caught the Frenchman and punched him on the chin, dropping him to the ground. Freddie bundled Barbara into the car and they drove off. Renauden eventually recovered and was delighted to find that his companion photographer had captured the whole thing. The pictures were the sensation of Paris the next day when *France Soir* ran them. The photos showing Freddie bopping the photographer made it to the United States, where it was pointed out that the car Freddie and Barbara were driving had CD plates – it was a car from the Diplomatic Corps. It wasn't clear which embassy lent the car to the couple, but Freddie had contacts everywhere and Barbara was, after all, the richest woman in the world and could easily have bought a couple of small countries.[7] Renauden said it was the most humiliating and satisfying moment of his career. He wished he'd had a chance to sit down with Freddie to laugh about it. Barbara later commented: 'It was one of the funniest things I've seen in my life.'[8]

One gossip writer went too far when *The Tatler* reported: 'Barbara Hutton and her latest husband, Freddie McEvoy, have the super suite at the Carlton in Cannes.'[9] Freddie chuckled and joked about it. He'd just opened his mysterious office, called The French Purchasing Agency, on the Champs-Elysees, where he arranged under-the-counter deals on art and jewellery, conducted black-market currency exchanges and performed shadowy tasks for the likes of military surplus dealer George Dawson. Freddie figured the publicity of being linked to the richest woman in the world would do him no harm. But Barbara was furious. Not only was she not married to Freddie, but she'd never stayed at the Carlton. She dispatched her lawyers to *The Tatler*. The gossip magazine wrote a grovelling apology to 'Mrs Grant' in its next edition.

But word of the new 'Mr Hutton' had reached the United States, and now it was Mrs Irene McEvoy's turn to turn on the fury. In a blaze of publicity, she got on a plane in New York with baby Stephanie bound for Paris, telling reporters: 'Freddie's so-called affair with Barbara doesn't mean a thing . . . and between you and me, I don't give a damn.'[10] In Paris waiting reporters propped up the bar of the Ritz Hotel where Freddie had been staying with Barbara Hutton. They were hoping for fireworks when Mrs Irene McEvoy, still only 21, would storm through the swank hotel doors to confront her cavorting husband.

American journalist Graham Miller witnessed the reunion of Mr and Mrs McEvoy. Miller had followed Freddie to the airport at Orly and saw him greet his wife:

> with all the solicitation that a good husband should show, [he] escorted her back to the Ritz and fussed about her gently as she had some tea. The happy family then proceeded upstairs to their single room, tucked the baby into a crib and unpacked Mrs McEvoy's personal luggage.[11]

Miller wrote that he visited their room and got a brief interview. Freddie told him:

Of course I'm an old friend of Barbara's. I've known her for years. I think she's somewhere in Switzerland just now, but there's no suggestion my wife and I are separating or that I am going to marry her [Barbara]. I'm happily married and intend to stay that way. It is all silly gossip.[12]

Miller had his story; not the one he was hoping for, but then Freddie had learned from Errol Flynn how to play newspapermen – give them a few quotes to make them happy for the next day's paper, and they'll be on your side, until the next deadline.

However, Irene's flight of fury failed to wrest Freddie from the company of Barbara. A short time later she flew back to New York, minus baby Stephanie, and sued for divorce. Freddie made a quick trip to the United States, ostensibly to try to patch things up, but in reality to ensure he would get custody of little Stephanie. The toddler was staying with Freddie's mother Violet at her Paris apartment. Freddie believed Irene was unable to cope with motherhood because of her drinking problem. He also didn't want Stephanie's domineering grandfather Charles Wrightsman getting his hands on her. That was Freddie's term for a quick divorce. In return for Irene agreeing to him having custody, Freddie offered no defence against Irene's claim of cruelty. She told the court Freddie had deserted her on their wedding night, leaving her alone while he joined a party with his friend Errol Flynn. She also said that when the baby was born Freddie refused to stick around; he went fishing instead. These accusations may well have been true. Freddie was frustrated he'd married an oil heiress whose fortune had been cut off. Irene told the divorce court in Los Angeles that, for the time being, she was 'satisfied to permit McEvoy to have custody of their daughter, but may ask that he be directed to return the child from France at some future time'.[13]

Irene's father had worked behind the scenes to end the marriage from the very start. Gossip columnists noted he'd visited Beatrice Cartwright several times, apparently trying to compile a dossier of Freddie's dirty deeds. However, Beatrice retained a great deal of affection for Freddie and was still sending him money as part of their divorce settlement. Freddie managed to stay friends with most of his lovers long after their intimate relationships had broken up. Putting aside his obsession with chasing easy money, Freddie wasn't mean or greedy. He spent any money he acquired at the casino or on having a good time with fast cars, fast yachts or yet more fast women. Having a young daughter didn't slow him down. His mother was happy to look after two-year-old Stephanie while Freddie spun his magic at his dodgy wheeler-dealer office in Paris.

With his divorce from Irene fast coming through, Freddie once again entertained the prospect of marrying Barbara. But he made the mistake of introducing her to one of his friends – Prince Igor Troubetzkoy, one of many Russian aristocrats whose families had fled, penniless, from the communist revolution. Igor was one of Freddie's agents in the black-money market, his princely title roping in impressionable wealthy Americans to assorted scams and shady deals. Igor wasn't the typical suave European titled playboy that Barbara had encountered before. He was 35, had never been married, was charming and polite, a bicycle-racing champion and a thorough gentleman who appreciated art, yet he had a shyness that attracted Barbara. She asked

Freddie about Igor, and Freddie spoke of him in glowing terms. If Freddie couldn't snare Barbara, at least if a friend did, he might still have a doorway to her money. Barbara moved to Badrutt's Palace Hotel in St Moritz along with Freddie, Prince Igor and her entourage of female assistants. Badrutt's was, of course, Freddie's childhood home and the place where he learned to bobsled. He loved to show Barbara all the places he had played as a child. But Barbara had eyes only for the prince. Freddie, after all, no matter how good a companion and satisfying a lover, was a mere commoner from the colonies. After a whirlwind romance, in February 1947 Barbara and Igor were married in a little Swiss village. Only two others were present as witnesses – Freddie as Igor's best man, and a female friend of Barbara's.

Barbara parted from Freddie as a good friend. Hutton biographer Dean Jennings said Freddie was the absolute good sport about losing to his friend Igor. He knocked on her door and when she opened it he looked taut and serious. He reached for her hands and said: 'Barbara darling, I just came to wish you happiness and everything good in your life with Igor.'[14] She gave him one of her luxury limousines, bundles of cash and some other property on top of the mansion in New Hampshire. Asked years later how she felt about Freddie, Barbara said: 'No matter what people thought of Freddie or what they said, I was for him. He helped me when I needed help.'[15]

Despite his gallant behaviour over Barbara, Freddie was in a bit of a bad way. He'd only just recovered from a serious gastric ulcer and continued to suffer from amoebic dysentery he'd picked up in Mexico years earlier. He'd been the victim of a silly prank by a friend who'd got a masseuse to give Freddie a

Good friends: Prince Igor Troubetzkoy, Barbara Hutton and Freddie McEvoy.

particularly hard going-over, unaware he had a bleeding ulcer. Tough guy that he was, Freddie didn't complain, but two hours later he was rushed to hospital, where for three weeks his life hung in the balance.[16] When Freddie finally re-emerged on the nightclub scene, friends said he appeared gaunt and lacking his usual energy and bonhomie. Missing out on marrying Barbara certainly didn't help his mood.

When Freddie heard that Barbara had offered Igor a million dollars in cash as a wedding present, his mood darkened further. He didn't care that Igor was said to have refused the offer. A million dollars on offer is a million dollars. It's what Freddie had been striving for all his adult life. A story went around the gossip columnists – some said it was true, others that it was made up by malicious society gossips who didn't like Igor or Freddie.

New York gossip writer Elsa Maxwell said that after Barbara and Igor's honeymoon, Freddie demanded a 'finder's' payment from Igor for singing his praises to Barbara. Maxwell wrote that Igor handed Freddie a cheque for US$200,000[17] – that's US$2 million in today's money. Other gossips embellished the story, saying Freddie hired a couple of thugs to put the hard word on Igor, but the thugs beat up Freddie in a pub brawl when he failed to pay them for their efforts. Others said the thugs were mafia who were demanding a slice of Freddie's black-market racket.

Regardless of whether any of these stories were true, Freddie was in a hole. His curious business on the Champs Elysees was slackening off as France was getting back on its feet. The black-market trade fares best when times are tough and goods are scarce, and the world economy was on the upswing by late 1948. One day a bit of good luck came his way. Freddie had always been a snappy dresser, often setting the trend in men's fashion. The story goes that Freddie was strolling along the Cannes waterfront dressed in sandals, crisp white shorts and a brightly coloured Hawaiian-style shirt when he was stopped by a rich Argentinian. The man wanted to have a close look at the sandals, so Freddie took them off and showed them. The Argentinian was fascinated and asked where he could get a pair. And the shirt, he just loved the colourful shirt. No worries, said Freddie, and took off the shirt and gave it to the Argentinian as well. 'All yours, mate, keep them.' Flabbergasted, the Argentinian reached into his pocket and pressed $2000 into Freddie's hand. Freddie wandered off laughing, as did the Argentinian. The story hit the Cannes newspaper, and thus Freddie stepped into legend as the man who gave the shirt off his back and started a Riviera fashion for men's colourful shirts.[18] Just as well the Argentinian didn't want the white shorts as well.

Freddie's business renovating luxury yachts was his best source of cash. He spent most of his time on the French Riviera with occasional flights to the Bahamas to meet up with his good mate Errol Flynn. *The Palm Beach Post* reported that Freddie was focused extensively on spear fishing for an underwater movie he was working on. Every day he took his catch to holidaying attractive blonde Janet Malley Paterno, heiress to a department-store fortune. However, Freddie lost out once again to a good friend. This time it was the wealthy Briton Steve Raphael, who had been part of the shared mansion in Bel Air during the notorious party that landed Errol Flynn on trial for statutory rape. There were no hard feelings. Freddie had made Raphael godfather to baby Stephanie. As the columnist unkindly said, Freddie 'had to chalk up Janet alongside Barbara Hutton Troubetzkoy as one of his more conspicuous failures'.[19]

Love and good fortune – the money variety, that is – seemed to have deserted Freddie McEvoy. He was still living the high life as part of the glamorous Riviera party set, but he was no longer at the centre of the action. Freddie had just turned 40 and, while still fit and attractive, he wasn't a movie star. Nor was he a prince, a duke, a count or even a lowly baron. He didn't have money. Sure, he had style and grace. He was witty and charming. He had a yacht. He played successfully at the casinos. But that dashing air of danger that attracted women like a magnet when he was in his 30s now appeared a bit worn. Suicide Freddie was now starting to look like Settled Freddie. Wealthy women rolling into the Riviera playground looking for sexual excitement had new – and much younger – prospective lovers to choose from.

Life magazine devoted eight pages to the 1948 summer scene on the French Riviera. The magazine showed pictures of girls in 'scanty bathing suits known as a "bikini"'. It gushed about glamorous parties hosted by Ali Khan, handsome son of the Aga Khan, and the Shah of Persia. 'Once a week this season Alberto Dodero would invite every available member of the new set to a colossal dinner where he provided pyramids of lobster and sometimes fireworks.'[20] Residents such as the Duke and Duchess of Windsor swanned around in limousines and yachts, crowded the best restaurants, jammed the casino gambling tables and lazed on patios sipping cocktails. Hollywood had moved in, including movie moguls Jack Warner and Darryl Zanuck. Hot actor of the day Orson Welles was enjoying a 'wonderful' reunion with his almost ex-wife Rita Hayworth. She in turn was being swooned over by Dodero. Linda Christian – the ex of Errol Flynn – was there with her fiancé Tyrone Power.

Freddie may have had old friends among this twittering troupe, but they had little time for him. Yet there was still life in old Freddie. He noticed a young blonde woman on the beach, her curvaceous body almost naked in the tiniest bikini one could wear in public. Freddie was instantly smitten. An invitation to his yacht, a walk along the beach promenade, a drive through the coastal mountains, a swank dinner, a night at the casino . . . the Freddie charm was turned up to full force. Her name was Claude Stephanie Filatre. She was 24. Freddie was 40. She was born of French parents in Algiers, where her father was a tobacco merchant. Her family was moderately well off, but not rich like

Freddie's previous targets. She had done some work as a model in Paris and was attractive without being a great beauty. There were no millions to be had from this romance, but Freddie didn't care. For once he was wooing a woman because he had fallen in love with her. And the joy of it all was that this slip of a young woman, 16 years his junior, loved him too. Freddie was excited that at long last he was seeking to marry a woman he actually loved and was wholeheartedly attracted to. As one writer who met her said: 'She had a quiet, undramatic beauty, her dark eyes giving the look of the eternal innocent.' Her miniscule bikini and diaphanous clothing left little to the imagination, 'but she carried herself with such unconscious grace that women did not resent it, and wolves respected it.'[21]

At the time Freddie met Claude, she was the mistress of a wealthy French watch manufacturer, Maurice Anguenot. She had a daughter from a previous marriage, Romaine Caroline, who was the same age as Freddie's Stephanie. Anguenot had showered quite a bit of wealth on young Claude in the form of jewellery, paintings, a couple of racehorses and stocks in his company. This was not an unusual arrangement in France, and Anguenot considered Claude to be virtually his second wife, her child an unofficial part of his extended family. So, it came as a shock to Anguenot when Claude told him she was leaving him to marry Freddie McEvoy. Anguenot knew of Freddie. All of French society knew of Freddie. He hit the roof, angrily telling Claude that Freddie was a penniless gigolo, always out to marry for money. The only possible reason he could be interested in her was the small fortune that he, her benefactor, had bestowed on her out of the goodness of his heart. It quickly developed into a blazing row. Claude shouted at her sugar daddy that she knew Freddie was poor; he was down to his last yacht in fact. But she cried that Freddie was marrying her because he loved her, and whatever money she might have was irrelevant to him. Anguenot scoffed at that, laughing that Freddie wouldn't marry her if he took away her racehorses, the company shares and the jewels. Well, that really made Claude blow up. She tore up the stock. She told him to take the horses. She'd keep nothing but the jewels, which she figured she'd earned for services rendered.

'I will prove that Freddie is marrying me for love alone,' she cried. Claude and Freddie flew off to the Bahamas, where Errol Flynn promised to be best man at their wedding. *The Palm Beach Post* reported it was surprising news that Freddie's fiancée was not an heiress or rich divorcee, but a young French model. Yet it was all warmth and sunshine. 'Sophisticates will be intrigued to learn that Freddie's first wife Beatrice Cartwright will entertain for him and his fiancée shortly after their arrival.'[22] Beatrice sure had a lot of class. The paper suggested Freddie and Claude's wedding could be delayed until Barbara Hutton and Prince Igor Troubetzkoy could join them. The wedding took place in the spring of 1949 in full view of Freddie's best friends. Errol was best man. It was a glorious moment for Freddie. He had found love and happiness with a beautiful young woman. Their two daughters, stepsisters now, could grow up as friends. Life was looking up. He understood Claude had a bit tucked away from her time with the French watch manufacturer, and that could help them launch a new life together.

Shortly after the ceremony, Claude chose a quiet moment to breathlessly tell Freddie that she knew he had married her

Newspaper clipping of Freddie and Claude.

purely out of love. They had no money, she said, but they would be together, happy. Ah, she was so young. Freddie, somewhat confused, asked her what she was talking about. Claude then proudly told Freddie what had happened with Anguenot, how he had said Freddie only wanted her money and how she had given Anguenot back the stocks and racehorses. Claude probably expected Freddie to pick her up laughing with joy, and dance around the bedroom with her in his loving arms. According to writer Michael Stern, a stunned Freddie blurted incredulously: 'What? You mean you gave it all back to him?'

'I flung it at him,' Claude said triumphantly. She didn't get the reaction she expected.

'Freddie hit her a short right to the mouth, dropping her like an ox,' wrote Stern. 'A friend who witnessed this incident said, "I don't think it was the loss of the money that bothered him, as much as the bourgeois morality she displayed."'[23]

A lifetime of pursuing moneyed women was obviously hard to leave behind. Freddie, of course, was devastated by what he had done. He carried Claude to bed and apologised profusely when she recovered. He couldn't believe he'd reacted like that. When she told him she still had the jewels and they were worth a fortune, Freddie laughed and then cried. He had done a terrible thing to her, and he realised she had only thrown away the stocks and racehorses in a bizarre effort to prove her love for him. However, the violent reaction demonstrated that Freddie still had a deep, dark side. That dangerous drive to succeed on the Alpine slopes and in motorcar races was a permanent part of Freddie.

It wasn't the last time Claude witnessed Freddie's dangerous side. She was with him at one of the most fashionable nightclubs in Paris, Chez Florence, when he got into an argument with playboy Jacques Cals. The pair had tangled over a card game in Nassau a year earlier, and Freddie had lost $9000 ($100,000 in today's money) to Cals in a marathon gin rummy game. Freddie wasn't used to losing. As gossip writer Charles Ventura wrote: 'Freddie's wizardry at any of the games played for money among the idle rich is an international legend.'[24] Freddie's resentment still ran deep. Gossip writer Cholly Knickerbocker said they quickly came to blows and were belting into each other on the dance floor. Claude came to the assistance of her husband, plunging into the battle and hurling a champagne bottle at Cals. It sailed over Cals' head by half an inch. Friends and waiters were finally able to separate the gladiators, and a doctor had to bandage up both men before they were escorted from the premises. Freddie had found a fellow warrior in his lovely young wife.

Freddie was learning that he had to dial back his old habits. Errol Flynn was about to leave Hollywood for Paris to meet up with Freddie when he bumped into Troubetzkoy. The prince warned Errol it might not be a good idea to just drop in on Freddie. 'I'm just back from there and Freddie's French gal blacked his eye when she caught him flirting with somebody. Oh, they are very happy.'[25]

Errol Flynn was once again single – or, to be more accurate, between women – and in early 1950 he decided to visit Freddie and Claude in Paris. Errol liked Claude. He felt she had a warmth and vivaciousness that made her ideal for Freddie. He was glad, too, that Freddie had finally married for love. They, in turn, were pleased to see him. Freddie said he had some work to do, but suggested Errol should look over the Louvre for the afternoon, and take Claude with him, but be back for dinner. Errol guessed Freddie was setting up a surprise date for him, but he later recalled he had a very pleasant afternoon discussing paintings with Claude. That evening when they returned to the McEvoy apartment, Errol was stunned by the sight of the dining partner Freddie had arranged for him. In his memoirs Errol described the dark-eyed woman as a 'dream'. 'She was beautifully dressed. She sat composedly, like a woman in a Goya painting. I gaped.'[26]

Freddie introduced her as Princess Irene Ghica. Flynn was awestruck. She was just 20 years old, which was sort of still within Errol's preferred age group, but a Romanian princess!

Freddie could only smile as he watched his friend, the great movie-star womaniser, do his best to impress the cool, somewhat aloof princess. Errol devoted weeks and months trying to seduce Princess Irene. He drove her around France in a flashy new white convertible Cadillac, the only one in France at the time. People stared wherever the couple went in the romantic limousine, crowding around every time they stopped. Errol had his yacht, the *Zaca,* sailed over to the Riviera, and he hoisted the sails to take Princess Irene to the most romantic spots of the northern Mediterranean. It took a long time but at last Errol was able to fulfil his moniker and was 'In Like Flynn'. The gossip pages said they were engaged, but Errol thought the princess was still rather cool and distant. She flew into a huff if she thought Errol was even looking at another woman. This annoyed Errol, because he looked at other women all the time. So, Errol was taken aback when he dropped anchor near a pretty little island beach to discover it was a nudist colony – and that though he was reluctant to reveal the full Flynn to all and sundry, the withdrawn princess had no such qualms about showing her crown jewels. She ripped off the bikini and ran around the beach revealing her regal attributes to all and sundry.

Errol was intrigued, but not totally sold on this bewitching lady. One evening a crew member alerted Errol to a trickle of blood coming from under Princess Irene's cabin door. They forced it open to discover blood everywhere. 'She had so many razor cuts on her wrist, it looked like a washboard,' Errol later wrote.[27] This disturbed Errol immensely. Warning signs flashed, the episode reminding him of his volatile first wife Lili, and he didn't want to go through that again. Nevertheless, Errol took

Irene to the United States with him to stay in a small town in New Mexico while nearby he filmed a western called *Rocky Mountain*. It didn't go well. The princess didn't like the desert of New Mexico or the attention Errol was giving his co-star Patrice Wymore, and she returned to Europe. Errol didn't care – he had already decided Pat was his real love. He wrote in his memoirs that not only was she beautiful and talented, a great dancer and heaps of fun, she could also cook great curries. As soon as the movie was finished, they decided to marry in France. Pat had never been to Europe, and Errol wanted to impress her. The *Zaca* was still tied up at Cannes, and Errol wanted Freddie to be his best man. After all, they'd become quite skilled at performing the role for each other. Freddie and Claude had made a home for themselves on the French Riviera, mostly living on the yachts that Freddie was renovating, including a stunning yacht Freddie called the *Kangaroa*. He'd wanted to call it *Kangaroo*, but that name was already taken in the registry so he just changed the last letter. Everybody called it the *Kangaroo* anyway. Freddie was intent on stamping his Australian identity on the Riviera, perhaps as an up-yours larrikin reaction to the snooty princes, faux aristocrats and rich folk who thought Riviera society belonged to them.

The civil ceremony at Monte Carlo was a modest affair – just the entire French press with flashbulbs popping. Errol still had star power. Monaco's Prince Rainier attended with the entire court of the tiny tax-free principality. Monte Carlo's mayor gave them a medal. The parents of both Errol and Pat were there, and Freddie signed the marriage book as witness. A day later, 23 October 1950, they were married at the French Lutheran Church in Nice. This was a huge affair – flowers filling the church, fleets of limousines dropping off wedding guests from around the world, a mammoth wedding cake and French police holding back gawking crowds of more than 3000. The reception at the Hotel de Paris in Nice was the party of the year.

However, in the middle of the celebration, Errol got a tap on the shoulder from a pale and shocked-looking Freddie. 'There is a man at the door who wants to see you. He says he has some kind of warrant for your arrest.'[28] Errol told Freddie this was no time for tricks. He challenged Freddie to show him the papers. He wasn't going to be fooled; they'd played too many pranks on each other for Errol to fall for this one. Freddie came back with what appeared to be a genuine document from the Monaco police, alleging Errol had 'lustfully, lasciviously, and carnally had intercourse with a young lady aged seventeen named Denise Duvivier . . . on board the *Zaca* a year earlier'.[29] The warrant ordered Errol to attend the Monte Carlo Town Hall to answer the charges, the same place where he'd had the civil ceremony the previous day.

Errol was outraged. While he was all for storming into the Monte Carlo Town Hall to strongly deny the charges, Freddie rustled up a lawyer friend attending the wedding. The lawyer looked at the charge sheet and quickly warned Errol not to return to Monaco. There was no such thing as bail for serious charges in Monaco, and Errol could be locked in a cell until the trial was over. Errol returned to the party, joking with his new bride that he'd just been charged with rape yet again. He said it was a stitch-up, somebody trying to extort money. Not to worry. On with the party. Errol and Pat retired to the *Zaca*, trying to put it behind them.

In the morning, he was woken by claps of thunder and the sound of heavy guns. Errol immediately thought Monaco police were storming the boat to arrest him, and he bolted on deck to see that a couple of launches from the US Navy had surrounded his yacht and were firing rockets in salute. The sailors were being ferried to shore from an aircraft carrier and escort fleet moored out at sea. Errol had worked closely with the US Navy during the filming of the 1941 movie *Dive Bomber*, and servicemen had great admiration for the gallant movie star. The sailors cheered him, asking how his wedding night had gone. Errol waved, and shouted back, 'Never better, sailor!'[30] The sailors cheered even louder when Pat joined him on deck. They hugged and waved to the saluting fleet. It was a glorious start to the day after the shock of the police charge the night before.

Unfortunately, later that day Errol badly injured his back in a fall while jumping into a boat. The US Navy came to the rescue, ferrying Errol out to the surgeons on the aircraft carrier. Sailors had a field day joking about Errol doing his back on his wedding night. It laid him up for more than a month. Meanwhile, Freddie told him pressure was growing on Monaco police to take action. French newspapers published a photo of the accusing girl in Errol's arms on the deck of the *Zaca*. They were both fully clothed, but Errol couldn't remember her at all and wondered how she had got on board his yacht. A letter arrived demanding $3000 – around $100,000 in today's money – compensation that she said she would give to charity. Oh, sure. Errol decided he would not let this haunt him any longer and, like Nelson sailing into battle at the Nile to destroy the enemy fleet, Errol pointed *Zaca* to Monte Carlo and, with all flags flying – including the crowing red rooster – sailed right into port. He tied up at the wharf and, with Pat holding his hand, strode right up to the Town Hall. The lawyer Freddie had supplied wasn't allowed in the court room as the judge read out the charges in French. It was alleged Errol Flynn had forced the girl into a shower on his yacht and then had pressed himself into her, pushing a button to close an electronically operated door to trap her inside.

Errol demanded to see his accuser. He couldn't believe it when in walked a plain-looking girl dressed in flat heels, white bobby socks, a child's smock, and even pigtails. Errol burst out laughing. They'd copied photos of Peggy Satterlee in the 1942 trial. Then he noticed she had hairy legs. Ha, he knew he'd never touched this girl. He'd posed for photos with hundreds of girls on the railings of his yacht, in the streets and in bars and nightclubs; the photo of him with this girl proved nothing. Errol invited the judge to venture on to his yacht, where Errol could prove she was lying. The judge and officials duly trooped out of court and down the pier to climb on board the *Zaca*. Errol showed the judge and the assembled court officials the tiny shower, which could barely fit one person, never two. There was no electric door. The judge turned on the shower tap and got a blast of cold sea water. Hardly the place for passion. The judge and the lawyers marched back up to the courtroom, where the judge promptly banged his gavel and dismissed the case. The girl's father was jailed for fraud and she was ordered out of Monaco, never to return.

That evening, Errol and Pat celebrated his freedom with Freddie and Claude. It was one of the greatest parties ever seen on the Riviera. A few days later, Freddie waved goodbye to

Errol, who had to return to the United States to make another film. They planned to meet up again in 12 months' time in the Bahamas, where their children could play together.

It was the last time Errol saw his best friend alive.

CHAPTER 13

THE MYSTERIOUS DEATH
OF FREDDIE McEVOY

By the summer of 1951 Freddie had finished restoring his yacht *Kangaroa*. It was a beautiful craft, 104 feet (31.7 metres), its two masts defining it as a ketch, and it had an auxiliary motor. On the bow was a carved wooden Negress with a white turban and huge golden earrings. Some took her as an evil omen, but Freddie loved the boat. He'd picked it up for a bargain price of $15,000 – around $150,000 in today's money – and transformed it into the most luxurious yacht on the Riviera. When it wasn't rented out to wealthy visitors to cruise up and down the coast, Freddie and Claude lived on board the boat moored at Cannes, Monte Carlo or the charming little fishing village of St Tropez, which was fast becoming the hot spot for the glamour set.

With summer coming to a close, the market for renting out the *Kangaroa* had dwindled, and Freddie decided to sell the vessel. Demand for such large sailing boats had also declined, because the millionaires preferred massive motor launches tied up stern-first at the docks where they could be seen by the passers-by, not to mention the greater deck space to hold parties. Freddie planned to sail the *Kangaroa* across the Atlantic Ocean to Nassau in the Bahamas, where he could meet up with his old friend Errol. It was also the best market for luxury sailing yachts, aimed at rich Americans popping over from the United States.

Freddie wanted to have something to come back to on the Riviera, so he bought another yacht, the smaller *Echappe.* She was a pretty 20-ton, 60-foot yacht built in Great Yarmouth. He fitted it out with luxury furnishings and rented it to the head of the giant Fiat car-manufacturing concern, Gianni Agnelli, until his planned return in the spring. Agnelli was a dedicated playboy in his own right, pursuing Linda Christian and Pamela Churchill – daughter-in-law of Winston. Men turning up for a business meeting with Agnelli were stunned to see the statuesque Swedish actress Anita Ekberg standing stark naked on Agnelli's desk, completely unperturbed at their arrival.[1]

Despite Freddie's extensive sailing experience, he had never attempted a major ocean crossing like this before. He'd sailed around the Mediterranean as well as around the Bahamas and Californian coast, always choosing to sail in good weather. But crossing an ocean, especially the treacherous Atlantic, was a very different proposition. Freddie knew he needed an experienced navigator to skipper the boat, along with a decent crew in case of bad weather.

Freddie usually skippered the *Kangaroa* himself when it was just a calm run along the coast, but when he wanted to sail across the Mediterranean to north Africa, or east to Italy or Turkey, he turned to Bruno Hertel, an experienced German seaman, to act as boat captain and navigator. Hertel was reluctant to undertake the long voyage but, like many who knew Freddie, he felt he couldn't refuse him. Hertel had done a lot of other jobs for Freddie, including dressing up and acting as chauffeur, valet, doorman and cook whenever Freddie needed to impress someone. Freddie only paid Hertel $11 a week ($100 in today's money), but no money had been forthcoming for the past five months. Six years after the war, it was still hard for Germans to find work in France, so Hertel stuck by Freddie. Despite Freddie's promises of a big cash payment once he sold the *Kangaroa* in Nassau, Hertel was doubtful, but he felt he couldn't let Freddie down.

Freddie asked around the harbours of Cannes and Nice but could not find an experienced sailor willing to skipper the *Kangaroa* across the Atlantic on the promise of payment after the voyage. Some looked over the ketch and warned Freddie that the vessel wasn't suited to deep-ocean sailing. Errol Flynn later wrote that he had warned Freddie that sailing the Atlantic was a huge step up from knocking about the Mediterranean. Errol asked one of his experienced Cuban sailors to help out on the voyage, but after the Cuban had looked over *Kangaroa* he too refused to go. He said said the rigging was all wrong for heavy seas. The ketch's engine was weak and capable of making only five-and-a-half knots. She was too much of a pleasure boat, and the luxury fixtures Freddie had added in the cabins risked making her top heavy.[2] A former Royal Navy skipper, Commander John Christian from Sussex – who, like Errol Flynn, claimed to be a descendant of Fletcher Christian of HMS *Bounty* – also knocked back the offer to captain the *Kangaroa*.

There is a grapevine in the yachting world at Cannes and certain things were said. I was advised to be very careful about taking the job. I noticed that the sails were in bad condition and told McEvoy he would have to refit before attempting the Atlantic.[3]

He couldn't reach an agreement on pay with Freddie, so knocked back the offer. 'His crew looked tough but none seemed to know anything about deep sea navigation.'[4]

Freddie dismissed the warnings. He set out to find a crew in the dark back alleys and bars of Cannes. Like any port city, once you walk inland from the fancy yachts tied up at the piers and the expensive shops and restaurants along the promenade, life can get seedy and even dangerous. In 1951 there were still many Nazi and Fascist war criminals desperately searching for a way to escape justice and get away from Europe. At war's end the top ranks of the Nazis had the money and connections to get out quickly, using what became known as the ratline route, which included assistance from prominent Catholic clergy to flee to South America. But the lower ranks, the privates and corporals, the SS, sadists and murderers who did the bloody hands-on dirty work in the concentration camps and execution squads were left to scramble over borders any way they could.

It was in these grungy back-street bars and dark cafes that Freddie finally found his crew. He was short of cash, and so could offer only a small amount up front to sign on. Instead, he promised full payment when they reached the Caribbean. He knew he'd only get those desperate to flee from Europe, but what choice did he have? He was broke, and once again he was prepared to take a risk. Besides, he was confident he could knock down anyone who got out of line. The first to sign up was a tough-looking Austrian who gave his name as Walter Praxmarer. Unbidden, he quickly produced a passport to prove who he was. That should have aroused Freddie's suspicions – very few people in these bars volunteered their real names – but Freddie accepted him immediately. The French may resent Germans, but Freddie didn't. He had no reason to hold grudges from the war. After all, some of his past friends and lovers had been ardent Nazis. Praxmarer confided to Freddie he'd been in the Waffen SS, the elite military fighting branch of the SS, not the black-uniformed fanatical Nazi SS that committed most of the atrocities.

Frankly, Freddie didn't care. He also signed up Praxmarer's Austrian pal, Franz Krotil. Neither had much experience sailing apart from weekend jaunts on lakes. Krotil had been convicted of smuggling cigarettes over the border from Italy, but that didn't worry Freddie, who had done quite a bit of smuggling himself. In fact, deep in the hold of the *Kangaroa* Freddie had stashed 40 wooden crates that were marked simply 'Scotch'. What was really in them was to become a key part of the looming mystery of the last voyage of the *Kangaroa*.

German seaman Willi Gehring said he had plenty of ocean-sailing experience, and a relieved Freddie signed him on as boatswain. Gehring was shocked to discover he would also effectively have to be the navigator and sailing master. For such a crucial job, Freddie really should have checked Gehring's credentials more carefully. Journalist Michael Stern, who investigated what happened on the ill-fated voyage, wrote that the captain of George Dawson's luxury vessel *Mimosan* told him Gehring had come around five days before *Kangaroa* put to sea asking for help. The *Mimosan* captain told Stern:

> He [Gehring] said he didn't know much about seamanship, but that McEvoy had told him to study up on it, and he asked me what book he could read. I loaned him my sea manual, but warned him that you don't learn seamanship from a book.[5]

Freddie signed on two local young men seeking adventure to act as crew. Jean Buisson, 20, joined as apprentice seaman, and 19-year-old Robert Guillat as cabin boy. The final crew member to sign up was the most experienced professional of all but it wasn't in sailing. Martinez 'Toledo' Galleriano was a highly paid Spanish chef working at Cannes' very swank Carlton Hotel who came aboard one night seeking to sign on as cook. Obviously, Toledo had a reason for wanting to get away from the Riviera as fast as possible. Freddie didn't ask. Toledo wasn't the first person to go to sea to escape problems ashore.

One of Freddie's old bobsledding buddies, American Jack Heaton, signed on as a paying passenger all the way to the Bahamas. Freddie also wanted to take Claude, his six-and-a-half-year-old daughter Stephanie and Claude's daughter of the same age, Romaine Caroline. He thought it would be a great adventure for the family, and felt he hadn't really spent enough time with Stephanie. Freddie's mother Violet had been looking after the young girl, and both girls had just started attending school in Switzerland. At the last moment Freddie's Riviera friend and business associate George Dawson succeeded in persuading Freddie not to take the children on the long ocean voyage.

Dawson, despite his extensive trade in military surplus with dodgy dictators, was a strong family man and adored the children. He feared they were too young and could come to harm. Freddie relented. Claude also took her French maid Cecille Brunneau, bringing the number on board to nine.

A week before the *Kangaroa* set sail from Cannes, Freddie was seen in the company of a mysterious American who was suspected by French police of being involved in a diamond-smuggling ring. This wasn't particularly noteworthy for police at the time, because Freddie was often seen in the company of suspect characters. Freddie had long been suspected of smuggling jewels and contraband such as liquor and cigarettes between France and north Africa. Police had turned a blind eye because he was, well, Freddie McEvoy, and he had friends in high places. That included the Riviera police, and the people who had influence over the top cops. Besides, this was to be a one-way trip with the *Kangaroa,* so Freddie wouldn't be smuggling anything back into France. It wasn't their problem.

Intelligence agencies had a different attitude. British military Intelligence and MI6, along with French Special Branch and the newly formed American CIA, had heard reports and gossip along the waterfront that Freddie had smuggled guns on some of his runs around the Mediterranean. They'd had a good long look at Freddie during their investigations into George Dawson's murky operations selling war surplus material, but they hadn't stopped him.[6] There were many clandestine operations carried out by intelligence organisations in the late 1940s early 1950s in the cause of the Cold War. Even today the operations are still classified secret. What MI6 knew about Freddie's jaunts is still buried deep in the vaults somewhere under Whitehall.

Just before he left Cannes, Freddie wrote to nightclub owner and Hollywood man-about-town Felix 'Fefe' Ferry. Freddie said he hoped the weather would be fine, that he had crammed up on navigation and he hoped they would reach their destination. Freddie wanted Ferry to ask around movie producers and directors whether they could use the *Kangaroa* in a movie. 'She is beautiful and looks like an old-fashioned ship with a lovely head on her bow of a Tahitian girl.'[7]

The *Kangaroa* set sail from Cannes on 1 October 1951. All looked good – fine weather and a calm sea. Freddie's concerns about not having a proper crew started to evaporate. However, after just a day at sea, Hertel revolted. As they passed Nice, Hertel demanded to be put ashore. He'd taken a look at the motley crew that Freddie had brought on board and he didn't want to spend months in their company, depending on their lax seamanship. He also had grave doubts about the Germans and Austrians Freddie had hired, particularly the former SS man. 'Praxmarer gave me the creeps. I had not the slightest wish to serve with him. He was a quiet one – a deep one,' Hertel later said.[8] Hertel got off *Kangaroa* at Nice. Once again Freddie could find no experienced skipper in the port city willing to sail across the Atlantic on his yacht. Freddie was now in real trouble, having such an inexperienced crew for the long and perilous voyage. Ten days into the voyage Heaton received a radio message to return to France for an urgent business meeting. He got off the *Kangaroa* at Ibiza. Like Hertel, Heaton had a lucky escape from what was to come.

The first port of call after sailing through the Strait of Gibraltar was Tangier, the exotic city of intrigue on the northernmost tip of Morocco. Freddie knew the city well as the trading market for all sorts of smugglers' delights. Precious gems, tobacco, liquor and arms were all to be bartered for smuggling around the Mediterranean, including behind the Iron Curtain in Yugoslavia and into the Black Sea. Freddie was still looking for a qualified sailing captain and went ashore to seek help from a friend, a certain Captain Welding. He also spoke to Jimmy Ward, who called himself a ship's broker but was said to have more shady goods to trade.[9] For days the trio scoured the port for a suitably experienced skipper, but they had no luck. By 4 November Freddie felt he could wait no longer. The weather was turning towards winter, and crossing the South Atlantic would only get more difficult the longer he waited.

The *Kangaroa* left Tangier and headed south, hugging the Moroccan coast. Freddie's route would take him along the coastline before heading westwards, out to the Canary Islands where he would take stock and prepare for the long voyage across the southern Atlantic. Perhaps he could find a skipper on the islands. Freddie kept in touch with Captain Welding via radio. Freddie had passed Casablanca and the port town of Safi when Welding warned him via radio of reports that a heavy storm was forming in his path. Welding urged Freddie to get into a safe harbour if he could. The warning came too late. It was mid-morning on 5 November, and Freddie watched ominous black clouds building further out to sea. Onshore winds were picking up. If Freddie had had more ocean experience, he would have headed further out to sea to ride out the coming storm. Instead, the most experienced seaman on board, Willi Gehring, urged Freddie to turn the ketch around and head back up the coast to try to reach the port of Safi. Freddie agreed. It was a fatal mistake.

The southwesterly wind grew in fury. *Kangaroa* was hit by a sudden squall with winds of 60 knots an hour (111 kph). The ketch keeled over, its spars touching the water. Waves washed right over the deck. Freddie had ordered everyone below apart from himself and Gehring at the wheel. They'd reefed the sails as the winds struck, but they'd left it too late. Mountainous waves breaking over the yacht made it impossible to further reduce sail. They now risked being driven towards the shore. The engine was running on full, trying to propel them towards the safe water of Safi. But it had insufficient power to fight the incredible force of the wind. The boat heeled over again and again as the wind struck with terrifying force. The noise of the sudden gusts of wind became an unrelenting howl. Water poured down the companionway, half-flooding the cabins below. Claude and her maid were terrified. The novice crew weren't faring much better. Cabin boy Robert Guillat feared the boat was sinking, and fled on to the deck, hoping to find safety there. A huge wave slammed into the yacht, lifting it high by the bow. When it cleared, the 19-year-old lad was gone. His body was never found. Absolute fear now gripped all those on board.

The crew looked to Freddie standing at the wheel. Survivors later said he instantly inspired confidence as he stood calmly, feet planted wide to balance against the wild tilting of the deck, hands gripping the wheel to steer the ketch to safety. One later remarked Freddie looked like a Greek god, his white shirt flapping furiously in the wind, salt water flying off his face, eyes peering into the wind looking for a passage through the storm. He looked almost like his mate Errol Flynn in *The Sea Hawk*. The truth was that Freddie probably didn't have a clue what he was doing. He'd already erred in his failure to reef down sooner, and he should have been riding out the storm with a sea anchor much further out to sea. As it was, having decided to reverse course and sail back up the coast, he was being driven by the fierce winds right toward the treacherous shore. He was running out of deep water.

As the yacht rose and crashed like a cork on the heaving ocean, Freddie saw through the driving rain white bursts of waves breaking over rugged black rocks. If Freddie had properly consulted the charts of this Moroccan coastline he would have seen a long, saw-toothed reef stretched for miles 150 to 200 metres out from the beach. And the *Kangaroa* was being driven right towards it.

Night was fast approaching. They had been battling the storm for more than eight hours. All on board were exhausted and terrified. Freddie managed to manoeuvre *Kangaroa* around a spit of land, and he thought Safi harbour must be in the next bay. They could make it. But on the other side of the land spit, the wind tore at them from a different direction with ever-increasing fury, driving them back. Suddenly a massive wave lifted the ketch up and slammed it down hard on the reef. One mast crashed down, hanging over the side. Another wave picked them up and drove them even higher up on the jagged black rocks with a sickening thud. Everyone raced up from below. The terrified cook 'Toledo' Galleriano, who had left the splendour of the Carlton Hotel for this ocean voyage, took one look at the rocks and leapt over the side into the sickening swirling water. Perhaps he thought they had reached land. His body was never found.

Freddie knew they were stuck fast. The hull had been breached. The ketch was marooned high on the reef. It was starting to get dark, but the beach was still visible about 200 metres away. For the time being, this was the safest place to be. Claude was keeping her nerve. She had absolute belief in her husband's ability to get them out of this crisis. But her maid Cecile Brunneau became hysterical. She screamed and screamed until Freddie and one of the crewmen tied her to the remaining mast. It sounded crazy, but it was the best way to stop her throwing herself overboard or being swept away by the giant waves that still crashed down on them.

Surviving crewmen later described Freddie as the epitome of the calm captain, going about his duties without showing a trace of excitement. He made it appear that battling storms and shipwrecks were natural to him, that he'd done it hundreds of times and come through. This was the same 'Suicide' Freddie who had stared death in the face many times in the course of his life – on the 1936 Olympic bobsled run and many crazy runs after that. He'd driven dangerous racing cars against the world's best. He'd stood up to brawlers in countless nightclubs. If this were to be the end, Freddie was ready to meet his fate. But he had his wife Claude to think about. Thank goodness he hadn't brought Stephanie and Romaine on this doomed voyage. He asked Walter Praxmarar whether he could reach land and seek help. The former SS soldier looked at the heaving waves between the reef and the beach. Yes, he could swim that. He dived in. Freddie watched until he was lost in the darkness. The former SS soldier did make it to the beach, exhausted. He found a road and headed north hoping to find someone who could bring a rescue boat.

Meanwhile, through the rain, Freddie saw the lights of a vehicle travelling along the coast road. He ordered Gehring to swim for shore and bring help – a boat, a long rope, anything that could be used to get the two women, Krotil and young Buisson ashore. Hours went by and he heard nothing from those who'd set out to swim to the beach. Freddie thought maybe they didn't make it. According to Michael Stern, who reconstructed what happened from survivor and witness interviews and statements, Freddie was a very strong swimmer and at this point decided to head for shore himself. Freddie thought the *Kangaroa* was stuck hard on the reef, and those still on board would be safe for a while. He reassured them he would be back with help, and dived over the side, striking out for the beach 200 metres away. He dragged himself up the beach, but he was more sapped by the effort than he realised. He was weakened by the ulcer operation he'd had the year before. He found himself on a stretch of coast that was completely deserted. He jogged along the road for a while, but there was no one to ask for help. There was no sign of the men he'd sent ashore. Perhaps they'd drowned or been washed further along the coast.

Freddie realised that no help was coming. The boat would eventually break up on the rocks, and he had to get those still on the stranded yacht to try to swim for the beach no matter how risky it was. Freddie ran back down the beach and threw himself into the waves. He battled through the pounding surf and struck out for the wreck. Through the lashing rain he could see the lanterns on the boat. He made it, breathing heavily as he dragged himself up the rocks and back on board. Claude threw her arms around him, sobbing with relief. Freddie looked around. The maid he'd tied to the mast was gone. Young Buisson had also vanished. Only Krotil and Claude remained. He told Krotil to swim for it. He would bring Claude. Krotil dived into the water and swam for land. Freddie put Claude in a cork life ring, and together they jumped overboard. Though he was tiring, Freddie pulled her towards the shore.

Accounts differ over what happened next. Krotil said he waited for hours on the beach, walking up and down hoping to catch sight of them, without luck. Some Moroccan tribesmen told reporters they saw Freddie almost reach the beach, and when he could stand he turned around and caught sight of Claude struggling in the water just 20 metres from shore. He ran back in to the surf to reach her. They didn't see whether Freddie found her in the confusion of the pounding surf, but he disappeared beneath the waves. Freddie was dead at age 44. He had just performed the most selfless act of his entire life, trying to save the life of the only woman he'd ever really loved.

Praxmarer, Krotil and Gehring were the only survivors. They joined up and made their way to Safi where they notified the local French authorities of the wreck, and the apparent death of their crewmates. The account of the battle against the storm, the wreck on the reef, the desperate swim to shore, the hero's death of Freddie McEvoy, the tragic death of Claude McEvoy and the rest of those on board all came from these three survivors.

It wasn't long before doubts started to emerge that the survivors' dramatic tale was the whole story. There appeared to be far more to this story than just a tragic shipwreck.

The badly battered bodies of Freddie and Claude were found by locals washed up on the beach two days later. French police immediately sent officers to investigate. The body of Freddie McEvoy was almost impossible to identify. The head had been badly pulverised. Seawater and heat had begun the process of decomposition. He was identified by a belt strapped around his torso and his swimming shorts. The head on the body of his wife Claude was similarly unrecognisable. Her clothing was completely gone. The bodies of the maid Cecile Brunneau and young crewman Jean Buisson were found washed up kilometres further down the beach. They were both naked. Their bodies were decomposing, but their heads weren't so badly disfigured.

Local Moroccan officials had the bodies moved to the morgue in the nearby historic Portuguese built town of Mazagan (today called El Jadida). A doctor examined the bodies and was surprised to find that the heads of both Freddie and Claude appeared to have been scalped. Even if they had been bashed against rocks, it was highly unlikely that they would both have received exactly the same head injuries.

By this time, news of the tragic shipwreck and Freddie's heroic attempt to save his wife was making headlines around the world. Newswire-service correspondents based in Casablanca sniffed a good yarn and jumped in vehicles to drive the 270 kilometres down the coast to the wreck site. On 8 November the news reached Australia. 'Australian drowned when yacht sinks' reported the *Newcastle Herald*. The Australian Associated Press, picking up the story from Reuters and other newswire services, quoted the survivors saying Freddie was 'swimming through 30 foot high seas and was only 6 feet from the shore when he turned back to aid his wife who was some distance behind. As he neared her side their strength failed and they both sank.'[10]

The news swept across Britain and Europe. It was particularly big news in the United States where Freddie was well known for his raucous adventures with Errol Flynn and his scandalous divorces from rich American heiresses.

'Millionaire, wife missing as yacht dashed on rocks' headlined the *Los Angeles Times*, and the next day followed up with, 'Playboy McEvoy heroic in death, sailors say'.

'A millionaire dies trying to save wife – dies a hero', cried the *Des Moines Tribune*.

'Society Yachtsman drowns vainly trying to save wife', said the *New Jersey Courier-News*.

'Playboy McEvoy, wife, drown as yacht goes on Africa rocks', reported the *New York Daily News*.

'Survivors tell of night of terror in McEvoy yacht', said the *Chicago Tribune*.

However, over the next few days, police, journalists and embassy officials realised that several aspects of the survivors' accounts didn't add up. Their initial story was they had gone along the road to seek help at the next village – so, how could they have seen Freddie almost reach shore and then turn back into the waves to try to rescue his wife? Why were the bodies of the two women and the young man found naked? Why had Freddie's head been stoved in, even scalped? Why hadn't the crew of the *Kangaroa* seen the danger of the reef and stayed well out to sea? What was the yacht doing off this desolate part of Morocco?

The British Embassy in Casablanca, which represented Australia diplomatically in Morocco, was immediately involved in the incident. A British consular official travelled down to Safi as soon as word reached them that *Kangaroa* was registered to an Australian and that his body had been found. The British diplomat coordinated with local French and Moroccan police and made burial arrangements for Freddie and his wife. French officials took over arrangements for the bodies of their citizens. However, as soon as the British official's cables reached the Foreign Office in London, alarm bells started to ring.

Britain's foreign Intelligence service, MI6, had a thick file on Freddie. According to several sources, it dated back to 1936 when Freddie McEvoy carried the British flag into the Winter Olympics in front of Adolf Hitler. At the time, it was important to know whether the Australian playboy would do the right thing and behave. British spooks kept an eye on Freddie throughout the 1930s in the lead-up to the war. After all, he mixed in elite circles, including rubbing shoulders with the Duke and Duchess of Windsor, and he had friends among the top echelon of European society. British agents were aware of Freddie's presence in France after the German invasion. What he did in Occupied France and Vichy France is still cloaked in mystery, but US officials did suggest he was some sort of double agent for the British. After Freddie managed to make his way to the United States with an exit visa from Vichy France, British Intelligence certainly would have received dossiers from US Intelligence on Freddie's activities in America. Since the war, MI6 and the British domestic spy service, MI5, had kept a close watch on Freddie and his suspected smuggling activities in the south of

France, particularly his dealings with military war-surplus dealer George Dawson.

Elements of the British Intelligence dossier on Freddie McEvoy were leaked to the *Daily Express*, Lord Beaverbrook's mass-circulation patriotic working-class newspaper. On 14 November 1951, just a week after the wreck, the *Daily Express* ran a massive headline across its front page: 'The MacEvoy [sic] Mystery – MI5 inquiry into yacht wreck – arms deal link'. The paper said in an Express Special Investigation that it could reveal that Britain's MI5 and Secret Service agents of three other countries

Daily Express front page 14 November 1951.

had become interested in the past activities of Freddie McEvoy. It reported that Freddie was thought to have become wealthy through his marriages to wealthy women but he claimed he made much of his money buying and selling yachts.

> But a quick survey of wartime and post wartime dossiers in military intelligence divisions has shown MacEvoy's [sic] name linked with arms deals and the disposal of surplus army stores. These dossiers are now under closer scrutiny. The French police have now been informed, and this sidelight on the mysterious MacEvoy [sic] is being kept in mind while the wreck of his yacht is being investigated . . .[11]

The *Express* story went on to link Freddie to George Dawson, 'the cockney who made a fortune in surplus war goods'. It said the two men were 'seen together frequently on the French Riviera'. The paper said it tried to contact Dawson for comment, but he had left Cannes six days earlier for a trip to Athens to sell vehicles. Citing Intelligence sources, the *Express* reported that before he left Cannes, Freddie was seen talking to an American who was suspected by the French Sûreté of being involved in a smuggling ring. 'This ring was taking contraband from Tangier to France and taking back jewels and foreign currency.'

The *Express* story was carried by many other newspapers in the United States and Australia. The *Barrier Miner* newspaper in Broken Hill asked in its headline: 'Was McEvoy a dealer in arms?'[12] At least the remote mining town's newspaper spelled Freddie's name correctly.

Someone in British Intelligence was clearly intent on turning up the heat on those investigating the wreck. Their motive for leaking Intelligence on the smuggling ring was a puzzle. After all, Freddie was dead. However, George Dawson was not; he was the real target. By publicly exposing Freddie's suspect smuggling activities and hinting darkly at arms deals, they were hoping to put pressure on Dawson over his selling of war-surplus equipment to the communist east bloc. His Majesty's Treasury was miffed too: it was missing out on taxing Dawson's massive profits because he was living in tax-free Monaco.

When Dawson was eventually asked by a journalist about being linked to Freddie's alleged smuggling activities, he was characteristically blunt. 'Utterly ridiculous,' he told a reporter, who probably had to censor Dawson's Cockney vernacular:

> There is as much chance of finding smuggled diamonds on McEvoy's yacht as there is of me finding an atom bomb in my stocking. I've known Freddie for fifteen years, and during the past two years have been close to him. I know him well enough to say outright that the stories they're spreading about him are vicious lies.[13]

The plot thickened when German and Austrian police saw Praxmarer's photo in newspapers telling his tale of his dramatic escape from the stricken yacht and the heroism of Freddie McEvoy. Four days after the wreck, while Praxmarer and his two fellow survivors were sipping coffee in Moroccan cafes, Austrian police sent an urgent request to French authorities in Morocco to arrest and hold Praxmarer, pending an extradition application. The former Waffen SS soldier was wanted on a six-year-old murder charge. The arrest warrant said Praxmarer wasn't his real name at all. He was in fact Manfred Lendner, aged 32, wanted in Berlin for the post-war 1945 murder of a woman, Lisbeth Holbeck. In 1950, while being held in Austria for extradition to Germany, he had escaped, shooting a prison guard. He was also wanted on two charges of bigamy.

French police arrested Praxmarer/Lendner and ordered him held in a prison cell in Marrakesh, 200 kilometres from the site of the wreck. The other two survivors were told not to leave the little Majestic Hotel in Safi. However, Moroccan prisons can develop flexible visiting rules with the right *baksheesh*, and journalists who managed to talk to Lendner before he faced an extradition trial said he told them that he'd informed Freddie he was wanted on murder charges but Freddie hired him anyway. His story of his escape from jail differed from that of the Austrian police. He claimed he'd been held in a Soviet forced-labour camp in Austria to work in a Soviet factory near Vienna – a factory that was making atomic weapons. He claimed he had to shoot the guard in self-defence. 'I met McEvoy in Cannes and told him everything. He hired and protected me,' Lendner told journalists from his Marrakesh cell.[14]

Lendner didn't tell the reporters that back in Berlin he had blamed a friend, Walter Rangfel, for the murder of the woman, nor that Rangfel had already been tried and executed. Before Rangfel faced the hangman, he provided police with evidence that Lendner was just as complicit in the killing. Lendner escaped Berlin by stealing the passport of dead Austrian soldier Walter Praxmarer. It was not clear whether Lendner had killed

Praxmarer to get his passport. Lendner also did not volunteer the information that, three years earlier, his name had been linked to a harbour murder in Tangier. French Countess Marguerite 'Marga' D'Andurian was a colourful and mysterious woman who had been a spy for both sides in World War II, and had herself been linked to several murders, including two husbands and a nephew who were all poisoned. She was never convicted. Freddie knew her as a fellow sailor along the Riviera Coast, and might have known her during his time stuck in Vichy France. On 5 November 1948, D'Andurian was asleep in her cabin on her yacht *Djelian* tied at the Tangier pier when a German called Hans Abel bashed her head, slit her throat, tied heavy weights around her body and tossed her corpse into the water. Abel was questioned by French police, and during their persuasive interrogation, he confessed. Abel was serving 20 years in a Tangier jail when local police heard of the *Kangaroa* case and thought there might be a link. They sent their files on Abel to Casablanca, which showed that Abel had told his inquisitors he had a friend called Manfred Lendner who was trying to secure a set of false papers for the pair of them to go to Australia, or some other British 'colony'.[15] This is quite possible, because Australia was taking thousands of migrants from war-devastated Europe at the time, including many former Nazis who were given false identities to get past security checks.[16]

A series of front-page articles in the UK *Daily Express* raised more murky questions about Freddie's activities in the year before he died. The newspaper found a first mate on an Italian schooner based in Genoa who said Freddie was up to no good. Guido

Pascale claimed Freddie came to Genoa every five or six weeks, driving a blue Alfa-Romeo saloon car with Rome number plates.

> He was driven by a foreigner – I think an Algerian. And Freddie was certainly not the boss. He seemed to be an employee of the cheroot smoking Algerian. What he came for and what he did I do not know but his business was often with a shady bunch of hoodlums.[17]

Pascale told the *Express* Freddie stayed at the lush Excelsior Hotel above the port, and always went down to the dockside and sat alone at a cafe for hours, waiting for someone. 'He would stand drinks for his contacts. Freddie's business may have been cigarettes, maybe gold, maybe anything. When business is straightforward it is done in shipping offices in the town, not secretly on the dockside.' Pascale said his captain once remarked as his schooner passed the *Kangaroa* in a Riviera port at 2am: 'Cigarettes are going to be cheaper along this coast for a few weeks.' 'And the captain was right. There is big money in cigarettes. A trip from Tangier to the Italian coast brings in about $20,000 [around $500,000 in today's money].'[18] Police questioned several black-market operators, and they all knew Freddie, the *Express* reported. One explained that black-market deals were preferably done in precious stones because they were easily transportable and untraceable.

The mystery of the death of Freddie McEvoy deepened even further when his brother Theodore turned up at the British Embassy in Casablanca. Freddie and Theodore had never been close. They'd been stuck together as young children in St Moritz during the war, then both went to the British upper-crust Jesuit school Stonyhurst. They saw little of each other in adulthood. While Freddie was outgoing and sporty, and loved parties and socialising, Theodore was quiet, introverted and preferred to live an isolated life in tiny French villages. Theodore told the consul he had come to claim Freddie's body, then asked how he could make a claim on £15,000 worth of jewellery that Freddie had in his possession on the *Kangaroa*. It was a massive amount – almost A$2 million in today's money. Theodore stunned the UK officials by producing a long list detailing the jewellery that he said Freddie carried in the ship's strongbox.

The paper, written in French, listed 40 very expensive items. It included gold cufflinks with rubies and diamonds worth 800,000 French francs (A$38,000 today), Cartier watches worth 100,000 francs, a pearl-encrusted broach worth 625,000 francs, a gold statuette worth 200,000 francs, a gold pendant with emeralds, rubies and diamonds worth 250,000 francs, pearl and gold earrings worth 400,000 francs, a gold ring with pearls valued at 2 million francs, and finally, a 2-million-franc mink coat – that's around A$100,000 today.

But how did Theodore come to have this list in his possession? The British consulate wrote in its files: 'Generally speaking, we gained the impression that Theodore McEvoy was unfamiliar with his brother's affairs.'[19] Freddie wouldn't have given it to him – he barely spoke to his brother, certainly not about money. It's unlikely it had been lodged with an insurance company – smugglers tend not to insure their contraband. It could have been Claude's jewellery left over from her time as a mistress. She may have given the list to a friend such as George Dawson, or to Freddie's mother who was minding their children while they were sailing, who then gave it to Theodore to try to retrieve the valuables from the wreck. Freddie and Claude were awaiting burial when Theodore arrived. Theodore said he couldn't pay for the burial because he didn't have enough money, but he agreed to sign a guarantee that he would reimburse the British consulate for the cost of the burial of his brother and sister-in-law, and for hiring local Moroccans to guard the wreck. Theodore signed the agreement to reimburse His Majesty's government £802, 6 shillings and fourpence. In today's money that amounted to A$37,314.02.

Journalists found Theodore and asked him whether it was possible Freddie was doing some smuggling and whether the 40 crates could have contained guns destined for Moroccan rebels. 'Ridiculous,' snorted Theodore. 'You can rest assured that the cases contain liquor. Freddie needed it for his own personal use. You see, he was a heavy drinker.'[20] This answer from Freddie's brother raised another question – was Freddie drunk when the *Kangaroa* hit the reef?

Daily Express correspondent Thomas Clayton reported from Casablanca that the mystery was being closely watched at the top level of police and intelligence organisations in Paris and London. Clayton questioned Gehring and Krotil while they were under house arrest in Safi. They both told him they had a good balance in their Casablanca bank account and had been paid £25 a month by Freddie. This conflicted with earlier statements that they had been recruited in back-street bars in Cannes. They also told Clayton they knew George Dawson well. 'He was often on board the *Kangaroa*. Both he and McEvoy talked of the very big deals,' they told Clayton.[21] Clayton said at that point the pair realised they had said too much and suddenly had difficulty understanding English.

When the sea finally calmed down, a team of divers went out to the wreck. They were supervised by the French police and watched over by a British consulate official. Millions of dollars in booty was at stake – and what was really in those 40 crates? For several days the divers looked over the wreck and the surrounding rocks, and dived to the bottom around the wreck. They found nothing. Or at least they said they found nothing. No jewellery, not even the 40 crates labelled 'Scotch'. It was a valuable treasure they were looking for, and it would have been easy for the divers to hide it to recover later, when supervising eyes had left. It was also possible the divers were too late, and enterprising locals had already braved the waves to search the wreck.

Once the search of the wreck proved fruitless, Theodore did what any self-respecting member of the McEvoy family would do when presented with a bill: he bolted. Theodore left Casablanca without telling a soul, especially not the British consul officials who had gone out of their way to assist him. Theodore hadn't even paid for a gravestone for his brother. When British consulate officials called at Theodore's hotel, they were surprised he had left without paying his hotel bill or leaving the consulate a cheque. It was terribly ungentlemanly conduct. Typical for a colonial. But the British consulate had Theodore's signed note guaranteeing reimbursement. It was a note that would have repercussions for many years to come. The British approached Australia House, the Australian High Commission in London.

Australian officials in London in turn approached the Australian Embassy in Paris, because Morocco was in their bailiwick.

Sir Keith Officer, Australia's ambassador to France at the time of Freddie's death, had a long and distinguished career behind him. He looked every inch the military officer, with his clipped moustache and a monocle. He had been an army captain in World War I, serving at Gallipoli, and was promoted to Major for the Western Front. In the 1930s he was a senior Australian diplomat. In 1941 he was in Tokyo and received Japan's declaration of war. Despite diplomatic immunity, he was confined until he was allowed to leave Japan in 1942. He was Australia's wartime diplomatic representative in Moscow in 1944, and Peking in 1945. After the war he was appointed ambassador to France. He therefore wasn't the sort of person who would tolerate bureaucratic nonsense. In December 1951 he sent a stern letter to the Foreign Affairs Department warning that if they kept shilly-shallying about paying for the burials in Casablanca, Freddie as well as Mrs McEvoy could end up in a pauper's grave. He cited a 1947 decision by the British Foreign Minister Ernest Bevin that British consulates could pay for the burials of British subjects (that included Australians). If possible, the consulate was to get a signed undertaking from the next of kin to repay the expenses. Officer said that had been done in the McEvoy case, so please just get on with burying them. Still bureaucratic paperwork held up the burials. Freddie, his wife and the three crewmen found on the beach weren't buried in a Casablanca cemetery until 28 December 1951.

Meanwhile the deepening mystery of the wreck and the death of Freddie McEvoy was garnering more world headlines. The senior French Sûreté detective in Casablanca, Commissioner Jean Leandri, known as the Maigret of Morocco, who had a remarkable likeness to Claude Rains in the film *Casablanca*, took over the investigation.[22] First, Commissioner Leandri wanted to know where the 40 boxes labelled 'Scotch' had disappeared to, and whether it really was whisky inside. At the time there was a very lucrative smuggling racket funnelling guns to a rebellious tribe of desert Moroccans who were fighting for independence against the French colonialists. They were the Riff, the same tribe that had been depicted as the rebel fighters in the 1942 Warner Bros film *Desert Song* in which Freddie had a bit part playing a Vichy French officer alongside his actor friend Bruce Cabot. Perhaps Freddie held some sort of romantic attachment to the Riff fight for freedom that he'd learned about from his part in the movie. On the other hand, there was a lucrative trade in smuggling liquor to American workers who were building air bases in southern Morocco. A single bottle of whisky could fetch $20 – around $200 in today's money – so 40 cases would have given Freddie a profit of more than US$4000 (US$50,000 in today's money).

It's also possible that the story spouted by Praxmarer and his two fellow survivors was a lie to cover up a mutiny and a robbery, even the murder of Freddie McEvoy and the rest of the crew, as well as the rape and murder of Claude and her maid. Author Charles Higham, who accused Freddie of being a key Nazi spy during the war, wrote that Freddie kept the key to the cargo around his neck, and several crew members had tried to grab it off him. Higham wrote that they beat him badly, and that it was Praxmarer who saved him by fending off the attackers. Then the storm hit, putting an end to the mutiny.[23] A thorough search of Higham's research papers found no evidence to support this story. The source was likely to have been Praxmarer, a liar and murderer. It is one more element in the unsolved mystery of what happened that night on the Moroccan coast.

But it was a scenario that Commissioner Leandri found credible. He argued to prosecutors that a mutiny by the crew to get the jewellery and whisky crates could explain Freddie's strange head injuries. If the women were raped, it could also explain why the bodies of the women were found naked. When French police learned of Praxmarer's violent past, and that he'd lied about his identity, the survivors' version of events became highly suspect. Police in Cannes interviewed Bruno Hertel, who told them he had left the *Kangaroa* in Nice because he 'felt something was wrong', particularly with Praxmarer.[24]

Police also tracked down the passenger Jack Heaton, who had debarked at Ibiza for business reasons. Heaton told the *Daily Express*:

I have read suggestions that Freddie might have been engaged in the smuggling of arms, diamonds or currency. I can assure you, from my knowledge of the man and from what I saw on the yacht that this is not the case.[25]

Heaton said the crew members were inexperienced but he added that he thought it was 'queer' that the crew seemed particularly fond of Praxmarer. He knew nothing about the murder charge Praxmarer was facing in Germany.

Two weeks after the wreck in which 19-year-old Jean Buisson died, Madelaine Augustine, living in the back streets of Cannes, received a postcard. It was from Jean, her ward. It had been posted in Tangier. Jean had left home to find adventure, and he worshipped Errol Flynn and liked Freddie McEvoy. But he sent a cryptic message to Mme Augustine: 'Tonight we leave for the Canaries. He is always the same. I desert him at the Bahamas.'[26] Mme Augustine had no idea who young Jean was referring to. Was it Freddie, or was it Praxmarer? It was another piece of the puzzle that was the sinking of the *Kangaroa*.

Commissioner Leandri certainly had his suspicions. He presented the conclusions of his investigation to the prosecutors. In an explanation to the mystery that could have been lifted from the closing pages of a Maigret or Poirot novel, Leandri argued to the Marrakesh court that there was enough evidence to suggest Freddie McEvoy had been murdered. Leandri questioned why Freddie and Claude, both strong swimmers, perished when the three survivors who made it to shore were weak swimmers. Leandri said the apparent disappearance of the valuable jewellery and the mysterious cargo of 40 crates labelled 'Scotch' pointed to a conspiracy. He argued that the valuable cargo and diamonds provided a motive to seize the yacht, smash it on the reef, kill the rest of the crew, hide the booty and then claim they were the only survivors. In a sensational turnaround, on 16 November the French court sitting in Marrakesh recorded a formal verdict of murder 'against persons unknown'.[27]

CHAPTER 14

DEAD FREDDIE HAUNTS PRIME MINISTER MENZIES

Errol Flynn was devastated when he heard his best friend Freddie McEvoy and his wife Claude had died in the yacht wreck off Morocco. Flynn immediately sent a cable from Hollywood to police in Morocco offering to fly from the United States if he could assist in the investigation. He had read reports of Freddie's bravery in turning back into the storm-tossed waves to try to rescue his wife, and he was stunned, writing in his memoir:

> It was really unlike him. He was such a selfish fellow, not one to lay down his life for anyone. Not really heroic. And yet, as I have always said, you never can tell what people will do in special circumstances – especially when you love, truly love.[1]

Errol said he would always remember Freddie for making that gallant rescue effort out of love.

There was a certain gift which not many have. I had been close to him for twenty years and his passing was a hard blow to me. I could have understood if he went out like a cheat, a gambler, a ne'er do well – but not in that gallant way.[2]

Errol noticed in the reports what Freddie was wearing when his battered body washed up on the Moroccan beach. The belt Freddie was wearing was one Errol had given him. 'It had a gold buckle on it – which he'd swiped from me!'[3]

A grieving Errol told a newspaper reporter:

Freddie was one of the great livers of life. He lived it the way he saw it. He didn't give a hoot. And the people who knew him knew that he was a brave and generous spirit. He went out the right way when his time came – with courage.[4]

Errol volunteered to adopt Freddie's daughter Stephanie. But he guessed that Irene, Stephanie's mother, would probably take custody of the six-year-old girl. Errol then asked authorities whether Freddie's stepdaughter Romaine had family who would take her in. Errol told reporters:

I don't know if there are any relatives left to care for Romaine. She is at school in Switzerland with Freddie's daughter Stephanie. If not, I will look after her, and if possible, adopt her. I have telephoned my mother who is in Wiesbaden, Germany, to go to Geneva to investigate the matter.[5]

It proved not to be necessary, because Claude's family stepped in.

Freddie's wealthy English stockbroker friend Stephen Raphael told reporters he was shocked at the stories Freddie could be involved in smuggling. 'Freddie was upright and honest,' Raphael told the *Daily Express*. 'He was a gentleman. All this talk of dope, diamonds and arms smuggling is ridiculous.' Raphael's wife, actress Eve Ashley, said: 'It's beastly the way his former friends now delight in whispering evil things about him. Yet both Steve and I think something dastardly may have happened on that yacht before it went down.'⁶

Errol Flynn wrote a tribute for Freddie, published in the UK *Daily Express*.

Freddie's first wife – Beatrice Cartwright – the one he had wronged so many times but who still held him in her affection, wrote to a friend: 'I am terribly shocked by Freddie's death. He died like a gentleman, fighting for the life of his wife and others like him. It was a gallant end.'⁷ She expressed regret that her health did not permit her to attend a mass that was organised for Freddie at New York's St Patrick's Cathedral on 19 November 1951.

Journalist George Frazier recorded that around 15 people attended the 9.30am high requiem mass held to commemorate Freddie in the chapel of St Patrick's Cathedral on Fifth Avenue. The mourners included a handful of international playboys, several teary anonymous women, a clutch of nightclub owners, a couple of press agents and several gossip columnists – who would now have huge gaps to fill in their columns. Freddie's fabulous frolics had filled their tattletale columns for more than a decade. 'Their faces were white and drawn after a night that had ended but a few hours before. Kneeling there, they prayed for Freddie McEvoy. May his soul rest in peace.'[8]

A long string of American newspaper gossip columnists over the previous 60 years had written under the pseudonym Cholly Knickerbocker. One of the longest serving was Igor Cassini, who had known Freddie and Errol for many years even before he started writing under the Cholly nom de plume in 1945. Hollywood gossipers lived in a small world. Cassini's brother was married for a while to the sister of Freddie's second wife, Irene. Cassini had had frequent tussles with both Errol and Freddie as he wrote about their troubled love affairs, nightclub brawls and financial flops. Not always a charitable chronicler of the foibles of the rich and famous, Cassini – in his alias byline of Cholly Knickerbocker – wrote of 'handsome Freddie McEvoy', his 'friend' who had led a 'legendary life':

Freddie had finally found the love of his life. This man who had been a playboy and a libertine, became a different sort.

He showed he was a champion when he died to save his wife. They died as they had lived – together.[9]

George Dawson, Freddie's good friend and multi-millionaire business associate on the French Riviera, did his best to rubbish stories about Freddie smuggling contraband. 'He just didn't need to make himself a few peanuts by smuggling,' Dawson told a journalist.

> He was always in a position to introduce one very rich person to another rich person; get the two to do business, and take his commission. Why, if he wanted $10,000 there were a thousand people on the Riviera ready to lend it to him at once, and without security.[10]

Dawson said he'd warned Freddie about his crew on the last night before he sailed, that they were a tough-looking bunch. Dawson said Freddie just laughed and said he could handle them. 'That was Freddie, just plain reckless.'[11]

Dawson's wife Olga, a former Russian model, told the journalist: 'Freddie was a great guy. He took his friends out of Debrett's [the guide to British peerage] and the gutter with complete disregard for convention. His only fault was generosity.'[12]

Not so ready with kind words about the late Freddie McEvoy was the father of his second wife, Irene. Multi-millionaire Texas oilman Charles Wrightsman moved quickly as soon as he got the news that Freddie was dead. He set lawyers on Freddie's mother Violet, who had been looking after six-year-old Stephanie in Switzerland. Within days of Freddie's death, Wrightsman, his daughter Irene and a phalanx of lawyers arrived to take custody of Stephanie. While Irene took custody of her daughter in Switzerland, Wrightsman and the lawyers headed to the Riviera. The lawyers seized Freddie's yacht, the luxury 60-foot *Echappe*, waving papers claiming it was Stephanie's inheritance. This was the yacht to which Freddie had planned to return after he'd sold *Kangaroa* in the Bahamas. Acting in Stephanie's name, Wrightsman's lawyers quickly sold the *Echappe* and anything else belonging to Freddie that they could get their hands on. Wrightsman was intent on wiping out any skerrick of Freddie McEvoy from the lives of his daughter Irene and granddaughter Stephanie.

A gossip column under the Cholly Knickerbocker name reported that a year earlier Wrightsman had – through lawyers – approached Freddie, offering a large sum of money for him to relinquish custody of Stephanie. 'But Freddie loved his child too much to let her go,' wrote Knickerbocker.[13]

In Morocco, the investigation into the death of Freddie, his wife and the crew continued for several months, but it rapidly drifted into farce. Seven months after the *Kangaroa* slammed into the reef, it was still perched high on the rocks. Reports were leaking out from frustrated police investigators that counter-espionage authorities in both London and Paris knew very well what was in the 40 crates marked 'Scotch', but for some secret reason decided it was best to leave the contents at the bottom of the reef. 'Best informed sources say the yacht was loaded with guns for African tribesmen bent on gaining their independence from France,' wrote correspondent Birt Darling in July 1952.[14] Someone in power concluded that it was far more convenient to all involved to let the sunken booty remain a mystery. Freddie was Australian, but he was also a British subject. It would be very awkward and probably upset British relations with France if it were proved that he was running guns to Moroccan rebels in a land France was desperate to hold on to as a colony. British knowledge or even involvement in the smuggling racket can only be guessed at, because the files on Freddie McEvoy held inside Britain's Secret Service vaults are still sealed. Requests to examine Freddie's files in the British archives have been met with the reply that they don't exist, were probably destroyed as part of file sorting or can't be found.

French Special Branch were quick to board and search Freddie's second yacht *Echappe* at Cannes. They remained tight-lipped at what they found, but it was reported that they wanted to question the Italian industrialist who had leased the yacht, Fiat boss Gianni Agnelli. Agnelli had also leased *Kangaroa* during the summer for £400 a month ($200,000 in today's money).

Meanwhile, Praxmarer/Lendner languished for years in a Marrakesh police cell. He awaited his fate on the extradition request from Austria to face trial for murder of Berlin woman Lisbeth Hobeck. The other two survivors of the wreck – Krotil and Gehring – were forced by police to stick around Safi until they were cleared to leave. At one stage it appeared they would be charged along with Praxmarer for the murder of Freddie, but the investigating magistrate determined that there was insufficient evidence to charge any of the three. A forensic report on Freddie's body determined that he died of immersion. Despite the damage done to his head, the forensic surgeon ruled out foul play. Krotil and Gehring were allowed to return to Germany. There were never heard from again.

In May 1954, almost three years after the fatal shipwreck, Praxmarer/Lendner went on trial in Salzburg for murder under his real name of Manfred Lendner. It was an extremely quick trial, lasting just two days. On 7 May he was found guilty and sentenced to 15 years in jail. As an added punishment, he would be locked in solitary confinement every 3 October, the date he murdered Lisbeth Hobeck. For three months of the year Lendner would be ordered to sleep on a hard bed in his cell. Lendner was also convicted of the two charges of bigamy.

In 1955 film producer and director Barry Mahon set out to make a film based on a search for the hidden treasure lost when Freddie's luxury yacht went down. It was to be called *Deep Waters* and he'd signed up sultry Corinne Calvet to play the damsel in distress and her husband Jeffrey Stone, fresh from playing D'Artagnan in *The Three Musketeers*, to play gallant hero Cap'n Freddie. Hollywood gossip queen Hedda Hopper said it should be 'quite a yarn, if the truth were told'.[15] For reasons unknown, the movie was never made.

That should have been the end of the saga of the death of Freddie McEvoy. But that did not take into account the slow wheels of international diplomacy, pedantic form-filling accountants or a vindictive Australian prime minister, nor the obstinacy and outright meanness of top Australian bureaucrats. The death of Freddie McEvoy was destined to become one of the longest, most drawn out, petty, ridiculous and unnecessary bureaucratic battles, totally devoid of reality and common sense, ever witnessed in the sheltered offices of the Australian public service in sleepy Canberra.

The communiqué that started years of bickering and sheer bastardry arrived in the Department of Foreign Affairs in Canberra on 27 July 1955. The British Foreign Office in London had politely asked its Australia House counterparts whether they could please finalise the expenses bill left after Freddie's burial. Almost four years had passed, and the British consul in Casablanca wanted to clear the bill from their office accounts. The British reminded the Australian Foreign Office that in November 1951 the Australian Embassy in Paris had asked the British consulate in Casablanca to take control of the burial arrangements for Freddie and his wife, as well as matters relating to the wreck of the *Kangaroa*. The total bill amounted to £820, 6 shillings and fourpence – around $37,000 in today's Australian dollars.

It was hardly a large sum. The matter could easily have been resolved by dipping into petty cash. Far weightier matters should have been occupying the minds of the Foreign Office and Treasury in Canberra. In 1952 Australia started paying the huge cost of assisting Britain to test its atomic bombs on Australian soil. In 1954 Australia paid the substantial cost of the first royal visit to Australia by the new Queen Elizabeth II and Prince Philip. In 1955 Australia forked out vast sums to pay for its share of military involvement alongside Britain in the Malayan Emergency.

But bureaucrats live by paperwork, and this small bill was destined to become one of the most notorious cases of buck-passing and pig-headedness ever seen in Canberra – so much so that the 3-centimetre thick file on Freddie McEvoy's burial bill was strictly classified, not allowed to be seen by the public for decades. Only a concerted effort by this author in 2017 and 2018 managed to get the file dragged out of the depths of the National Archives in Canberra and finally declassified so that it could be revealed for the first time in this book.[16]

The first communiqué from London to Canberra came in July 1955, summarising what had happened to the *Kangaroa* and the burial of Freddie McEvoy and his wife. It included a copy of the guarantee signed by Theodore McEvoy that he would pay for the expenses incurred by the British consulate. It said insurance on the *Kangaroa* had covered the repatriation to Hamburg of two of the surviving crew, as well as placing a guard on the wreck. It recounted how Freddie's daughter Stephanie had been taken by her grandfather Charles Wrightsman and that he, not the child's mother, Irene, had legal custody of the child, along with any inheritance from her father, Freddie McEvoy. The diplomat summarising the case, CO Adams, said Wrightsman had been 'evasive' when asked about his claim that he had the right to sell Freddie's yacht *Echappe*. 'What title Mr Wrightsman had to do this has never been explained by his lawyers,' the communiqué said.[17] Wrightsman told the British consulate official that all the proceeds from selling *Echappe* had gone to people Freddie owed money to in France and insisted there was nothing left over to cover Freddie's burial expenses. Adams said Wrightsman offered no evidence to prove this was the case.

Adams said the only other asset in Freddie's estate was his share in a trust fund left by his late father. When Theodore was in Casablanca, he had written to the Melbourne lawyers administering the trust fund to ask whether the burial expenses could be met from Freddie's share of the trust fund. The trust estate provided a monthly income to Freddie's mother, Violet, as well as a smaller amount to Freddie and Theodore; only after Violet's death would the two sons receive what was left in the trust. Freddie's heir, his daughter Stephanie, would receive her late father's share of the trust fund. Theodore, therefore, could not get money from the trust fund to pay for Freddie's burial. Theodore didn't have enough of his own, so the British consulate paid the cost on the basis of Theodore's promise to reimburse them. As stated previously, Theodore not only skipped Casablanca without honouring that promise; he also didn't pay his hotel bill nor for a notice of the death of his brother he'd placed in the local newspaper.

Thus began the Australian government's long pursuit of Freddie McEvoy's estate to reimburse the British government for the cost of his burial in Casablanca. Throughout 1956 and 1957, letters flew back and forth between the British and Australian Foreign Offices arguing over who should foot the bill, and whether the bill couldn't be met by Freddie McEvoy's estate. The Australians questioned whether the British were right to pay for the funeral of Mrs McEvoy because she was born French, but if they were married after a certain date she might be considered a dual citizen. Frustrated Australian official in London, MGM Bourchier, wrote back to Canberra: 'The whole affair McEvoy has been wrapped in mystery, and facts are the most difficult things to pin down.'[18]

In 1958 the bean counters in Canberra's Treasury stepped in, and things got even murkier. They demanded to know why consular officials should pay for funerals of Australian citizens, let

DEPARTMENT OF EXTERNAL AFFAIRS, CANBERRA.

Name of Paper *Sunday Telegraph.*   File No......................

Published at .... *Sydney.*   Date *17-2-63*

asked by
Alan to help
of Dr. Bugle
erpol also was
to investigate on . . .
requested in 1951

Aust. playboy's voyage with a vicious murderer

LONDON, Sat. — Australian playboy-adventurer Freddie McEvoy set sail on his last voyage not knowing that his engineer was a vicious murderer sought by every police force in Western Europe.

This is revealed in a new book "Inside Interpol" which throws a new and sinister light on the mystery surrounding McEvoy's death.

Freddie McEvoy was a tough, charming international knockabout who rubbed cocktail sticks with the rich and famous from Monte

Carlo to Las Vegas.

He was a close personal friend of Errol Flynn, who admitted in his memoirs that McEvoy had cured him of his addiction to opium by challenging him to an all-in brawl.

Flynn's death was the one universally accepted at the time.

When McEvoy's yacht Kangaroo foundered off the coast of north-west Africa.

Flynn wrote that McEvoy had drowned trying to gain safety with his wife. He said: "In turn a dis-

They took 30,000 marks from the body, buried it and escaped.

After they had lived on women and the black market for some months the police caught Fritz Laub, then Schröder.

They were held pending trial in separate

side territorial waters and took on board three large packing cases, passed up from a small boat.

Once the cases were stowed Kangaroo headed for the open sea, Did Schröder know what was in those cases? Whatever it was, it was valuable

chasing among themselves in German the secret cargo on board the yacht.

Suspecting smuggling, the keeper phoned the police and Schröder's goose was cooked.

The local detectives recognised him from an Interpol circular and sent him back to face

McEVOY with his third wife, Claude.

Government bureaucrats knew all about the adventures of Freddie McEvoy, placing newspaper clippings in their files.

alone their non-Australian spouses. Treasury wanted to know why Freddie's mother hadn't been approached to pay the burial costs of her son. Foreign Affairs replied it had become the standard practice to pay for Australian citizens who died overseas. Twelve months later, the Melbourne lawyers again told Foreign Affairs it could not use the trust to pay the funeral costs, but they did supply the address of Violet McEvoy – the Hotel Beausite, Lausanne, Switzerland – a modest little pub on the city outskirts. Foreign Affairs promptly sent a letter to Freddie's elderly mother care of the Lausanne Hotel asking whether she was prepared to pay the bill. If not, could she supply Theodore's address?

In 1959 Foreign Affairs asked Treasury to make a decision about whether to reimburse the British consulate the £802, because the matter was 'rather irritating'. Foreign Affairs pointed out that 'a major point of principle' was involved because British consuls act on behalf of Australian citizens in posts where Australia is not represented. 'Irrespective of the formal position as to liability for expenses, the Australian government should feel obliged to reimburse the British government.'[19]

Treasury then proved how mean it could get when pursuing money from dead people. In documents marked RESTRICTED, the bean counters proposed the Crown Solicitor take legal action against the McEvoy estate to force it to pay the burial bill. Treasury felt the Australian government should not accept responsibility for the cost of the burial of Mrs Claude McEvoy, because she was not an Australian citizen.

Four months after writing to Violet McEvoy at the Hotel Beausite and getting no reply, the Australian Embassy in Geneva was instructed to send someone to the hotel to front the elderly lady about paying the bill. Mary McPherson, second secretary in the embassy, discovered that Violet McEvoy had skedaddled. For a while she was in another hotel in Lausanne, then said she was going to Florence, leaving no forwarding address. At the same time, the Melbourne lawyers produced Theodore's address – the tiny hamlet of St Cassien-Des-Bois, 20 kilometres north-east of Cannes.

On 10 June 1959, CL Hewitt, first assistant secretary of the Treasury, finally told the secretary of the Foreign Affairs Department it would reimburse the United Kingdom for Freddie's burial costs, but not those of his wife. Treasury insisted there be 'vigorous' action to pursue Theodore and the McEvoy estate to recover the amount. It even quibbled about the expense of the British Vice Consul's journey to Safi to recover the bodies from the sea; it would pay only half of it. Australia's Foreign Affairs Department duly sent a cheque for £396, 15 shillings and eight-pence to the British High Commission in Canberra – half what was owed to the British for their efforts in arranging the burial of Freddie and his wife eight years earlier.

If the misers in Treasury thought that was the last they'd hear of the corpse of Freddie McEvoy, they were very mistaken. Australia's High Commissioner in London, Sir Eric Harrison, joined the fray. Harrison was a former government minister and a close ally of Prime Minister Robert Menzies. In a long 'Dear Bob' letter, Harrison stressed the importance of Australia receiving assistance from friendly consulates in countries where it had no diplomatic representation. 'This is a case that frankly amazes me,' he told Menzies and spelled out the long saga of Freddie's burial costs. He said the British consulate in Casablanca had acted in good faith in burying Freddie and his wife, and had approval to do so from the Australian embassy in Paris:

> If by our actions we cause the British to warn their consulates that the Australian government is likely to prove ungenerous in reimbursing the UK government for assistance given, we are buying ourselves in the process of saving a few pounds, a lot of potential difficulty.[20]

Harrison warned that if this saga became known publicly, 'some real awkwardness' might result.

Finally, the stench of dead Freddie rose all the way to Prime Minister Robert Menzies. Instead of seeing the pettiness of the whole affair and simply ordering his public servants to pay the damn bill, Menzies sided with the penny pinchers. On 28 August 1959 Menzies replied to Harrison saying he had spoken with his top departmental secretaries 'about the case of Freddie McEvoy', which is 'complicated as well as long'.

Menzies pointed out that Mrs McEvoy and the crew were not Australian, 'therefore perhaps not everything the British consul did at Casablanca was done as agent for Australia'. Menzies said, 'we have not yet got to a final view' about paying the full bill. 'What interests us more is getting the money from the McEvoys. Personally, I would not over-rate the chances of success in this – but hope has by no means disappeared and will perhaps remain alive for some time yet.'[21] Menzies had just ordered the full might of the Foreign Office, Treasury and government lawyers to pursue to the bitter end Freddie McEvoy's relatives, as well as any inheritance for his daughter.

Menzies told Harrison to tell the British that Australia would 'in due course make a response' to their bill for £802 even though 'a great deal of time has passed'. This was an understatement – eight years had passed. Menzies said the government should continue trying to get the money from Theodore McEvoy because they now had an address for him. It just so happened that at this time Paris embassy officials reached Theodore at St Cassien-des-Bois. He declined to reach into his pocket to pay up, and again referred the bill to the Melbourne trust lawyers. Theodore told them Freddie's daughter Stephanie, now aged 13, lived in the St Pierre Hotel in New York with her grandfather, Charles

Wrightsman. She had dropped her McEvoy surname, and went by Wrightsman. Freddie had truly been wiped from her life.

Menzies' decision not to make a decision over McEvoy caused uproar and frustration in Foreign Affairs. More memos flew. The head of the Prime Minister's Department, Sir John Bunting, said the discussion in the PM's office over McEvoy concluded that the government 'may need to wait until after the death of Freddie's mother to see where we stand'. The head of Foreign Affairs, Sir Peter Heydon, warned in a strongly worded memo to Bunting, marked CONFIDENTIAL, that any further delay in paying the McEvoy bill in full would damage Australia's standing with the British government. If Freddie knew that his rotting corpse lying in a Casablanca cemetery would cause such a huge stink in Canberra he'd have laughed his head off.

Menzies and his top bureaucrats certainly knew of Freddie's colourful history. Newspaper clippings of Freddie's exploits with Errol Flynn were stuck into the McEvoy file that was distributed around the departments. American adventurer and author Robert C Ruark wrote on the occasion of Flynn's death in October 1959 that Errol's buddy Freddie was one of the 'true swashbucklers – just as wild as Flynn, just as handsome, just as reckless, and just as careless of public opinion'. Ruark told *Daily Telegraph* readers that the men's love of boats 'made both tall, handsome gentlemen striking figures at any place where the sun shone warm, there was booze to be drunk and women to chase'.[22] Ruark suggested that McEvoy died a hero trying to rescue his wife, an act that was out of character for the 'freebooter'. He wrote under the headline 'A rascally pair who could raise the devil':

They were both of a stripe – handsome, dashing, beloved by women, great admirers for the bottle, and invested with a great sense of levity concerning their own personal dignity. If there is any such thing as hereafter, this rascally pair will be together, and there will, in a word, be hell to pay with the devil catching the cheque . . .

Obviously that didn't go down too well with the conservative stuffed shirts in Canberra. They increased their efforts to make the McEvoys pay. The Crown Solicitor was ordered to start action against the McEvoy estate held by lawyers in Melbourne. The embassy in Paris was told to start planning legal action against Theodore McEvoy, even though it could cost 250,000 francs in legal fees – more than $5000 in today's money.

But that plan ended on 3 March 1960 when the Paris embassy received a letter from Theodore's wife saying he had died on 12 January. His widow said they had not lived together for the past three years, and she found the embassy demands for payment when she cleared out his home. She had been living in Lausanne with their seven-year-old son Sebastian because Theodore had no income and could not support the family. 'My husband was not very responsible and when he took this engagement [guaranteeing to pay for his brother's burial] he knew this could not be paid out of his brother's share of the trust.' She pleaded with the government not to take money from the trust because it was sorely needed by Sebastian.

The Crown Solicitor sat down with the Melbourne lawyers administering the trust and found that Charles Wrightsman had been doing his best to get Freddie's share as well. 'There is little doubt that Charles Wrightsman has intermeddled in the estate of the late Frederick James McEvoy,' the Crown said in its report to the Attorney General.[23]

As the McEvoy fiasco dragged into its tenth year, officials complained that Menzies had tied their hands by ordering that the McEvoys pay the bill. The officials therefore now had to wait for Violet to die. 'She is about 87 so we could be able to close the file before too long,' wrote senior diplomat Ralph Harry. He said in a furious note to a colleague that the McEvoy case had tied up at least £2000 of officers' time and warned him not to be drawn into it. Senior diplomat Sir Keith 'Mick' Shann wrote to Harry: 'the ghostly ship *Kangaroa* sails on'. 'I thought she was nearing port but the rockbound ugly coast of Treasury cuckoo-land now seems as cold and unreceptive as before.' Shann was at a loss what to do, except maybe pass the hat around and pay the bill out of their own frustrated pockets.

Harry suggested someone track Violet down in Florence to see how she was going. In March 1961 the consul in Florence reported there was no sign of anyone named Violet Coral McEvoy in the city, but on 5 July 1961 the Geneva embassy reported they'd found Violet living with her daughter-in-law in Lausanne.

At the end of July 1961, Menzies stepped in again. 'I want this case closed this year,' Menzies wrote to his department head. He ordered the Geneva embassy to speak to Violet McEvoy to see whether she would pay the remainder of the bill. Menzies also wanted a report on her age and health. Geneva replied on 13 October that Violet seemed to be avoiding them: every time they called she had just left for somewhere, now believed to be Gstaad in Switzerland. A month later they finally cornered her, and the embassy's first secretary, PGF Henderson, interviewed her on a day that was close to the tenth anniversary of the death of her eldest son. She was younger than the bureaucrats had estimated – 75 years of age – but she told Henderson she didn't expect to live long. Asked if she would pay the money, she said no. 'The reason for this is not so much that she is unwilling to pay it, but simply that she cannot afford to do so.'[24] Violet told Henderson she had been in Gstaad trying to see her grand-daughter, Stephanie. The teenager was there with her mother, Irene, who spent her days in hotel bars drinking. Irene refused to speak to Violet, even though Violet had raised Stephanie as a young child.

On 14 December 1961, 10 years after the death of Freddie McEvoy, Treasury finally agreed to reimburse the British govern-ment the full amount. But Treasury decided to keep open the option of getting money from the estate after the death of Violet McEvoy. 'The Geneva consulate might please be asked to notify your office in the event of her death,' signed CL Hewitt, Treasury first assistant secretary. Diplomat Ralph Harry saw the note on 22 December and commented on it: 'Glory be.'

On 28 February 1962 a UK official 'happily' thanked Australia for the cheque that enabled them to close their 10-year-old file on Freddie McEvoy. But just when you'd think that was the end of the matter and Freddie McEvoy had finally been laid to rest, the Canberra bureaucrats rose from the dead like zombies in a horror movie. In January 1963 Treasury asked Foreign Affairs for the present whereabouts of Violet McEvoy. In January 1964 Treasury again asked: Where was Violet McEvoy? The Geneva

The Australian government file on Freddie was finally closed
in 1964 – 13 years after he died.

consul said they hadn't heard a thing. Six months later, Treasury
asked whether she was still living in Geneva.

The very last memo in the massive file on the death of Freddie
McEvoy came from the second secretary in the Geneva consulate, RJ Greet. 'Police inform us that Mrs McEvoy left Lausanne

on 30 April 1964 to go to Stresa, on the Italian side of Swiss–Italian border. She gave her address as the Hotel du Simplon.'[25] Violet had skipped over the border. Treasury would have to get the Australian consul in Italy to pursue her. At this point sanity prevailed somewhere in the bureaucracy, and they decided to call it a day. Violet McEvoy, now aged 78, had beaten them. Thirteen years after Freddie drowned in mysterious circumstances off a deserted Moroccan coast, the bulging government file on him was sent to the basement stamped: FILE CLOSED.

CHAPTER 15

THE SUN SETS ON FREDDIE'S WORLD

Freddie's daughter Stephanie, now aged 73, says she knows very little about her father. 'I was six years old when he died, and I have no memory of him,' she told me in a telephone interview from her home in the United States.

> I don't have anything that belonged to him, no letters, no mementos, not even any photographs. After he died I spent all my school years in a Swiss boarding school. I was in a convent as a charity ward. I had to work for the nuns to pay my fees. I was abandoned. When my mother eventually picked me up I was taken to hospital in Paris sick with pneumonia and asthma. I spent my childhood in boarding school. I didn't even speak English. I do know my father was a colourful character, but I haven't ever heard more than that.[1]

She certainly doesn't have any positive feelings towards him. 'My father put me in boarding school when I was three years old. What does that tell you?'[2]

Stephanie didn't know that her father had won a medal at the 1936 Winter Olympics, and quite frankly didn't care. When she was young she was told her father was a smuggler who was killed at sea by pirates, and his body never found. She'd never heard about the wreck or the story told by the surviving crew. She didn't know that her father was buried at Casablanca. She knew nothing of the McEvoy trust fund, and certainly never inherited anything from it. She said her grandfather didn't get on with Freddie. It's clear from what she said that her grandfather did all he could to turn Stephanie away from her father. Just three months after Freddie died, her mother Irene changed both their surnames to Wrightsman in the Los Angeles County Court. She never met her cousin Sebastian; she didn't know he existed until he called her out of the blue for her 70th birthday. She saw no reason to meet him. She has had no contact with her step-sister Romaine since they were parted in 1951.

Stephanie married four times. She said the first husband was arranged in 1964 by her mother when she turned 18. The gossip columns leaped into action. 'So, who is Stephanie's father?' asked the gossip writer in the *Philadelphia Inquirer*. 'Stephanie's father was the late sportsman Freddie McEvoy, one of the most colourful figures who ever dashed Errol Flynn-like from one fleshpot to another in the high old days when a playboy was a playboy.'[3] The wedding, which took place in front of high society in Lausanne, didn't lead to a happy marriage. Stephanie said she felt her first few husbands were only after the Wrightsman money. It was only when she was in her 70s and single that she felt happy. 'I have loads of good friends and at last I have made my life a happy one, and I don't have to listen to assholes,' she said.[4]

•

Freddie's first wife, Beatrice, died in 1956 in her beloved Casa Estella villa on the French Riviera. She was remembered as a much respected and admired matriarch of New York society.

Freddie's second wife, Irene, was not so fortunate. After her stormy divorce from Freddie, she careened around Hollywood, joining up with a series of handsome movie stars including Robert Stack and Kirk Douglas. It got quite serious with Douglas – but then he met her father, Charles Wrightsman.

'He was one of the richest men in the country, and one of the meanest . . . what her father was doing to her was criminal. He was cruel and selfish,' Douglas wrote in his memoir.[5] The actor said Wrightsman demanded his two daughters be 'ornamental and obedient . . . if they did not please him he would cut them off without a cent, keeping them in a constant state of turmoil'. Douglas said every time Irene visited her father's house she fell ill and couldn't move from her bed. As soon as they left, she was fine. Douglas added that Wrightsman forbade him from marrying Irene. Douglas believed it was because he was Jewish. Wrightsman shocked Douglas when he pressed upon him that Irene was mentally sick. Douglas could see her father was the sole reason for her problems. Douglas broke off their relationship when he found her in bed with Sydney Chaplin, son of Charlie.

Irene drank more and more. She became thin and pallid. Douglas saw her a year after they broke up and said she looked like a cadaver. Irene's mother drank herself to death in 1963. A month later Irene's sister Charlene committed suicide, aged 36. In 1965 Irene took an overdose of pills and alcohol and died, aged 40. Charles Wrightsman died in 1986 aged 90. A *New York Times* obituary praised him for his multi-million-dollar gifts of art to the Metropolitan Museum of Art, where eight halls are named after him. There was no mention of his two daughters or his first wife.

The marriage of Freddie's close friend and lover, Barbara Hutton, to his friend and one-time partner in shady business deals, Prince Igor Troubetzkoy, didn't last long. They divorced after three years, just before Freddie died. Igor had great fun with Barbara's money, racing a Ferrari in the Monaco Grand Prix, and when the marriage was over he received a sizeable payout. Barbara's next marriage was to much-married Latin American playboy, racing driver, polo player and one-time friendly rival to Freddie McEvoy, Porfirio Rubirosa. A Colombian diplomat and supporter of right-wing dictators, Rubirosa's legendary reputation as a lover was up there with that of Freddie McEvoy. They were rivals for the ladies, but Rubirosa's reputation for being hung like a horse was such that Parisian waiters named gigantic pepper grinders as the 'Rubirosa'. It wasn't a happy marriage. Gossip writer Phyllis Battelle said of the wedding: 'The bride, for her fifth wedding, wore black and carried a scotch and soda.'[6]

Rubirosa moved fast – so fast that Barbara divorced him after just 58 days of wedded bliss. To say goodbye she gave him $2.5 million, polo ponies, jewellery and a converted B-52 bomber. Barbara married twice more – to a German baron, and to a penniless Prince of the Orient. Perhaps she was happiest with Freddie McEvoy and, had they married, their wedding vows may have lasted longer than the other grifters who buzzed around her like bees at a honey pot – at least, so long as her money flowed. She and Freddie were close friends until he died, and she was greatly saddened to hear he was gone. Barbara had a sad death. Her only son, Lance, died in an air crash in 1972, aged 36. Barbara died in 1979 aged 66. She'd been ripped off by so many men and been such a spendthrift that she was down to her last thousands.

Errol Flynn parted ways with Patrice Wymore in 1958. He never could stick with one wife for long. 'Nobody ever tried harder than Pat to make me happy,' he wrote.[7] In yet another scandal, Errol took up with blonde teenage actress Beverly Aadland, whom he'd met on the set of *Cuban Rebel Girls*. She was only 15 years old. Without her making a complaint, the cops did nothing. Ever ready to make a joke at his own expense, Errol announced at a party for Beverly's 17th birthday: 'I'm looking about for another girl. Miss Aadland is getting rather old for me.' In good form, Errol joked: 'I may be too old for young girls, but they're not too young for me.' When a reporter asked what women saw in him, Errol shot back: 'I have no idea, old bean, I never question success.'[8] But his life was descending into a spiral of alcohol and drugs. Blocked from the bar at the Hollywood Publicists' Ball for being drunk, Errol was indignant. 'I demand to be arrested,' he cried. 'I want the whole world to know of the injustice of this deed – that Errol Flynn was arrested as a drunk before he even got to the bar!' When police threw the famous Aussie actor into the West Los Angeles drunk tank, the plastered Mexicans in the cell rose as one and cried, 'Viva El Kapitan Blood.'[9]

Beverly was with Errol in Vancouver to lease his beloved yacht *Zaca* to a rich man to cover his debts when he fell seriously ill. Errol died in Vancouver on 14 October 1959. His death certificate listed so many causes of death it didn't fit onto the form: myocardial infarction, coronary thrombosis, coronary atherosclerosis, fatty degeneration of liver and portal cirrhosis of the liver. At age 50, decades of hard living had finally caught up with the Aussie swashbuckler.[10]

Months after Errol's death, his hilarious and controversial memoir *My Wicked, Wicked Ways* was published. It became an instant bestseller, selling more than a million copies and has never been out of print. In the memoir, Errol wrote very fondly of Freddie McEvoy. He described his friendship with Freddie as a 'deep, a real sporting relationship . . . he made life appear a thing of gaiety'. Freddie was, wrote Errol, a true international playboy, charming, debonair, a talented diver, big-time card-playing gambler, a man who made and lost fortunes without really caring. 'His profession? Anything. He made a fortune, he married wealth, he raced cars, he was a leader in his set. People like me had to work. Freddie didn't in order to live high.'[11] Errol could imagine no greater praise for his best friend.

As for Errol Flynn, there will always be the glowing black-and-white misty image of one of the best looking men ever to grace the silver screen. His movies are still adored by movie buffs, and new fans find his films on late-night television and movie classics on cable. Errol's son with Lili Damita, Sean, an adventurer and promising photojournalist with his father's good looks, was 28 when he disappeared in Cambodia in 1970 while covering the war in Vietnam and was presumed dead. Errol lost Mulholland Ranch in 1955 after a long pursuit for alimony by Lili. It was bought by composer of religious music Stuart Hamblen, who turned the orgy room into a small chapel. Singer Ricky Nelson took it over but he died and it went to rack and ruin. In 1988 Mulholland Ranch was torn down. Justin Timberlake now lives on the site in a new building.

Blonde Nazi Mata Hari spy Hilde Krüger went on to be the companion of a string of wealthy and powerful Mexican and Cuban men – married and unmarried. She was credited with using her influence to keep Mexico exporting valuable minerals to Germany along with refuelling spots for German U-Boats. She appeared in a few forgettable Mexican films but after the war became a respected historian of Mexico's past. Reports had her decades later living quietly in New York. Some say she died there in 1991, others that she died during a trip to Germany.

Freddie's female equivalent, Sandra Rambeau, got into a bigamy tussle with George Hearst, wealthy son of billionaire publisher William Randolph Hearst. In 1951 they married in Mexico only to find George was still married to wife number three. Sandra waltzed into the sunset carrying a large alimony payout for her heartbreak.

Countess Dorothy di Frasso, who helped launch Freddie on the US social whirl in 1941 by bragging of his sexual prowess, died of a heart attack in 1954. The socialite and matchmaker for movie stars was in a compartment on a luxury Union Pacific train between Las Vegas and Los Angeles. She had just spent Christmas with Marlene Dietrich. She was found dressed in her customary mink coat and $3 million worth of jewels. Her interior decorator friend Tom Douglas told reporters she had been popping nitroglycerin pills 'like popcorn' six at a time.[12]

George Dawson, Freddie's Riviera partner in murky post-war deals, got into all sorts of financial strife and legal action over debts and tax in the late 1950s. In one 1958 bankruptcy court battle Dawson claimed to have been burgled 13 times and that's why he wouldn't reveal where he kept his money. But he did admit to keeping £20,000 (US$6.5 million in today's money) in jewels under his bed and had 'black market money in France'.[13] A London court declared Dawson bankrupt in 1957. In 1959 he was convicted of fraud and sentenced to six years' jail. Dawson told the judge: 'I have always thought I was doing just ordinary business – perhaps a little bit sharp, but not criminal.'[14]

The nightclubs in which Freddie caroused and had a roaring good time have all gone. Club Mocambo and Ciro's in Hollywood, El Morocco in New York, Chez Florence, Club Scheherezade and Le Ciel in Paris all either closed or were transformed into crass discos by the 1970s. The once exclusive reserve of the promenades of the Riviera are now choked with scantily dressed tourists taking selfies in front of the massive motor yachts moored by multi-millionaire merchant bankers, rap singers and Russian oligarchs. All the class and élan of the 1930s, 40s and 50s seem to have disappeared, replaced with vulgar displays of ostentatious wealth. The sun has truly set on the fashionable era in which Freddie thrived.

Many look back on Freddie's era on the Riviera with nostalgia – the fashion, the style, the ease of living, the decadence, the hidden danger. It is captured in popular art-deco posters and the movie stars of the day, such as Grace Kelly and Cary Grant in *To Catch a Thief,* Brigitte Bardot in *And God Created Woman* and Michael Caine in *Dirty Rotten Scoundrels.* Ian Fleming set his first book, *Casino Royale,* on the Riviera, and he could have had Freddie in mind when he described fictional Riviera playboy Count Lippe for his ninth James Bond 007 novel, *Thunderball*:

> The man was extremely handsome – a dark-bronzed woman-killer with a neat moustache above the sort of callous mouth women kiss in their dreams. He was an athletic-looking six feet . . . a good-looking bastard who got all the women he wanted and probably lived on them – and lived well.[15]

You can exhaust a Thesaurus finding words to fit the legendary playboy that was Freddie McEvoy – rogue, bounder, cad, rake, grafter, scoundrel, anti-hero, opportunist, rascal, rapscallion, lothario, gigolo, smuggler, black marketeer, brawler, predator, philanderer, reprobate . . . the list of negatives is long. But then there are the adjectives: witty, charming, amiable, elegant, debonair, daring, dashing, swashbuckling, carefree, fearless, seductive, fascinating, devil-may-care, considerate, courteous, polite, impeccably mannered, versatile, gallant, attractive, liberterian, likeable, loyal. They all fit.

Freddie had exactly the right personal qualities that placed him above the great playboys and charming rogues of his time. He led the high life without any visible means of support. Women of all types found him irresistible, and he could pick and choose among the most beautiful – and those with the most money. Others in Freddie's world of luxury yachts on the French Riviera, exclusive ski chalets in Switzerland, high stakes in casinos and frolicking in the nightclubs of Paris, Monte Carlo, Havana, New York and Hollywood managed to live up to the life in varying degrees, but only Freddie made it without the backing of an upper-crust family, an old European aristocratic title or money of his own.

Freddie was no coward or pacifist, yet he disdained war as an inconvenience – something that should not involve him. War, he concluded, was a total waste of life, and life was meant to be enjoyed to the full. He told anyone who asked him what he did for a living and he meant it when he replied: *Pleasure is my business.* He spent very little of his life in Australia and never returned after his teens, yet he proudly displayed the Australian flag on his racing cars and made a point of telling the snooty high-society set he mixed in that he came from a land Down Under.

Andreas Zielke – German chronicler of the playboy world of the post-war decade – wrote that Freddie McEvoy, Porfirio Rubirosa and Prince Aly Khan (the polo-playing racing-car driving son of the wealthy Aga Khan) had the same male chemistry.

First, they loved women, and would not let a chance go by to seduce beautiful women of all kinds. Second, they possessed a readiness to recklessly risk everything, even their lives, for nothing more than a bet, a dare or one night with a beautiful woman. It is no coincidence that these three playboys all died in the prime of their lives in deadly accidents.[16]

Rubirosa died aged 56 when he crashed his Ferrari into a tree racing through the Bois de Boulogne in Paris. Aly Khan, once married to Rita Hayworth, died in a car crash aged 48.

'Freddie McEvoy was a shining light for all professional playboys by being totally fearless and having no regard for the danger to his greatest asset; his body,' wrote Zielke:

> Freddie developed a unique level of recklessness and enthusiastic risk-taking as he had an insatiable appetite for intrigues and adventure. He was reputed to have killed a man in a bar fight, thus earning a notch on his belt that increased his reputation for danger. Freddie was the rough variety of playboy that held enormous appeal to many women.[17]

Freddie certainly deserves a place in the history of extraordinary Australians. He was a sporting hero who should be up there with other great Australian sporting heroes. He was the first Australian to win a medal at any Winter Olympics. He was the world champion bobsledder for two years running at a time when no other Australian even thought of sliding down an ice tunnel at breakneck speed. He proudly displayed the Australian flag on his racing car on tracks around Europe and the United States. He may not have won those pre-war races, but he was competitive against the best in the world, and he did it on his own. Unlike his competitors, Freddie had no family wealth, no aristocratic title and no backing from a big car manufacturer.

Freddie McEvoy was by no means a politically correct hero of the sort society demands today. But he was a man of his time – a time of male machismo. A time that allowed him to advance into international high society when, as a penniless Australian, he had no right to be there. He rose to the heights of society through his wit, his charm and his Aussie sense of humour. He possessed an extraordinary ability to seduce women and legendary sexual prowess, yet somehow he managed to stay best friends with the cuckolded husbands. He wheeled and dealed, doing dodgy black-market exchanges for whatever was needed or desired. Often his only asset was his charm. The rich would give him huge loans they never expected him to repay, simply because they loved having Freddie around.

Freddie succeeded in hard times with what he had: his personal flair and his physical skills. He did it at a time when great turmoil swept the world in the face of incredible evil being done under the cloak of crisp black SS uniforms and swastikas. Did he collaborate with the Germans after they invaded France? Did he act as a Nazi spy in America? He certainly took several female Nazi spies to bed, but it's doubtful that they discussed the virtues of Adolf Hitler. Freddie was not ideologically inclined. He thought it was ridiculous to fight a war over ideology or territory. Did he scout out spots in the Caribbean for German U-Boats to refuel? It is possible that in return for cash Freddie may well have swapped some sailor talk of remote and isolated bays in the Caribbean with German agents. But that was never proved. Apart from running Nazi Mata Hari agents up and down his own flagpole, there is no evidence he did anything more for the Third Reich. After years of investigations and monitoring his every move, the FBI cleared him of 'alleged political subversive activities'.[18] Some US counter-intelligence officers suspected Freddie was a British double agent, using his wiles to infiltrate the Nazi underground network to plant false information – a James Bond before Ian Fleming even thought of writing tales of 007. Freddie had friends in the US Navy in strategic positions who helped him make a film on underwater spear-gun fighting – hardly the thing the US Navy would do with a suspected enemy spy.

There are many mysteries still surrounding Freddie McEvoy. British Secret Service files on his activities in France, both during and after the war, have gone missing or are still classified as secret. Perhaps in those files lies the answer to what Freddie really had in those 40 crates on his yacht, and why they were never allowed to be discovered. Freddie truly was an international man of mystery.

AUTHOR'S NOTE

The more I dug into the incredible life of mystery man Freddie McEvoy, neglected Australian sporting hero and dashing international playboy, the more I wished I could have met this remarkable man. I knew little about him when I started researching this book – just that he was a great mate of Aussie screen legend Errol Flynn, that he'd been accused of being a Nazi spy, and that he'd won a medal at the 1936 Winter Olympics in front of Adolf Hitler and held the title of world-champion bobsledder for several years running.

Nobody who knew Freddie is still alive. His daughter, who was six when he was killed in mysterious circumstances off the coast of Morocco, knows nothing of him. So I had to rely on official records and documents and, most of all, on newspaper reports of his exploits written at the time. Gossip columnists loved Freddie – probably because he was such good material and he never denied anything.

There was a great need to separate the rumour and claims about Freddie from what could be proved in documents, files and official records. My search for documents took me from Los Angeles to Washington, from Berlin to Paris and London. What they revealed was extraordinary, and I thank all the archivists who helped me navigate the miles of files. Thanks to those who worked to put thousands of newspapers online. It's a huge help for history hunters like me.

A special thanks to archivist Ned Comstock, who was extremely helpful at the Cinematic Arts Library and Archives at the University of Southern California, Los Angeles. Along with Sandra Garcia-Myers, Ned is custodian of the Charles Higham Collection, the documents gathered by Higham for his controversial book on Errol Flynn included a lot of FBI and State Department files held on Errol's partner in debauchery, Freddie McEvoy. Ned persuaded Higham to donate the dozens of boxes of documents he'd accumulated over the years to the Library, and it proved extremely useful. In the files I found that Higham had often added up one and one and got three or four. Higham described his book on Errol as a 'deductive biography'. There was no need for him to exaggerate – the story of Errol and Freddie's lives was already larger than life.

Louise Hilton and Rachel Bernstein at the Margaret Herrick Library at the Academy of Motion Picture Arts and Sciences in Beverly Hills helped the movie part of my research, along with the records of Hollywood gossip writer Hedda Hopper.

Ruby Talbot and Jessica Delfs at the Mullin Automotive Museum in Oxnard, California, kindly allowed me to have a good look at Freddie's amazing and beautiful Talbot-Lago Teardrop car, which he drove from Paris to Cannes in under 10 hours in 1936.

In Washington, DC, Haley Maynard and Cate Brennan at the US National Archives and Records Administration were very helpful in showing me how to find the myriad FBI and State Department files on Freddie McEvoy, as well as all those suspected Nazi spies he mixed with – some more intimately than others.

In Berlin, researcher Dr Christian Schoelzel dug his way deep into the wartime files searching for any sign of Freddie McEvoy in the Nazi records. His name wasn't there. He could have had a code name, or he was just never on the books. We don't know. My thanks to him for his search, and for supplying valuable material on the 1936 Winter Olympics.

In London, researcher Simon Fowler discovered Freddie's school records and helped with approaching the Foreign Office for files on Freddie – all of which mysteriously can't be found or were destroyed.

In Canberra, Australian government files at the National Archives of Australia were finally declassified and dusted off from the basement at my request with the help of archivists William Edwards and Megan Vasey. Those files exposed many years of petty small-minded meanness and outright vindictiveness regarding the bill for burying Freddie that went all the way up to Prime Minister Menzies.

A special thanks to my old journo mate Maggie Hall in Washington who introduced me to her interesting drinking buddies and listened while I ranted about the search for Freddie.

Photo researcher and long-time friend Annette Cruger used her skills to find some excellent historic pictures of Freddie.

Thanks to Betsy Bush in New York who helped with research, Barbara Hall in Los Angeles who gave advice on how to research movie history, Agathe Merceron and Joelle Andreoli Dietrich for their help with French swear words, my wife Esther for German translations, Ole Böttner for help with jpegs and pdfs, and Philip Sholl for advice on sailing terminology. Thanks to my brother Peter who read through the manuscript and once again gave birth to many commas and full stops, and pointed out repetitions.

Thanks to publisher Vanessa Radnidge, Head of Non-Fiction at Hachette Australia, for seeing the potential in Freddie's story, copy editor Claire de Medici for cleaning it up, editor Tom Bailey-Smith for sewing it together and Isabel Staas for her work on the photographs.

Finally, a big thank you to my family who put up with me during my search for Freddie and writing his story. And thanks to Di, Karim and the other dawn dog walkers who kept me going by asking every morning what chapter I was up to.

I can be contacted through my website, www.frankwalker.com.au

Frank Walker
Sydney, 2018

ENDNOTES

Prologue

1 Cholly Knickerbocker, 'Heroic end of the fabulous playboy', *The American Weekly* magazine, 30 December 1951, page 5.
2 Robert C. Ruark, 'A rascally pair who could raise the devil', *Daily Telegraph*, 29 October 1959.

Chapter 1

1 Robert Upe, 'Australian medal-winner "Suicide Freddie" McEvoy was a killer on the slopes', *Sydney Morning Herald*, 21 January 1994, page 29.
2 David Clay Large, *Nazi Games – the Olympics of 1936*, WW Norton and Co, New York, 2007, page 125.
3 Anton Rippon, *Hitler's Olympics – the story of the 1936 Nazi Games*, Pen & Sword Military, Barnsley, Yorkshire, 2006, ibook, page 1241.
4 *Die Tagebucher von Joseph Goebbels*, Part 1, 1923–1941, edited by Elke Frohlich, KG Saur, Munchen, 2005, pages 376–77.
5 Large, op. cit., page 58.
6 Max Fisher, *The Atlantic Magazine*, 10 May 2012.
7 Large, op. cit., page 107.
8 Andreas Meyhoff and Gerhard Pfeil, 'German ski resort represses memory of 1936 Winter Olympics', *Der Spiegel Online*, 22 January 2010.
9 ibid.
10 Large, op. cit., page 122.
11 ibid.
12 ibid., page 123.

13 Organisationskomitee fur die IV Olympische Winterspiele 1936 Garmishc-Partenkirchen, *IV Olympische Winterspiele 1936 – Amtlicher Bericht* [Official report of the German Olympic Organising Committee for the 1936 Winter Olympics], Reichssportverlag, Berlin, 1936, pages 235–36.
14 'Nazi "sportsmanship" in the Olympics', *Wisconsin Jewish Chronicle*, 14 February 1936.

Chapter 2

1 *Stonyhurst Magazine* No. 256, April 1925, page 61.
2 www.badruttspalace.com/en/120-years-badrutts-palace/dancer-to-millionaire.
3 George Frazier, 'The golden playboy', *Esquire*, February 1954, page 104.
4 ibid.
5 Dean Jennings, *Barbara Hutton*, WH Allen, London, 1968, page 187.
6 ibid., page 188.
7 Michael Stern, *No Innocence Abroad*, Random House, New York, 1953, page 11.

Chapter 3

1 Bobsled times, places and details from *Amtlicher Bericht IV Olympische Winter-spiele 1936*.
2 www.sports-reference.com/olympics/athletes/mc/freddie-mcevoy-1.html.

Chapter 4

1 www.archive.org/details/1936-Jugend-der-Welt.
2 Large, op. cit., page 138.
3 ibid., page 143.
4 ibid., page 144.
5 Rupert Matthews, *Hitler: Military commander*, Arcturus Publishing, London, 2003, page 115.
6 ibid., page 135.
7 ibid., page 141.
8 Philip van Rensselaer, *Million Dollar Baby: An intimate portrait of Barbara Hutton*, Hodder & Stoughton, London, 1979, page 232.
9 The bet between Freddie McEvoy and Barbara Hutton is detailed in the book *French Curves*, page 202, published by the Mullin Automotive Museum in Oxnard, California.
10 Racing results taken from the website Racing's Golden Era, www.kolumbus.fi/leif.snellman/dm.htm#MC
11 Vanderbilt Cup Races website, www.mail.vanderbiltcupraces.com/blog/article/thursday_december_29_2010_exclusive_starting_lineup_for_the_1936_vander-bilt.
12 Frazier, op. cit., page 104.
13 Cholly Knickerbocker, 'Heroic end of the fabulous playboy', *American Weekly*, 30 December 1951.
14 *Yorkshire Post*, 15 February 1937, page 11.
15 *Daily Express*, 2 February 1937.

16 www.independent.co.uk/sport/rugby/rugby-union/captain-who-swapped-white-shirt-for-black-proves-sport-and-politics-an-unhappy-mix-6895.html.

Chapter 5

1 Susanna de Vries, *Royal Mistresses of the House of Hanover-Windsor*, Pirgos Press, Brisbane, 2012; location 3218 in ebook format.
2 Cassandra Jardine, 'She was game for anything', *Daily Telegraph* (UK), 31 January 2003, www.telegraph.co.uk/news/health/3300215/She-was-game-for-anything....html.
3 Frazier, op. cit., page 104.
4 Charles Higham, *Errol Flynn: The untold story*, Granada, London 1980, page 185.
5 Gordon Greenwood, *The Modern World: A history of our time*, Angus & Robertson, Sydney, 1965, page 267.
6 Antony Beevor, *The Second World War*, Weidenfeld & Nicolson, London, 2012, page 49.
7 Charles Higham Collection, Box 33: 17, University of Southern California Cinematic Arts Library.
8 Charles Glass, *Americans in Paris: Life and death under Nazi occupation 1940–44*, Harper Press, London, 2009, page 1.
9 William Wiser, *The Twilight Years: Paris in the 1930s*, Robson Books, London, 2001, page 254.
10 Dialogue reconstructed from what is contained in official documents.

Chapter 6

1 Ian Ousby, *Occupation: The ordeal of France 1940–1944*, Thistle Publishing, London, 1997; location 791 of 5939 in ebook format.
2 ibid., location 801.
3 ibid., location 845.
4 US National Archives and Records Administration (NARA), Maryland, File 195.1, *Black Swan*.
5 ibid.
6 German Archives Berlin: R 100.131, Series 6886–6889, German Embassy in Paris files 1940–1941, Volumes 5 and 6.
7 Colin Smith, *England's Last War Against France: Fighting Vichy 1940–42*, W&N, London, 2010, page 137.
8 ibid., page 147.
9 Ousby, op. cit., location 2697.
10 ibid., location 3422.
11 Charles Higham Collection, University of Southern California Cinematic Arts Library, Box 33: 18.
12 ibid., Box 37 folder 2.

Chapter 7

1 *Minneapolis Star*, 1 June 1941, page 27.

2   Robert Matzen and Michael Mazzone, *Errol Flynn Slept Here*, GoodKnight Books, Pittsburgh, 2009, page 22.
3   Cousin Eve, 'Chicago society busy with autumn duties', *Chicago Tribune*, 19 October 1941.
4   Charles Higham Collection, Box 33:18, University of Southern California Cinematic Arts Library.
5   NARA File 800.20211, document 100-12556, McEvoy, Frederick G./2.
6   NARA File 800.20211, document 100-12556, McEvoy, Frederick G./2.
7   NARA File 800.20211, document 100-6441, McEvoy, Frederick G./3.
8   ibid.
9   ibid.
10 ibid.
11 ibid., page 5.
12 'Dancer denies wedding to Nazi General', *Fresno Bee*, 7 July 1941, page 14.
13 NARA file, 800.20211, document 100-6441, McEvoy, Frederick G./3, page 4.
14 ibid., page 5.
15 ibid., page 4.
16 ibid., page 5.
17 ibid., page 9.
18 ibid., G./13.
19 NARA File 800.20211, document 65-6441, Frederick McEvoy, page 2.
20 ibid., page 3.
21 ibid.
22 ibid., page 6.
23 Adam Higginbotham, 'Last of the big spenders', *Daily Telegraph* (UK), 23 November 2004
24 https://www.sports-reference.com/olympics/athletes/mc/freddie-mcevoy-1.html
25 NARA file 800.20211, document 100-12556, page 2.

Chapter 8

1   ibid.
2   Sander A Diamond, *The Nazi Movement in the United States 1924–1941*, Cornell University Press, Ithaca, NY, 1974, page 75.
3   *Life* magazine, 7 March 1938, page 17.
4   Video: *When 20,000 American Nazis descended on New York City*, by Marshall Curry, 10 October 2017.
5   Paul Roland, *Nazi Women: The attraction of evil*, Arcturus, ebook pages 126–31.
6   Jean-Denis Lepage, *An Illustrated Dictionary of the Third Reich*, McFarland Publishing, Jefferson, NC, 2013, pages 153–57.
7   Jana Richter (ed.), *Die Tagebücher von Joseph Goebbels, Teil 1 1923–1941*, KG Sauer, München, 2001, page 95.
8   Allan Hall, 'Joseph Goebbels: The Casanova of the Nazis', *Daily Telegraph* (UK), 8 January, 2011.
9   Richter, op. cit., KG Sauer, page 155.
10 'Hilde Krüger, Nazi Spy in Mexico, mexicounexplained.com/ hilde-kruger-nazi-spy-mexico.

11 Deutsche Welle, 'Oil Baron Getty revealed as Hitler fan', 2 September 2003, www.dw.com/en/oil-baron-getty-revealed-as-hitler-fan/a-961176.
12 Frank Walker, *Traitors*, Hachette Australia, Sydney, 2017, pages 116–40.
13 ibid., page 249.
14 NARA file Hilde Krüger 65-1157, 20 February 1941.
15 ibid.
16 Charles Higham Collection, loc. cit.
17 ibid.
18 Patt Morrison, 'How Hitler's Fascism almost took hold in Los Angeles', *Los Angeles Times*, 27 September 2017.
19 Author Steven J Ross, history professor at University of Southern California, interviewed in *LA Times*, 27 September 2017 on his new book, *Hitler in Los Angeles: How Jews foiled Nazi plots against Hollywood and America.*
20 FBI file 1 February 1941 #65-796.
21 Higham, op. cit., page 187.
22 Walker, op. cit., pages 249–56.
23 Michael Stern, *No Innocence Abroad*, Random House, New York, 1952, page 5.
24 ibid.
25 Stern, op. cit., page 6.
26 Higham, op. cit., page 188.
27 Stern, op. cit., page 6.
28 NARA FBI file 800.20211, document 100-12556 FAC, marked internal security, page 3.
29 ibid.
30 Charles Higham Collection, loc. cit.
31 NARA FBI files 800.20211, McEvoy G/6.
32 David Bamber and Chris Hastings, 'Errol Flynn spied for Allies not the Nazis', *The Telegraph* (UK), 31 December 2000.
33 Higham, op. cit., page 187.
34 ibid., page 188.
35 Thomas David Schoonover, *Hitler's Man in Havana: Heinz Lüning and Nazi espionage in Latin America*, University Press of Kentucky, 2008, page 87.
36 NARA FBI file RG38, McEvoy Box 23 in Records of the Chief of Naval Operations, 24 October 1944.
37 University of Southern California Cinema Arts Library, loc. cit.

Chapter 9

1 The 'Charming People' column in the *Washington Times Herald*, 19 June 1942.
2 FIBI archives on Errol Flynn, J Edgar Hoover letter dated 22 June 1942, www.archive.org/stream/ErrolFlynn/Flynn%2C%20Errol#page/n133/mode/2up.
3 FBI archive file on Errol Flynn, 3 July 1942, file number 25-2167.
4 Errol Flynn, *My Wicked, Wicked Ways*, G.P. Putnam's Sons, New York, 1959, page 276.
5 ibid.
6 *Philadelphia Inquirer*, 7 August 1953, page 19.
7 David Bret, *Errol Flynn: Satan's angel*, Robson Books, London 2000, page 107.

8 Flynn, op. cit., page 276.
9 ibid., page 277.
10 Higham, op. cit., page 272.
11 ibid.
12 *20/20*, American Broadcasting Company, 13 March 1980.
13 ibid.
14 Flynn, op. cit., page 347.
15 Jack Lait, 'Broadway and Elsewhere' column, *Honolulu Star-Advertiser*,
    4 February 1943.
16 Flynn, op. cit., page 370.
17 ibid.
18 Gregory Mank, *Hollywood Hellfire Club*, Feral House, Port Townsend, WA,
    2007, page 291.
19 Thomas McNulty, *Errol Flynn: The life and career*, McFarland & Co, London,
    2004, page 125.
20 Flynn, op. cit., page 293.
21 ibid., page 346.
22 FBI file, New York, marked 'internal security', document number 100-153670-93.
23 FBI report document number 62-75147-46-7.
24 ibid.
25 Flynn, op. cit., page 311.
26 ibid., page 312.
27 ibid., page 313.
28 ibid., page 314.
29 A grand jury performs a function similar to a preliminary hearing in the
    Australian legal system, but a prosecutor has to convince a jury of 16 to 23 lay
    persons that there is sufficient evidence to bring criminal charges against the
    accused.
30 Bret, op. cit., page 112.

Chapter 10

1 ibid.
2 Flynn, op. cit., page 315.
3 ibid., page 316.
4 Bret, op. cit., page 116.
5 You can see Errol and Freddie's scene at: www.youtube.com/watch?v=N9t29i5bRpo
6 Gene Ringgold and Lawrence Quirk, *The Films of Bette Davis*, Cadillac
    Publishing, New York, 1966, page 123.
7 Documents concerning machinations behind the movie are kept at the Margaret
    Merrick Library, Academy of Motion Picture Arts and Sciences, Los Angeles.
8 One of the founders was 18-year-old William F Buckley Jr, who became a leading
    conservative writer.
9 Bret, op. cit., page 117.
10 Flynn, op. cit., page 326.
11 Bret, op. cit., page 122.
12 ibid., page 117.

13 ibid., page 120.

14 ibid., page 119.

15 Thomas McNulty, *Errol Flynn: The life and career*, McFarland & Co, Jefferson, NC, 2004; location 2918 in ebook edition.

16 ibid., location 3110.

17 ibid., location 2928.

18 'Betty crashed party, Errol Flynn's host says', *Detroit Free Press*, 27 January 1943, page 4.

19 Bret, op. cit., page 123.

20 ibid.

21 ibid., page 124.

22 *Newsweek*, 15 February 1943, page 39.

23 ibid.

24 ibid.

25 ibid.

26 ibid.

27 McNulty, op. cit., location 3054.

28 *Wilkes-Barre Record*, 2 February, 1943, page 2.

Chapter 11

1 More on Charles Wrightsman in *Vanity Fair* magazine, January 2003, www.chicsavage.blogspot.com.au/2009/02/mrs-charles-b-wrightsman.html.

2 Michael Stern, *No Innocence Abroad*, Random House, New York, 1952, page 6.

3 FBI file SATF 12876 – released online as part of unclassified FBI files on Errol Flynn.

4 FBI file 31-68502-6, 3 September 1943. Report written by Special Agent BF Cartwright.

5 ibid.

6 Whitney Bolton, 'Looking Sideways' column, *Daily Press Virginia*, 14 November 1951, page 4.

7 Frazier, op. cit., page 104.

8 FBI file 31-68502, 27 October 1943.

9 ibid.

10 ibid.

11 Higham, op. cit., page 265.

12 Flynn, op. cit., page 281.

13 ibid., page 282.

14 ibid.

15 ibid.

16 ibid., page 345.

17 ibid., page 346.

18 David Niven, *Bring on the Empty Horses*, Coronet Books, London, 1975, page 127.

19 Higham, op. cit., page 324.

20 'Dawson tells jury about his life as a dealer', *The Guardian*, 11 March 1959, page 4.

21 Michael Stern, 'Chapter 4 – George Dawson', *No Innocence Abroad*, Random House, New York, 1952, page 115.
22 Stern, op. cit., page 12.

Chapter 12

1 Dean Jennings, *Barbara Hutton*, WH Allen, London 1968, page 190.
2 ibid., page 189.
3 Higham, op. cit., page 184.
4 Jennings, op. cit., page 191.
5 'Woolworth Heiress may marry Australian', *Courier-Mail*, 13 April 1946.
6 Jennings, op. cit., page 193.
7 'The New Barbara Hutton', *Atlanta Constitution*, 18 August 1946.
8 Jennings, op. cit., page 200.
9 ibid., page 194.
10 ibid.
11 Graham Miller, '"Secret treat" (or is it) rumoured in Paris between Babs Hutton and Freddy McEvoy', *St Louis Star*, 3 September 1946.
12 ibid.
13 'Oil heiress divorces sportsman McEvoy', *Los Angeles Times*, 23 December 1947, page 14.
14 Jennings, op. cit., page 208.
15 ibid., page 189.
16 Frazier, op. cit., February 1954.
17 Jennings, op. cit., page 219.
18 'The last gamble of the boy with the golden manner', *The Truth* (Australia), 2 December 1951.
19 'Society Begging in the Bahamas', *Palm Beach Post*, 11 February 1948.
20 'New International Set – movie celebrities swarm to the French Riviera to turn it into a Hollywood playground', *Life* magazine, 13 September 1948, pages 131–39.
21 Stern, op. cit., page 8.
22 Charles Ventura, 'Society Today', *Palm Beach Post*, 8 December 1948.
23 Stern, op. cit., page 9.
24 Charles Ventura, 'Society Today', *Palm Beach Post*, 5 April 1949.
25 Earl Wilson, 'It happened last night', *Newsday*, 29 November 1948.
26 Flynn, op. cit., page 373.
27 ibid., page 375.
28 ibid., page 377.
29 ibid., page 378.
30 ibid., page 379.

Chapter 13

1 Nick Foulkes, 'The Rakes of the Riviera', *The Rake* <www.therake.com/stories/icons/rakes-of-the-riviera>.
2 Flynn, op. cit., page 382.
3 'The MacEvoy [sic] Mystery', *Daily Express*, 19 November 1951, page 2.
4 ibid.

5   Stern, op. cit., page 15.
6   ibid., page 15.
7   Item in *Los Angeles Times* gossip column, 9 November 1951.
8   'MacEvoy [sic] yacht searched', *Daily Express*, 15 November 1951, page 1.
9   Stern, op. cit., page 16.
10 *Newcastle Morning Herald*, 8 November 1951, page 3.
11 'The MacEvoy [sic] Mystery', *Daily Express*, 14 November 1951, page 1.
12 *Barrier Miner*, Broken Hill, NSW, 16 November 1951.
13 Knickerbocker, op. cit., page 4.
14 *The Truth*, loc. cit.
15 Stern, op. cit., page 22.
16 Walker, op. cit., pages 80–107.
17 'MacEvoy [sic]: Police file murder charges', *Daily Express*, 17 November 1951, page 1.
18 ibid.
19 National Archives of Australia (NAA), Canberra, A1838, 1543/1/133, Part 1 – Death of Australian Abroad, McEvoy Frederick J.
20 Stern, op. cit., page 24.
21 Thomas Clayton, 'No. 1 Detective in Casablanca – Paris sends out urgent orders', *Daily Express*, 19 November 1951, page 1.
22 Frazier, op. cit., page 105.
23 Charles Higham, *Errol Flynn: The untold story*, Granada, London, 1980, page 336.
24 'Playboy McEvoy's head was scalped', *The Mirror* (Perth), 24 November 1951, page 15.
25 Denis Martin, 'Passenger in MacEvoy [sic] yacht now comes forward', *Daily Express*, 24 November 1951.
26 Frank McGarry, 'Yacht survivor cuts parole to meet mystery stranger', *Daily Express*, 21 November 1951.
27 'Startling turn in probe on Playboy's end', *The Truth*, 18 November 1951, page 1.

Chapter 14

1   Flynn, op. cit., page 383.
2   ibid.
3   ibid.
4   Knickerbocker, op. cit., page 5.
5   'Errol Flynn offers to adopt stepdaughter of McEvoy', *Los Angeles Times*, 8 November 1951.
6   Thomas Clayton, 'Yacht survivors made to re-enact escapes', *Daily Express*, 20 November 1951, page 5.
7   Knickerbocker, op. cit., page 5.
8   Frazier, op. cit., page 105.
9   *The Truth*, op. cit.
10 Knickerbocker, op. cit., page 4.
11 'I warned MacEvoy [sic] says Flynn', *Daily Express*, 15 November 1951, page 7.
12 Knickerbocker, op. cit., page 5.

13 *The Truth*, op. cit.
14 Birt Darling, 'When the postman calls', *Lansing State Journal*, (Michigan), 18 July 1952, page 20.
15 Hedda Hopper, 'Looking at Hollywood', *Chicago Daily Tribune*, 10 October 1955, page C4.
16 NAA, loc. cit.
17 ibid.
18 ibid.
19 ibid.
20 ibid.
21 ibid.
22 Robert C Ruark, 'A rascally pair who could raise the devil', *Daily Telegraph*, 29 October 1959.
23 NAA file on McEvoy.
24 NAA file on McEvoy.
25 ibid.

Chapter 15

1 Phone interview with Stephanie Wrightsman conducted by author, 5 September 2017.
2 Interview with author, 12 March 2018.
3 Suzy Knickerbocker, 'Still fooling them', *Philadelphia Inquirer*, 26 June 1964, page 21.
4 Interview with author, 12 March 2018.
5 Kirk Douglas, *The Ragman's Son: An autobiography*, Simon & Schuster, New York, 1988, page 179.
6 Phyllis Battelle, 'Dazed bride wears black, carries soda and scotch at Spanish ceremony', *Milwaukee Sentinel*, 31 December 1953, page 1.
7 Flynn, op. cit., page 434.
8 'Errol was sharp as a whip with a quip', *New York Mirror*, 18 October 1959.
9 ibid.
10 Beverley Aadland married four times and died in 2010.
11 Flynn, op. cit., page 383.
12 'Film stars' pal dies in train room', *Long Beach Independent*, 5 Janauary 1954, page 1.
13 'Mr George Dawson kept £20,000 under bed', *The Guardian*, 12 March 1958, page 3.
14 'Dawson sent to prison for six years', *The Guardian*, 28 March 1959, page 2.
15 Ian Fleming, *Thunderball*, Vintage Books, London, 1961, page 26.
16 Translated from the German book by Andreas Zielke, *Der Letzte Playboy*, LSD Publishing, Göttingen, 2015, page 50.
17 ibid., page 51.
18 NARA FBI file cover dated 31 May 1941.

BIBLIOGRAPHY

Anger, Kenneth, *Hollywood Babylon*, Dell Book, New York, 1975.

Anger, Kenneth, *Hollywood Babylon II*, Penguin, New York, 1984.

Bach, Steven, *Leni – the life and work of Leni Riefenstahl*, Alfred A Knopf, New York, 2007.

Beevor, Antony, *The Second World War*, Weidenfeld & Nicolson, London, 2012.

Bowers, Scotty, *Full Service*, Grove Press, London, 2012.

Bret, David, *Errol Flynn – Satan's Angel*, Robson Books, London, 2000.

De Vries, Susanna, *Royal Mistresses of the House of Hanover-Windsor*, Pirgos Press, Brisbane, 2012.

Diamond, Sander A, *The Nazi movement in the United States 1924–1941*, Cornell University Press, Ithaca, 1974.

Douglas, Kirk, *The Ragman's Son – an autobiography*, Simon & Schuster, New York, 1988.

Editors, Charles River, *Vichy France*, ebook.

Fleming, Ian, *Thunderball*, Vintage Books, London, 1961.

Flynn, Errol, *My Wicked, Wicked Ways*, Aurum Press, London, 2005.

Glass, Charles, *Americans in Paris – life and death under Nazi occupation 1940–44*, Harper Press, London, 2009.

Goebbels, Joseph, *Die Tagebucher von Joseph Goebbels*, Part 1 1923–1941, edited by Elke Frohlich, KG Saur, München, 2005.

Greenwood, Gordon, *The Modern World: A history of our time*, Angus & Robertson, Sydney, 1965.

Higham, Charles, *Errol Flynn – the untold story*, Granada Publishing, London 1980.

James, Richard, *Australia's War with France: The campaign in Syria and Lebanon*, 1941, Big Sky, Newport Australia, 2017.

Jennings, Dean, *Barbara Hutton*, WH Allen, London, 1968.

Large, David Clay, *Nazi Games – the Olympics of 1936*, WW Norton and Co, New York, 2007.

Lepage, Jean-Denis, *An illustrated dictionary of the Third Reich*, McFarland Publishing, Jefferson NC, 2013.

Lovell, Mary S, *The Mitford Girls*, Abacus, London, 2001.

Lovell, Mary S, *The Riviera Set*, Little Brown, London, 2016.

Mank, Gregory, *Hollywood Hellfire Club*, Feral House, Port Townsend, WA, 2007.

Matthews, Rupert, *Hitler – military commander*, Arcturus Publishing, London 2003.

Matzen, Robert, and Mazzone, Michael, *Errol Flynn Slept Here*, GoodKnight Books, Pittsburgh, 2009.

McNulty, Thomas, *Errol Flynn: The life and career*, McFarland & Co, London, 2004.

Morton, Andrew, *17 Carnations – the Windsors, the Nazis, and the cover-up*, Michael O'Mara Books, London, 2015.

Mullin Automotive Museum, *French Curves*, Oxnard, CA.

Niven, David, *Bring on the Empty Horses*, Coronet Books, London 1975.

Organisationskomitee fur die IV Olympische Winterspiele 1936 Garmishc-Partenkirchen, *IV Olympische Winterspiele 1936 – Amtlicher Bericht.*

Ousby, Ian, *Occupation – the ordeal of France 1940–1944*, Thistle Publishing, London, 1997.

Riding, Alan, *And the Show Went On – cultural life in Nazi occupied Paris*, Duckworth, London, 2011.

Ringgold, Gene, and Quirk, Lawrence, *The Films of Bette Davis*, Cadillac Publishing, New York, 1966.

Rippon, Anton, *Hitler's Olympics – the story of the 1936 Nazi Games*, Pen & Sword Military, Barnsley, Yorkshire, 2006.

Robertson, Patrick, *The Guinness Book of Movie Facts*, Abbeville Press, New York, 1988.

Roland, Paul, *Nazi Women – the attraction of evil*, Arcturus, London, 2014.

Rosenzweig, Laura B, *Hollywood's Spies – the undercover surveillance of Nazis in Los Angeles*, New York University Press, New York, 2017.

Ross, Steven J, *Hitler in Los Angeles – how Jews foiled Nazi plots against Hollywood and America*, Bloomsbury, New York, 2017.

Rugoff, Milton, *The Gilded Age*, New Word City, Boston, 2018.

Schoonover, Thomas David, *Hitler's Man in Havana: Heinz Lüning and Nazi espionage in Latin America*, University Press of Kentucky, Lexington, KY, 2008.

Shipman, David, *The Great Movie Stars – the golden years*, Angus & Robertson, Sydney 1979.

Shirer, William L, *The Rise and Fall of the Third Reich*, Simon & Schuster, New York, 1960.

Smith, Colin, *England's Last War Against France: Fighting Vichy 1940–42*, W&N, London 2010.

Stern, Michael, *No Innocence Abroad*, Random House, New York, 1953.

Van Rensselaer, Philip, *Million Dollar Baby – an intimate portrait of Barbara Hutton*, Hodder & Stoughton, London, 1979.

Walker, Frank, *Traitors*, Hachette, Sydney, 2017.

Weber, Ronald, *News of Paris*, Ivan R Dee, Chicago, 2006.

Whiting, Charles, *End of War – Europe 1945*, Random House, London, 1973.
Wiser, William, *The Twilight Years – Paris in the 1930s*, Robson Books, London, 2001.
Writer, Larry, *Dangerous Games – Australia at the 1936 Nazi Olympics*, Allen & Unwin, Sydney, 2015.
Zeilke, Andreas, *Der Letzte Playboy*, LSD Publishing, Göttingen, 2015.

Newspapers, journals

American Weekly
Atlanta Constitution
Barrier Miner (Broken Hill, NSW)
Chicago Daily Tribune
Courier-Mail (Brisbane)
Daily Express (UK)
Daily Press (Virginia)
Daily Telegraph (Sydney)
Daily Telegraph (UK)
Der Spiegel
Detroit Free Press
Deutsche Welle
Esquire
Fresno Bee
Honolulu Star-Advertiser
Lansing State Journal (Michigan)
Life
Los Angeles Times
Milwaukee Sentinel
Minneapolis Star
Newcastle Morning Herald (Australia)
Newsday (New York)
Newsweek
Palm Beach Post (Florida)
Philadelphia Inquirer
St Louis Star
Stonyhurst Magazine (UK school)
Sydney Morning Herald
The Atlantic
The Guardian
The Independent
The Mirror (WA)
The Truth (Australia)
Vanity Fair
Washington Times Herald
Wilkes-Barre Record
Wisconsin Jewish Chronicle
Yorkshire Post

Dossiers, documents, files

Charles Higham Collection, University of South California Cinematic Arts Library, Los Angeles.
Foreign Office Archives, London.
German Archives in Berlin, files on occupied France.
Margaret Merrick Library, Academy of Motion Picture Arts and Sciences, Los Angeles.
National Archives of Australia, Canberra.
US National Archives and Records Administration, Maryland – FBI, State Department, Defence files.

Websites

Badrutt's Palace: www.badruttspalace.com/en/120-years-badrutts-palace/dancer-to-millionaire
FBI declassified files on Errol Flynn: https://archive.org/details/ErrolFlynn
Hilde Kruger Mexico file: http://mexicounexplained.com/hilde-kruger-nazi-spy-mexico
Freddie McEvoy in biographies of Olympic athletes: www.sports-reference.com/olympics/athletes/mc/freddie-mcevoy-1.html

Motor racing golden era biographies of drivers (with incorrect photo of Freddie
    McEvoy): www.kolumbus.fi/leif.snellman/dm.htm
Vanderbilt Cup Motor Races 1936: www.vanderbiltcupraces.com/races/year/1936_
    vanderbilt_cup_race
The Errol Flynn blog: www.theerrolflynnblog.com
The Rake: https://therake.com

Videos, films

1936 Winter Olympics Garmisch-Partenkirchen: www.youtube.com/watch?v=
    t6NTbu5F1Uo
Hitler opening the 1936 Winter Olympics with sound: www.youtube.com/watch?v=
    ooxkC8ZJffA
Jugend der Welt 1936: www.archive.org/details/1936-Jugend-der-Welt
20/20, American Broadcasting Company
Thank Your Lucky Stars, Warner Bros, 1943.
The Desert Song, Warner Bros, 1943.
When 20,000 American Nazis Descended on New York City by Marshall Curry:
    www.theatlantic.com/video/index/542499/marshall-curry-nazi-rally-madison-
    square-garden-1939

INDEX